Praise for
The Emotionally Absent Mother

"With compassion and sparkling clarity, Jasmin Lee Cori describes the effects of being undermothered and what it takes to overcome them. Her book will be of great value to new mothers serious about creating a loving environment for their children, adult sons and daughters who want at long last to fill the holes in their hearts, and clinicians interested in understanding and healing the mother wound."

—**Evelyn Bassoff, PhD,** psychotherapist, author of
Mothers and Daughters: Loving and Letting Go

"This book is a revelation to those of us whose mothering was short of what we needed. The author sensitively and authoritatively weaves developmental principles into a compassionate understanding of what it means to be undermothered."

—**Connie Dawson, PhD,** coauthor of *Growing Up Again: Parenting Ourselves, Parenting Our Children*

"Jasmin Lee Cori has done a superb job of describing the importance of childhood attachment needs and the psychological wounds that get inflicted when an emotionally absent mother cannot meet those needs well enough. She has skillfully laid out clear steps wounded adults can take to identify their inner strengths and heal attachment wounds. I wholeheartedly recommend this book for anyone who wishes to understand and heal the wounds that can arise when parented by an emotionally absent mother."

—**Shirley Jean Schmidt, MA, LPC,** author of *The Developmental Needs Meeting Strategy: An Ego State Therapy for Healing Adults with Childhood Trauma and Attachment Wounds*

"With a compassionate and steady voice, Jasmin Lee Cori guides the reader through the difficult terrain faced by adults who have grown up without sufficient emotional mothering. Relying on personal experience and practice as a psychotherapist, she provides insight and tools to help readers overcome the challenges of a painful childhood and to move into the pleasures of living adult life fully."

—**Kathryn Black, MA,** psychotherapist, author of *Mothering Without a Map: The Search for the Good Mother Within*

"This book effortlessly intertwines neuroscience with clinical acumen in a lovely work of extraordinary depth. In her compelling, heartrending analysis of the importance of motherhood, Jasmin Lee Cori has created a work as significant as Alice Miller's *Prisoners of Childhood*. Easily accessible and very useful, it is a must-read for parents-to-be, those in the helping professions, and adults who have been wounded by a negligent parent."

—**Kate Crowley, OTD, OTR/L,** Adjunct Faculty, University of Southern California, Specialist in Infant Mental Health

THE EMOTIONALLY ABSENT MOTHER

UPDATED & EXPANDED SECOND EDITION

How to Recognize and Heal
the Invisible Effects of
Childhood Emotional Neglect

Jasmin Lee Cori, MS, LPC,

THE EXPERIMENT

NEW YORK

THE EMOTIONALLY ABSENT MOTHER: *How to Recognize and Heal the Invisible Effects of Childhood Emotional Neglect*—Updated and Expanded Second Edition
Copyright © Jasmin Lee Cori, 2010, 2017

All rights reserved. Except for brief passages quoted in newspaper, magazine, radio, television, or online reviews, no portion of this book may be reproduced, distributed, or transmitted in any form or by any means, electronic or mechanical, including photocopying, recording, or information storage or retrieval system, without the prior written permission of the publisher.

The Experiment, LLC, 220 East 23rd Street, Suite 301, New York, NY 10010-4674
theexperimentpublishing.com

This book contains the opinions and ideas of its author. It is intended to provide helpful and informative material on the subjects addressed in the book. It is sold with the understanding that the author and publisher are not engaged in rendering medical, health, or any other kind of personal professional services in the book. The author and publisher specifically disclaim all responsibility for any liability, loss, or risk—personal or otherwise—that is incurred as a consequence, directly or indirectly, of the use and application of any of the contents of this book.

Many of the designations used by manufacturers and sellers to distinguish their products are claimed as trademarks. Where those designations appear in this book and The Experiment was aware of a trademark claim, the designations have been capitalized.

The Experiment's books are available at special discounts when purchased in bulk for premiums and sales promotions as well as for fund-raising or educational use. For details, contact us at info@theexperimentpublishing.com.

Library of Congress Cataloging-in-Publication Data

Names: Cori, Jasmine Lee, author.
Title: The emotionally absent mother : how to recognize and heal the
    invisible effects of childhood emotional neglect / Jasmine Lee Cori, MS,
    LPC.
Description: Second Edition, Revised. | New York : Experiment, [2017] |
    Revised edition of the author's The emotionally absent mother, [2015]
Identifiers: LCCN 2017003974| ISBN 9781615193820 (pbk.) | ISBN 9781615193837
    (ebook)
Subjects: LCSH: Self-help techniques. | Inner child. | Self-actualization
    (Psychology) | Mother and child. | Adult children of dysfunctional
    families.
Classification: LCC BF632 .C647 2017 | DDC 155.9/24--dc23
LC record available at https://lccn.loc.gov/201700397

ISBN 978-1-61519-382-0
Ebook ISBN 978-1-61519-383-7

Cover design by Alison Forner | Additional cover design by Sarah Schneider
Cover photograph by Mark J. Barrett | Author photograph by Gail A. Bishop
Text design by Scott Harmon | Additional text design by Sarah Schneider

Manufactured in the United States of America
Distributed by Workman Publishing Company, Inc.
Distributed simultaneously in Canada by Thomas Allen and Son Limited

First printing April 2017
10 9 8 7 6 5 4 3 2 1

To the motherless child
who somehow survived
all that was missing,
even when Mother was there.
This book is for you.

Mommy, Where Were You?

My first steps
I stood there teetering, so proud
ecstatic as a baby bird learning it could fly.
When I looked back, my smile about to break my face,
I couldn't find you.
Mommy, where were you?

My first day of school
boarded onto that noisy, clackety bus
going to a strange place
kids crowding, adults peering
the whole world new to me.
Mommy, where were you?

The first time I came home crying
the butt of children's laughter
their words still stinging in my head
I would have liked some consolation
but you were silent.

You are there in old photographs
but in my memories, you are missing.
I don't remember cuddling or being comforted
no special moments, just the two of us
I don't remember your smell or the feel of your touch.

I remember the color of your eyes
and the pain deep inside them—
the pain usually hidden, like so much else
beneath the mask I couldn't get behind.

You looked but didn't see me.
Your warmth never reached my little girl's heart.
Why did we miss each other, Mommy?
Where were you?
Was it because of me?

—JC

Contents

PART III: HEALING MOTHER WOUNDS

Introduction to the Second Edition

FEW EXPERIENCES IN LIFE are as deep as the feelings we carry about our mothers. The roots of some of these feelings are lost in the dark recesses of preverbal experience. The branches go every which way, some holding glorious, sun-drenched moments, while others are broken off, leaving sharp and jagged edges that we get caught on. Mother is not a simple subject.

On both a cultural and a psychological level, our feelings about mothers are often inconsistent and tangled. Mom and apple pie are potent symbols, venerated in our national psyche but neglected in national policy, as reflected, for example, in our meager family leave policies in comparison with other developed countries. If we were really serious about mothering, we would provide more financial and in-home help as well as education for mothers. As it currently stands, mothers are held up on a pedestal with little support beneath them.

We are aware of this as adults. Few of us escape the feeling that mothers are to be honored, or the awareness that mothers are too often taken for granted and their sacrifices unappreciated. Yet, many of us are secretly (or not so secretly) unsatisfied with what we got from our mothers, and resentful that—whether their fault or not—they failed to provide important aspects of what we needed. And we're paying the price.

These are sensitive issues—sensitive for mothers and sensitive for all of us. Some, in a need to make mothers off-limits from criticism, become critical of those who are unsatisfied, blaming us for blaming our mothers, as if we are unfairly passing off the responsibility for our suffering. While I don't deny that some may use blame as a distraction and fail to take responsibility for the arduous task of healing, what I see more often as a therapist is the enormous guilt and resistance people have to work through in order to stop protecting their mothers. It is as if, even within the privacy of our own minds, we are afraid to criticize her. We are protecting the image of mother inside, protecting our fragile relationship with her by denying anything that might unsettle it, and protecting ourselves from the disappointment, anger, and pain that we've kept out of consciousness. As I will explain in the chapters that follow, many don't dare to uncover the painful truth of what was missing in their mothers because they are unprepared to deal with what this would mean.

Any relationship as complex as that between mother and child is going to include both love and hate. Most young children feel moments of hatred when their needs or wishes are frustrated, although many children wouldn't dare express this, their bond with Mommy far too fragile. And virtually all children feel love for Mother, even when that love is buried or walled off. As Robert Karen eloquently reported in his compilation of research on attachment:

> Virtually all children, even abused children, love their parents. It's built into the nature of being a child. They may be hurt, disappointed, caught in destructive modes of being that ward off any possibility of getting the love they yearn for, but to be attached, even anxiously attached, is to be in love. Each year the love may become a little more difficult to access; each year the child may disavow his wish for connection more firmly; he may even swear off his parents and deny that he has any love for them at all; but the love is there, as is the longing to actively express it and to have it returned, hidden like a burning sun.[1]

Karen's words show some of the complexity of this relationship. No one escapes wanting a mother's love.

Mothering is also a sensitive topic for those who are mothers. When I was first working on this book, I noticed some guilt and defensiveness when I would share what I was writing about with women who were mothers. They wanted to say, "Don't give me so much power. There are many other influences in a child's life. It's not all my fault how they turned out." All very true. We come in with individual differences that are stunning. And there are other childhood influences as well, including birth order, bonding with Father and his adequacy as a parent, environmental and genetic influences on a child's basic physiology, family dynamics and important events in the family such as a major illness, and the stresses in the larger culture.

Despite these many factors, the impact of Mother is unparalleled. An attentive, capable, caring mother can help make up for many other handicaps, and the absence of such mothering is perhaps the greatest handicap of all, because when Mother is not doing her larger-than-life job as it needs to be done, children have significant deficits in their foundations.

My focus on the mother is not because mothers need more guilt or responsibility heaped on, but because the quality of the mothering we receive so powerfully shapes our development. My hope is that understanding these influences will lead us to better understand ourselves and, most important, to complete the developmental tasks and heal the injuries that resulted from insufficient mothering.

For those readers who are mothers or who are becoming mothers, it is my hope that my breaking down the roles of mothering as I do here and highlighting the central importance of nurturing will help train your focus. Although there are aspects of mothering that are instinctive and are passed through the generations by women who were well mothered themselves, for many women mothering must be consciously learned. If you were inadequately mothered, your task will be twofold: to heal your own wounds and to open up a different way of being with your children than your mother was with you.

As I began working, I wanted to supplement my understanding of the undermothered adults I had experienced within my own circle and in my psychotherapy practice, so I put out a call for "undermothered" adults to interview. I was immediately flooded with responses. As might be expected, I found more women than men who were willing to talk with a stranger about their experiences, although I also had more access to women. There was nothing scientific about my sampling, so I can't claim to have captured the undermothered from a demographic or sociological perspective, but I think their brave and often insightful disclosures have some value for us all. Some of my findings are sprinkled throughout the chapters, but most of them are found in chapter 6, "Living with an Emotionally Absent Mother," where I describe both the childhood environments my interviewees experienced and the challenges they have faced as adults.

In the first edition of this book my focus was on the effects of having been raised by an emotionally disengaged mother. In the years since this book was first published I have learned more about the variety of emotionally absent mothers and how emotional neglect and emotional abuse often come intertwined. In this expanded edition, I go further into the abuse aspects and what is wrong with Mother that causes her to act this way.

The book now has three parts: Part 1 examines what children need from Mother. It looks at the elements of good mothering and the importance of this first attachment. In Part 2, we learn what happens when mothering goes wrong, what the impacts are from emotional neglect and abuse, and what leads mothers to fail their children in these ways. Part 3 tackles the subject of healing. After an overview of the healing process, chapters delve into psychotherapy, reparenting your inner child and making up for unmet needs, and negotiating your relationship with Mother as an adult.

There are a number of exercises in the book, which you are free to complete or not. There are also pauses throughout the book that invite you to digest the material and reflect on your own situation. I encourage you to take a moment to consider these, listening for what comes to mind as you read them, even if you don't choose to formally answer each question.

Since what you take away for yourself in terms of your own understanding and healing is an important benefit to reading this book, I invite you to take your time. You have to be your own gatekeeper here, so if working with particular material is distressing, consider what kind of support you may need. Practice being a good mother to yourself by taking on only what you can handle at any given moment. You can always come back to the material at another time. Some readers have found the first section on good mothering too evocative for them at the get-go, and prefer to return to it later. So, although each chapter builds on what came before, the book can be worked with however it best suits you.

My four goals in this book are:

- To help you get a clearer picture of what kind of mothering you received.

- To help you see the connection between the mothering you experienced and the difficulties in your life. What have been thought of as personal *defects* can then be linked to mothering *deficits*, relieving self-blame.

- To provide suggestions for how these missing elements can be made up for now—whether in therapy, through close relationships, or by providing them for yourself.

- To help you decide how to proceed in your relationship with Mother as an adult, giving you more tools and options than you may have started with.

The good news is that the deficits of inadequate mothering can be made up for later—maybe not completely, but more significantly than we usually dare to hope. We can heal the unloved child within and become empowered, loving adults. This is a journey worth taking.

PART I

What We Need from Mother

1.

Mothering

Mother as the tree of life

I will always remember an image in *The Family of Man*, a photo exhibit that traveled the world and was captured in book form. A tall, lanky black woman stood with two young children, their faces dark, caught in shadow. On the facing page, quoting Proverbs, were these words: *She is a tree of life to them.*

A tree of life. A tree providing shelter, home, protection. A tree you can climb on and eat from. A tree that seems big when you are many times smaller. A tree that is *your* tree.

In world mystical traditions, the tree of life is the vertical axis around which life revolves. In a similar way, Mother is the axis around which the family and the child's emotional life revolve. In the vast stretch of history before the Christian era, the tree of life was often depicted as a mother, and the Great Mother/Goddess was often depicted as a tree.

Thus the tree is a natural symbol for mothering. With its fruits and flowers, with birds and animals in and around it, it provides both shelter and supply. Growing in many directions, but particularly with its arc of outward expansion, it is like a fountain of abundance. Part of the tree-of-life archetype is this sense of bounty and of giving.

This archetype is captured in the children's book *The Giving Tree* by Shel Silverstein. Originally published in 1964, it is considered a classic parable of love and devotion. It is about a boy and a tree that loves him very much and gives him every-thing she has. She lets him swing on her branches, gives him shade to sit under, apples to eat, and branches to build a house. She even lets him cut down her trunk to make a boat. In the end, the tree only a stump and the boy an old man, she gives him a place to rest.

As many have clearly noted, the relationship between the boy and the tree is much like that between a child and mother. The tree puts the boy's needs first. It gives and gives and gives. This is part of the role of a mother, which competes at times with a woman's own needs to develop herself as a person apart from her mothering role and her relationship with others. Many women have lamented losing themselves in mothering and in being partners. Yet if a woman isn't ready, at least for a period of her life, to attend to the needs of others, she really isn't ready for the task of mothering.

There are many legitimate reasons a woman may be unable to fully take on the enormous task of mothering, yet unfortu-nately women have often not been given (or not felt) a choice about this. Because of either unintentional pregnancy or social expectations, women may slide into motherhood without choosing it. Often such women have not yet grown into full adults themselves. They are ill-equipped for what lies in front of them.

It is not easy to give of yourself if you still have many unmet needs. Yet, mothering requires constant giving. A good mother shares the warmth of her body when her child is cold, the milk from her breast when her child needs nourishment. She gives both the unborn child and the nursing child calcium from her bones. This is a very basic level of giving of oneself. No wonder "Mother" is a symbol of sacrifice!

Mommy is what we are made of

There are two important levels to the assertion that we are made of our mothers. The first is the obvious biological fact: We were made in her body, and we are made from her body. Then there is the psychological level where Mother is part of our personality, psyche, and structure. It's as if she is literally a layer of our being. You'll get a better understanding of this in the next several chapters.

How we are put together, how we see ourselves, our sense of self-esteem, our unconscious beliefs about relationship—all of these are strongly imprinted by our mother. She is not the only influence, but she and our interactions with her provide the basic building materials for all of these things.

Whether we feel that basic material as nourishing or toxic is largely determined by the quality of our interactions with our mother. It is not what Mother *does* that is so critical, but rather her energetic presence and her love that are so important. Is she angry or spaced out while feeding her baby? When Mother is really there in a loving way, then Mommy's milk and Mommy's heart don't feel separate. When she's not there, her milk is not as sustaining. The baby may feel not quite right taking it, perhaps because it is not so freely given or because there's something unwanted in the interaction that comes along with the milk.

As they would say in a children's rhyme, when this interaction is good, it feels very, very good, and when it is bad, it feels horrid. Of course this view is more black and white than things usually are, but young children experience the world with great intensity. You can feel Mother as an inner layer of support, a layer of love that is always with you, or you can feel as if there is something dead or toxic in you. This toxic substance is what you absorbed from your interactions with her and perhaps from what was toxic inside her.

Who can mother?

I use the term *mother* all through the book, yet I don't necessarily limit this to the woman who gives birth to a particular
child—although that relationship, even if it never goes beyond
birth (because the mother dies or gives the baby away), marks a
person's entire life. When I ask about your mother in this book,
I'm asking about the person who functioned in this primary
role, and the term *Good Mother* can refer to any adult who takes
on a caring, nurturing, protective role in your life, fulfilling the
functions described in the next chapter.

This can include an adoptive mother, grandmother, or step-
mother; even the right father can fill these shoes. Others further
outside the inner family circle can help meet some of the child's
needs (even into adulthood): teachers, aunts, mothers of friends,
therapists, partners. We can even meet some of these needs for
ourselves as we mature, understanding that the undermothered child is usually still alive in an adult, still needing what he
needed then.

Although not every woman adapts to the role of mothering, nature has done its best to give biological mothers every
advantage. Research supports the idea that mothers, as a
group, instinctively employ behaviors that infants prefer. Studies in Sweden found that even when a mother works outside
the home and the father is the primary caretaker, babies still
strongly prefer being with the mother.[1]

Nature also supports biological mothers through their hormones (especially oxytocin), which seem to put them in the mood
for bonding and are directly correlated with bonding behaviors.
Breastfeeding puts the infant at the perfect distance at which it
can focus on the mother's eyes. Of course the developing fetus
has already been forming a relationship with the mother in the
womb, responding to her heartbeat, her voice, her touch through
the abdominal wall, and her energetic presence.

Unfortunately these biological advantages aren't enough for some women to overcome the lack of readiness they show for taking on the tasks of mothering. It is a good thing, then, that people other than biological mothers can "mother."

The good-enough mother

Mothers don't need to be perfect, and can't be. The perfection, when there, is supplied through the eyes of the child—who, when the mother does a good-enough job meeting her basic needs, feels total adoration. This is helpful, because when you're totally dependent on someone, you want to believe that person can do the job. To overlook the slips and lack of perfect attunement and accentuate the positive is both good psychological strategy and good evolutionary strategy, since the child's good feelings also help the mother bond to the child.

The term *good-enough mother* was coined by the famous pediatrician and psychoanalyst D. W. Winnicott to describe the mother who provides enough for a child to have a good start in life. Winnicott sees the primary job of the good-enough mother as adapting to the baby. He describes how the good-enough mother starts off with almost complete adaptation to her infant's needs, and subsequently adapts less and less as the infant can tolerate more frustration. A mother who continued to satisfy all the infant's needs perfectly and immediately would rob the baby of the need to learn new behaviors, develop new skills, and be able to handle delay and frustration.

Recent research reinforces this notion that the mother doesn't have to be 100 percent attuned and available to her child to offer good-enough parenting. It suggests that what is needed is to be in sync (defined as in a harmonious state together, with the mother attuned to the child) 30 percent of the time.[2] Is that really so much to ask?

According to psychotherapist and author Diana Fosha, "What matters as much as (if not more than) the natural capacity to be in sync is the capacity to repair out-of-syncness so as to reestablish optimal connection."[3] The good-enough mother needs to repair the inevitable ruptures that occur in every relationship. She is not going to always behave just right, but she has to know how to make it right when she misses.

Research suggests that she has help in this from her child. Babies come into the world with an urge toward and capacity for maintaining a strong bond with their mothers. They are also wired to make the most of the mother's reparative efforts.[4] For a child to be able to rectify the inevitable disruptions in this relationship is empowering. Conversely, to not be able to get Mother's attention, to not be able to reconnect after there has been a disconnection, can leave the baby feeling profoundly impotent and discouraged about relationships and about getting her needs met.

When a mother is not attuned enough to respond to a child's needs, the child ends up adapting to the mother instead of the other way around. Losing touch with his core experience, the child then develops what Winnicott calls a *false self.*

Good Mother messages

How Mother responds to our basic needs tells us about our importance to her. Is she generous in giving to us (even joyful!), or does she meet our needs with a sense of burden and an attitude that says, *you're bothering me*? When she changes a diaper or dresses us, is her touch gentle and loving, or is it efficient and slightly brusque? Perhaps it seems mechanical. What do her eyes say? How about the expressions on her face? What do her actions and choices convey? All of these are a part of a mother's communication and shape our relationship to her. Together they form the basis of the messages we receive.

We start by looking at "Good Mother messages"[5] and then consider what those of us who are undermothered heard instead.

Here are ten basic Good Mother messages:

- I'm glad that you're here.
- I see you.
- You are special to me.
- I respect you.
- I love you.
- Your needs are important to me. You can turn to me for help.
- I am here for you. I'll make time for you.
- I'll keep you safe.
- You can rest in me.
- I delight in you.

Let's look at these in more detail:

I'm glad that you're here.

"I'm glad that you're here" is an important first message for a child to hear. This message is communicated through behaviors that tell the child she is valued and wanted.

Many believe that this fundamental sense of being wanted begins in utero. Certainly there are many moments in children's lives in which they feel either wanted or not. I would suggest that this is not an all-or-nothing experience but rather a matter of degree and that isolated moments of feeling unwanted can be counterbalanced to a great extent by a larger stream of experiences where the child feels valued.

The message "I'm glad you're here" helps *us* be glad that we're here. It helps us feel comfortable taking up space and being in our bodies.

I see you.

A mother conveys "I see you" primarily through accurate mirroring (see Mother as Mirror, p. 32) and attuned responsiveness. She knows, for instance, what we like and what we don't. She knows what our interests are and how we feel about things. Being seen is being known.

You are special to me.

The message "You are special to me" (usually not said in words) tells us that we are prized. As is true with other messages, this needs to be paired with the sense of being seen for who we are so that we do not associate specialness with some superficial, external quality or image.

I respect you.

A mother communicates "I respect you" when she supports a child's uniqueness, doesn't try to control when there is no need to, accepts the child's preferences and decisions, and communicates that she values what she sees in the child. Children who feel respected and loved in a genuine way will have permission to discover and express their unique self rather than mirror the parent(s) or conform to some parental blueprint.

I love you.

"I love you" is often conveyed by these simple words yet needs to be experienced as sincere and authentic in order to have meaning. Many children hear these words several times a day; others go a lifetime without them. It is important that they not be perceived as manipulative and not paired with requiring something of the child.

Love is probably most effectively communicated by nonverbal means, including touch, tone of voice, eyes and facial expression, body language, and attentiveness. When the environment provides a secure sense of holding and containment (such as provided through boundaries and rules), this also feels like love.

Your needs are important to me. You can turn to me for help.
"Your needs are important to me" expresses a sense of priority. It's not just that Mother is saying, "I'll take care of you because I have to" or "when I get to it," but "because this is actually important." With this message, we get the sense that Mother's attentiveness comes out of love and genuine caring. "You can turn to me for help" gives permission; it says you don't have to hide your needs or try to take care of them yourself.

I am here for you. I'll make time for you.
"I am here for you" is a way of saying, "You can count on me. I'm not going to disappear on you." Often this will relate to specific needs, but beyond that, it means "I am here as a consistent presence in your life." This supports a sense of relaxation and trust.

A related message would be "I'll make time for you." It expresses availability, priority, and valuing. Unfortunately, too many children feel that their parents don't have time for them.

I'll keep you safe.
"I'll keep you safe" could also be expressed as "I'll protect you. I won't let you be hurt or overwhelmed (unnecessarily)."

A sense of safety is essential for a child to be able to relax and explore. Without safety, we may never feel ready to go out into the world. Without our caretaker's protection, our only protection is to stay small and build defensive structures into our personality.

You can rest in me.
"You can rest in me" is a way of saying several things. First, it implies a protected space; if you have to be on guard, you can't really rest. It also implies availability (Mother needs to be here to rest in) and acceptance. It is a way of saying, "With me, you can be at home." We all want a place where we can be totally ourselves, where we don't have to perform, and where we feel soothed and comforted in the company of another.

I delight in you.

"I delight in you" provides an affirmation of the child's precious-ness. It says to the child, "you are a delight," "you are a joy to be around." We see this when Mother's eyes light up when she sees us, in her smile, her laugh.

What happens when Good Mother messages are absent?

When these Good Mother messages are absent, they leave specific "holes" or feelings of deficiency. Using the above list, it might look like this:

I'm glad that you're here.

When we don't feel welcomed or wanted, we may conclude, *maybe it would be better if I weren't here.* It can also lead to a great fear of abandonment. One woman who never felt wanted as a child was terrified every time she went to a restaurant or Laundromat with her mother that her mother would leave her and never come back. For a young child to not feel wanted is to have no solid ground.

I see you.

If Mother doesn't see or know us, then her responses will not feel on target. She may try to guide, for instance, but starts in the wrong place.

When we are consistently not seen, it can lead to feeling invisible and an uncertainty that we are real. The feeling of unreality can be subtle and generally unconscious, or it can be quite pervasive and disorienting.

You are special to me.

When we don't feel special to our parents, we don't feel cher-ished for who we are. We may even think, *Mommy might like it better if I were someone else.*

I respect you.

When we don't feel that our capacities, boundaries, and preferences are respected, we don't learn to respect these for ourselves. We may develop a sense of unworthiness and shame or fail to actualize our true potential. This can also set us up to be too accommodating to other people rather than stand behind ourselves.

I love you.

With an absence of sufficient loving, we may conclude, *I am unlovable as I am.* Consequently, we may contort ourselves in the hope, *if I conform to what others want, maybe they'll love me.*

Your needs are important to me.

When we don't get a sense that Mother wants to meet our needs, we can believe, *my needs are shameful or a burden. I shouldn't have needs.*

I am here for you.

Without a sense Mother is here for us, we feel alone. It leads to the sense that *I need to raise myself.*

I'll keep you safe.

Without the sense of protection, we can feel overwhelmed by life and conclude that the world is dangerous.

You can rest in me.

When being with Mother is not a safe place to be ourselves, we miss an important aspect of connection. Being with Mother then becomes a time we need to stay alert or perform, and we never fully feel at home with her.

I delight in you.

Without a sense that Mother enjoys us, we may conclude, *I am a burden that nobody wants. I wish I could disappear. I shouldn't take up so much space.* We shrink in ourselves and learn to hide our light.

The messages you received

• Go through each of the ten Good Mother messages, and for each one note your emotional response to it. Does this message feel familiar? (Remember these messages are communicated by behaviors more than through words.) Is this a message you think you received? How does it feel in your body?

• You might compare each message in the first list with the corresponding one in the second list and see which seems more true for you, paying attention as best as you can to thoughts, emotions, and sensations in your body.

As with any exercise in this book, this may bring up uncomfortable feelings, so you'll want to pace yourself. If you find yourself feeling overwhelmed, you might let it go for now and come back to it when you're ready, or do the exercise when you have a supportive person present.

What does it mean to be undermothered?

When you don't get enough good mothering, in terms of these Good Mother messages, the functions described in chapter 2, the secure attachment of chapter 3, or the nurturing touch and love and other building blocks in chapter 4, you are undermothered. Yes, you received enough mothering to survive, but not enough for the kind of foundation that supports healthy self-confidence, initiative, resilience, trust, healthy entitlement, self-esteem, and the many other qualities we need to thrive in this challenging world.

The more clearly you can see the ways you were insufficiently mothered, the more proactively you can make up for them. Let's learn more about what was missing.

2.

The Many Faces of the Good Mother

THE PERCEPTUAL WORLD (and specifically the visual world) of the infant contains many experiences of the same few objects, yet each experience is quite distinct and different—so much so that, from the infant's point of view, they seem to be different objects. In a somewhat similar way, we can take the image of the Good Mother and separate it into different experiences, which I call the many faces of the Good Mother. Each "face" represents a role that she fulfills or a psychological function important for the child's development.

After reading this chapter, you may wonder how one person can fulfill so many important and seemingly endless tasks. Of course no one can perfectly, which makes our picture of the Good Mother an ideal or model. By reflecting on how well your mother fulfilled each of these psychological functions, you will understand more about her fingerprint on your psyche and bring more insight into your feelings, beliefs, and behaviors. You'll understand why some parts of you need more shoring up than others.

You'll also notice that many of these roles overlap, and it may seem arbitrary at moments to try to separate them. They work together to do their magic and create the larger-than-life archetype of the Good Mother. In dissecting the Good Mother this way, we may take away a little of her mystery, but perhaps the cost is worth it if it helps us see our needs more clearly and get serious about meeting them.

Please keep in mind that although I am talking about these as functions of the mother, they can be fulfilled by any caregiver and are not strictly limited to biological mothers. Fathers, grandparents, nannies, day care workers, extended family members, and even mother figures found later in life can provide some of these important nutrients.

The ten faces are as follows:

- Mother as *source*
- Mother as *place of attachment*
- Mother as *first responder*
- Mother as *modulator*
- Mother as *nurturer*
- Mother as *mirror*
- Mother as *cheerleader*
- Mother as *mentor*
- Mother as *protector*
- Mother as *home base*

Mother as Source

"Mother" is what we come from and what we are made of. In mythology and religion, this source is often depicted as some kind of mother goddess, often an ocean goddess. Just as life is thought to have evolved from the ocean, human life evolves from the mother and, more specifically, the womb. Thus, at both the mythological level and the more mundane, the source of life is Mother.

When the child has a positive experience of Mother, he gets the sense, *I am* of *Mommy. I come from her. I'm part of her. I'm like her.* This becomes a building block of identity.

Unfortunately, not everyone has an experience of Mother as Source in a positive way. Some adults, through an experience of age regression in hypnosis or any kind of depth work, recover memories of the womb as a toxic environment they are trapped in. They have a strong sense of being "of"—but it's an icky *"of"* from which they would rather be separate. This also happens with engulfing mothers, who are not experienced in a positive way.

Then there is the experience of children put up for adoption whose source has, at least on a subjective level, rejected them. They are in the complex situation of being both *"of"* this first mother since she gave birth to them, and also "not *of"* her, because they do not continue to belong to her. Sometimes it's challenging for them to develop a firm sense of belonging to their adopted mother.

Having a sense of belonging somewhere is essential, and the sense of Mother as Source is only one part of it. As we'll see, it also comes into play when we experience Mother as the Place of Attachment.

Although some of this may be beyond Mother's control, there are things Mother can do to be experienced as source in a positive way. She can create a welcoming environment, from the first moments of life. She can be a positive energy that her children want to be around and are nourished by. She can draw similarities between herself and her child, while careful to give the child plenty of room to also be different. And she can be a positive role model that her children, throughout their lives, will be proud of.

Your mother as source

- When you think of your mother's womb, does it feel like an inviting place? If you can't imagine this, ask how it would feel to be enveloped in your mother's energy. Is that something you would like?

- Did you want to be like your mother or did you want to be as different as possible (or anything in between)? If someone said, "You are so like your mother!" how would you feel?

- Can you imagine feeling pride about being your mother's child? Do you identify yourself in relation to your mother?

Mother as Place of Attachment

Mother is our first connection to the world. Here we focus not on Mother as the ocean we come from, but as the more immediate place where we are attached, like the underside of a boat that a barnacle fastens to. Mother is the belly of the ship that a securely attached child clings to.

When you watch securely attached toddlers and young children with their mothers, they are in constant physical contact, climbing over, pulling on, sucking, and hugging the mother's body. Even an older child will take Mother's hand when scared. As we'll learn below, attachment is not created just through body contact, but also through the mother's attunement and responsiveness to needs. Attachment is so important that the whole next chapter is devoted to it.

Attachment for the young child brings the feeling *I belong to you. And because I belong to you, I have a place.* Without this, we are untethered, adrift well into our adult years. One woman felt like a piece of driftwood out at sea; another was so unbonded to her mother that she felt as if she must have been found under a cabbage leaf—or may as well have been. This can result in a profound sense of aloneness, alienation, and not belonging.

With secure attachment, a child feels securely held, safe. This function overlaps with Mother as First Responder because it is largely through this function of being responsive to needs that attachment is formed.

Your mother as place of attachment

- On a scale of 1 through 10 (with 10 being extremely connected), how connected would you say you feel to your mother?

- How has this changed throughout your life?

- What are your early memories around physical contact with your mother? Was she your jungle gym or was there more a sense of "Keep Out"?

- As a child, did you clearly feel part of your family? Did you feel bonded or adrift?

- Have you had feelings of being an orphan or motherless child?

Mother as First Responder

A very important role that secures Mother in her role as place of attachment is what I call Mother as First Responder. The "first responders" in our modern world are firefighters and police officers, the folks you call when there is an emergency. Imagine your home is on fire and no one comes. How would that affect you in terms of believing help will be there when you need it?

As many authors have convincingly shown, every need feels urgent to a baby, and thus is an emergency. As babies, we had no way of meeting our basic needs and were entirely dependent on others to be responsive to our calls for help. When our needs are consistently met, we feel secure and trust that help will be there. Without this, we learn that care is not available, the world doesn't feel friendly or supportive, and we feel more insecure and mistrustful. We don't know that we will have what we need, which jeopardizes our basic sense of trust.

The Good Mother messages related to this are "I'll take care of you. Your needs are important to me. I am here for you. You can rest in me."

Of course, to do this, a mother needs to be tuned in to her child in an accurate way. It doesn't help if the first responder goes to the wrong address, offers shelter when what's needed is food, or insists on giving you what you don't want. In psychological parlance we call this accuracy "attunement." Mother as First Responder will be helpful to the extent she is attuned to her child's needs. This is especially true for the early years before language.

This attunement and responsiveness to needs provides what is called a holding environment. With it, we feel held. This function is also what leads to *self-regulation* (described next in Mother as Modulator).

Your mother as first responder

- It may be hard to remember how your mother responded to you as an infant and small child, but often a telltale clue is how you feel about your needs now. Are you respectful and attentive to your needs, or so ashamed of needing that you try to hide them? Or perhaps you are demanding. How you respond to your own needs most often parallels how your mother responded to your needs, unless there have been a number of significant imprinting experiences that gave you a different reference point.

- What information do you have about how your mother responded to your needs? What stories have you heard? What do photographs show?

- Beyond your early childhood, what do you know about how your mother tended to respond to other people's needs? Was she Johnny-on-the-spot? Resentful? Not so competent? Gracious? Did people need to ask multiple times? Did she meet what she assumed to be others' needs rather than finding out what the real needs were?

Mother as Modulator

Mother as Modulator is very much interrelated with Mother as First Responder, but by tilting the picture just a little bit and giving it a different name, we see it in a different way.

When Mother is there as first responder, the fire doesn't rage out of control. To give but one example, the baby's hunger is met, and he can return to a state of homeostasis and rest. Imagine the intolerable discomfort when this is not true.

To *modulate* something is to make sure it's not too strong and not too weak, but falls within a more optimal range. The mother helps manage her child's physiological states, such as being hungry or cold, by meeting those specific needs. Most often when therapists are talking about regulation they are referring to our emotions. Without Mother as an effective modulator, we don't learn to effectively manage our emotions. Either we cut off feelings, or our emotional states tend to spiral out of control. Anger turns into rage, crying into hysteria; we can't contain our excitement, frustration, sexual impulses, or anything else.

Learning to modulate our internal states is called *self-regulation* or *self-modulation*. It is something the nervous system for the most part controls, but it is learned initially by the mother standing in for the developing nervous system and by meeting the child's needs before he gets totally overwhelmed. Mother as Modulator serves as a cushion to the child's fragile nervous system while it is developing.

There are a number of ways a mother can accomplish this. She can soothe the distressed child (whether through touch, words, or simply her caring presence), help the child identify needs and emotions, help turn the child's attention away from the distress, thus modulating it, and provide reassurance. One woman who has suffered lifelong anxiety told me that she never once heard her mother say, "It will be all right." Her mother never calmed her or helped her feel better.

When Mother is modulator, she helps us transition from negative emotional experiences to positive ones. One way she does this is by first empathizing with what is going on, and then leading us to more comfortable territory. She shows us how to let go of one emotion and move on to another, and in her own cheerfulness gives us something brighter to join with. We see this in the mother who meets her child's tears with a sad face and soon has her child laughing.

On a yet more subtle level, Mother modulates a child's distress through a process more recently called *limbic resonance* or *limbic regulation*. In limbic regulation, one person's emotional brain entrains another's, whose emotional brain shifts to match the first person's. All mammals have this capacity, and it is thought to be a major mechanism through which an infant or young child's inner state is directly modulated by Mother. Just by gazing into the child's eyes, the mother communicates brain to brain with her child, bringing the child's limbic system into coherence with hers. (This is helpful when Mother is in a positive, regulated state but not when she is fussy and upset herself.)

An inability to regulate physiological arousal is common in those whose childhoods match up with the description of complex trauma as found with emotionally neglectful and abusive parents. When people lacking modulation are triggered by something, they can get so upset that they can't think clearly or stay fully present. It's as if there isn't a regulator on their system, so they can't keep their physical and emotional responses within a manageable or optimal range. Although we can learn self-regulation later in life, it saves us a lot of grief if Mother helps us master this critical skill early.

Your mother as modulator

- What do you know about how your mother responded to your needs in infancy? How available was she? How many other children was she also caring for? Was she depressed or absorbed elsewhere?

- What philosophies shaped her parenting? Was she influenced by the school of thought that told parents to let their babies "cry it out"?

- Do you remember times when your mother provided reassurance or comfort when you were in distress? Did she help you through the hard times?

- Is your mother (or was she) good at regulating her own physiological needs—attending to hunger, thirst, need for sleep, or contact, for instance? Can she regulate her own emotions, keeping them in a moderate range while still truly feeling them?

- Was your mother good at tuning in to your emotional states? Did she seem to care about them? Did she teach you how to constructively manage emotions without simply suppressing them? Did she model healthy expression of emotions?

Mother as Nurturer

An essential aspect of the archetype of the Good Mother is to be nurturing. In her role as nurturer, Mother provides both physical and emotional nourishment. Often these are experienced together, as in breastfeeding. A mother feeds her baby her body and her love. Both are necessary for the baby to survive and to thrive.

Children seem to have an inherent ability to know when emotional nourishment is genuine (it truly does feed them) and when it's fake. A mother can profess to be very loving and involved with her child, and she can gain considerable recognition from the world for this, but the child will feel a hole in his soul when Mommy's love isn't genuine. It doesn't matter how many pronouncements Mother makes or how impeccable she is about physical care, if there isn't a sense of real contact and caring, the child will not experience Mother as a source of nurturance.

Since a child's first language is touch, much will be communicated by the mother's holding and handling of the infant as well as by the way she continues to touch her growing child. Does the touch communicate real caring and love, or is it simply accomplishing the task at hand?

The main message associated with this function is "I love you." This is crucial to the development of self-esteem. When it is present, the child thinks, *Mommy loves me, so I am somebody.*

Your mother as nurturer

- As a child, did you feel loved by your mother? What memories support this?

- What do you as an adult know about this? Perhaps you recognize that she did love you but was severely limited in her ability to express it, or that she was unable to love. Or perhaps you see that you were unable to let it in.

- On a scale of 1 through 10 (with 10 being extremely nurturing), where would you rank your mother in terms of being nurturing? How has she nurtured others?

Mother as Mirror

A mother's role in providing reflection is one of her most important. It is how children feel known and come to know themselves.

Mirroring happens both verbally and nonverbally, and there are several levels to it. The first is one where children feel contacted, met. When a child feels seen, she can recognize herself as a developing person. If the child feels invisible or not seen, often that child will feel not fully real. So the most fundamental message of mirroring is "I see you—and you are real."

Psychologists and others who study human development report that those qualities that are recognized in a child develop, whereas those that aren't often wither away. Think of the way children learn language: As linguists have noted, children start out making sounds from many, many languages, but only those sounds that are part of the parents' language are reinforced, and the other sounds fall out of the child's vocabulary. Similarly, emotions that are not seen, behaviors that are not seen, and qualities that are not seen or not supported either fail to develop or go underground.

Verbal mirroring involves saying things like "You're really angry!" or "You're sad right now." Verbal mirroring helps a young child identify feelings and helps people of all ages feel heard. The process isn't limited to feelings; qualities are mirrored as well. "You're a pretty girl" and "My, aren't you smart!" are other examples.

Before the child develops language, mirroring is much more physical. It involves replicating the child's expressions: laughing when the child laughs, frowning when the child frowns, and so on. Because the baby can't reflect on or sense himself at this early stage, he needs a mirror to see himself.

The basic message of "I see you" is modified by the tone involved. It can be "I see you, and you are good" or "I see you, and you are bad." The first we might call the admiring mirror; the second could be considered a shaming mirror. An admiring mirror helps us stand tall, feel proud of ourselves, feel that we have a right to be here and it's good that we're here. Our sense of value derives greatly from this positive mirroring. The admiring mirror (when sincere and realistic) helps us develop self-respect.

In order for us to really feel seen, mirroring needs to be accurate. Distorted mirroring can have several results. One is conforming to what others believe about you, whether the message is that you're a slow learner or a troublemaker. In addition, distorted mirroring can lead to an ongoing attempt to get accurate mirroring. Some children and adults get aggravated when not seen accurately and try very hard to be understood. Others give up and feel invisible. Admiration, powerful as it is, paired with distorted mirroring doesn't hit the target and therefore doesn't do any good.

A further refinement of Mother as Mirror is when Mother acts as a compass. In this role, Mother knows you so well that she calls you out when you are not being true to yourself, essentially saying, "That's not really you." As children, we try on many different costumes as we're coming to know ourselves, and having someone who knows us so well that she can (at the right time) say, "That doesn't quite fit you, darling," can be helpful. I use the word *compass* because in this role, Mother reflects to us when we're getting off course and seems to know what "true north" is to us.

Mirroring is so important that a lack of mirroring often leads to a lifelong craving for it.

Your mother as mirror

- Do you feel that your mother saw the real you? What gives you this impression?

- What nonverbal expressions, if any, stand out in your memory of your mother's response to you? (Tone of voice is also included in this category.) What did these communicate?

- Was she good at verbally naming and reflecting back your feelings and needs? If not, any ideas about why not?

- What are some aspects that she was best at mirroring, and what aspects did she miss? (For instance, she may have acknowledged your intelligence but not your feelings.)

- Did your mother know you well enough to serve as a compass, recognizing when you were not being true to *your* own nature?

Mother as Cheerleader

When Mother is functioning as cheerleader, she is providing encouragement. This has some similarities to Mother as admiring mirror. The role is expanded here to include more active encouragement, praise, and support. The message is "You can do it! I know you can. I'm behind you."

This support and encouragement is very important during the stage of exploration (eighteen months through three years of age) when the child is first moving into the world. We need someone who is not only behind us but also actively with us. In *Giving the Love That Heals: A Guide for Parents*, bestselling authors Harville Hendrix and Helen Hunt describe how a good mother does this. "She is consistently warm and available, taking time to allow the child to satisfy his curiosity and share it. She praises his successes and applauds his discoveries. She creates opportunities for him to discover more than he could on his own and makes a conscious effort for these explorations to be fun and filled with laughter."[1]

Cheerleader messages might also take the form of "I'm with you" or "I'm right here"—messages that are helpful when we're stepping into the world on wobbly feet.

We all need cheerleading at different times in life. It is especially helpful when we feel intimidated by a task. In cases where we may not have all the skills needed, it is most helpful when paired with Mother's role as mentor, which I discuss next.

A mother may have difficulty cheerleading for several reasons. She may be so undermothered and unsupported herself that she doesn't know about cheerleading, she may be more focused on her own needs for support, she may be unaware of her child's needs, or she may be threatened by her child's achievements and growing autonomy. She also may be too harried or depressed to have the energy to cheerlead.

Encouragement has to be tailored to the child and must be realistic. If there is encouragement but not enough support or if encouragement is paired with unrealistic expectations, it can be experienced as pushing. Encouragement for things already mastered, on the other hand, can leave us feeling patronized, as if Mother hasn't been paying attention and doesn't see our capacity.

When Mother does not celebrate our ordinary successes, we may feel invisible or that we have to accomplish extraordinary things (good or bad) to get her attention.

Your mother as cheerleader

- Do you think your mother was available and able to support your early discovery of the world?

- How was your mother at showing enthusiasm for your accomplishments?

- Do you believe that your mother had confidence in you? (You may have the sense that she believed in your capacities but just didn't don the cheerleading suit.)

- Can you think of a time when you needed more encouragement for something? What would you have liked to hear?

Mother as Mentor

Imagine how terrifying it would be as a four- or five-year-old child to have someone put you on a bicycle and simply walk away. When Mother is there as mentor, she functions much like a set of training wheels. The role of training wheels is to help steady you while you're learning, to provide support so you don't fall on your face.

The function we're focusing on right now is that of support and guidance—calibrated help. We could also talk about Mother as teacher or guide. The task may at times involve modeling, such as showing a child how to ride a bicycle. Developmental psychologist and author Louise Kaplan uses the analogy of a stagehand in the theater. The stagehand helps with the behind-the-scenes support that allows someone else to perform successfully. Mother as Mentor provides enough support and guidance for us to develop our capacities.

Here Mother is teacher not simply of some isolated subject but of a much bigger curriculum. She orients the child to successfully living in the world. She teaches her child how to get along with others, how to make good decisions, and how to manage time, meet responsibilities, and pursue goals. Mother is in this sense the first "life skills coach." Each of these capacities is huge, and any particular woman may be better at teaching some of them than others.

A mother will be more competent in some areas of life than others, and will also be helped or hindered by her teaching skills. Is she comfortable enough verbalizing that she can put skills into words, or does she teach only by example? Are her explanations clear and tailored to the child's needs and level of development? A good mentor does not simply go through her life hoping that others will pick up what she knows, but is actively engaged in helping others learn. She is tuned in enough to notice what skills are needed and is patient enough to teach them.

We all know that you can help too much or too little. If you help too much, you take over and deprive the other of the chance to learn; if you help too little, the person feels overwhelmed and alone. Our efforts should be calibrated by the needs of those we're helping. In the case of parenting, it should also be age appropriate. It's one thing to help a child with homework or call up an elementary school teacher when some kind of advocacy is called for, and entirely another to call up the boss of your adult child when you think too much has been handed to him.

The Good Mother's guidance honors the child's limitations without drawing attention to them and without an attitude that the child should be one step ahead of where he is. Skillful guidance feels comforting rather than controlling or invasive.

I would add a further requirement for Mother as Mentor: understanding children's developmental needs and capacities.

Many of the parents who have the most critical, punitive reactions to their children are those who expect too much and think the child is intentionally being obstinate—say, when she lacks the fine motor coordination needed to drink a glass of milk without spilling.

Being a good mentor thus requires several things:

- having developed skills yourself
- being able to break down a learning task into pieces and teach each step through clear verbal instruction and/or demonstration
- being attuned to the needs of the other
- having the time and patience required to mentor

This function has a great deal of overlap with Mother as Cheerleader: It takes encouragement and positive reinforcement for all of us to learn.

Your mother as mentor

- In what areas was your mother most engaged in mentoring you?
  - getting along with peers
  - learning to talk and articulate your experience
  - understanding and managing feelings
  - grooming and physical appearance
  - learning to deal with gadgets, tools, technology
  - showing respect for others ("manners")
  - learning various social skills
  - religious or spiritual education
  - developing academic skills
  - learning to take responsibility
  - athletics or fitness
  - good health habits
  - arts and crafts
  - homemaking skills
  - critical thinking
  - teaching you to be assertive and stand up for yourself
  - handling disappointment and frustration
- Where did you need more mentoring than you got?
- Was her help calibrated to your needs? Did she help too much or too little?
- What attitudes were communicated through her help? (For example, that you were a bother, that she treasured you and wanted to help, that you could need help and still be deserving of respect, that you were a slow learner or quick learner, that she enjoyed teaching you ...)

Mother as Protector

How a mother provides protection for a child varies with different developmental stages. At first it involves providing a safe enclosure. The womb is the initial enclosure, and the symbiotic (undifferentiated) relationship is the second. Within this, the child does not feel separate, so the qualities of the mother's being and her feelings for the child are all part of the environment the baby exists within. The child needs to feel safe there.

With separateness comes danger. In the best of circumstances, Mother is there providing protection. A very young child often senses Mother as all-powerful. She shatters the darkness, shoos away noisy children and barking dogs. If the mother consistently protects the child from intrusive and overwhelming stimuli, the child feels safe. Mother here is morphing from safe enclosure to Mama Bear.

With more development, the child gains autonomy and the freedom to roam and explore, but the mother is never far away and at the first sign of danger is there fiercely protecting her offspring. The message associated with this function is "I'll keep you safe."

Still later, the child is sent out into the world with a set of rules and boundaries that are like an invisible fence, intended to keep the child out of harm's way. If children are not given these rules in a way that they can accept, or if they reject the rules as part of rejecting parental control, children are cast adrift, as their own judgment is often insufficient to protect them. To fully carry out this role of protector, a mother must teach her children about boundaries and self-protection.

Of course a mother can also be overprotective, not allowing her children as much room as they need to experience the world, or she can be protective in ways that communicate her mistrust in the child's capacities or perhaps her own mistrust of the world. How well Mother fulfills this role of protector cannot be reduced to only *whether* she provided protection but must also include *how* she provided it.

Your mother as protector

- What is your feeling reaction to imagining your mother as safe enclosure?

- What frustrations and dangers did she not adequately protect you from?

- Can you identify ways she did protect you?

- Did your mother teach you about protecting yourself? In what kinds of situations?

- What do you wish she taught you about self-protection that she did not?

- Did her way of protecting you feel more comforting to you or suffocating? Did it feel caring?

Mother as Home Base

The message associated with this is "I'm here for you." When you really take that in, then even in adulthood you will reference Mother as the place you can always come back to for refueling, comfort, or support. When the world beats you down, when your marriage falls apart, when your feelings are hurt, you can always turn to Mother. This is similar to the period of development called *rapprochement*, where the child is first separating from Mother, venturing into the world, and yet goes back and forth, back and forth, returning to Mother for psychological refueling.

Mother is our first home base, later replaced (or partially replaced if she maintains that role) by subsequent relationships and whatever we identify as *home*—be it community, country, place, or something else.

If Mother is not consistently available, is self-absorbed or absorbed elsewhere, is erratic and unstable or unable to be emotionally present for the child, then we don't experience her as home base. There is no Mother's lap. This may show up in adulthood as difficulty establishing a sense of home.

Your mother as home base

- There may have been times both in childhood and in adulthood when you turned to Mother for help. What happened?

- If you do not feel comfortable turning to her, notice how that feels in your body and what self-protections come up. What do your inner voices say?

When any one of these essential functions is missing, it leaves a hole in our development. Understanding what holes are there is a first step in eventually filling that hole. We will return to the issue of making up for specific deficits later in this book.

Working through this chapter may have left you feeling a bit glum. The vast majority of the undermothered have known few, if any, of these faces of the Good Mother. Please don't despair! None of these holes needs to be permanent. While it is true they will likely not be filled by the mother you grew up with, we can experience all of these functions somewhere in our adult lives.

3.

Attachment: Our First Foundation

OUR FIRST INTERPERSONAL TASK in life is to bond with our primary caregiver, in most cases our mother. This is essential to our survival, since as babies we are totally dependent on someone to meet our basic needs. The term *attachment* is most often used when referring to this bond, and there has been a great deal of research into attachment behaviors and "styles." Attachment has a significant impact on our brain development, mental health, and future relationships.

Although a child's relationship with his or her mother is not the only contributor to these things, it is the original and in most cases the primary influence. Fortunately, we can also form secure attachments with fathers, grandparents, nannies, day care workers, and others in a caretaking role, and we can form secure attachments in adulthood with mother figures, therapists, friends, and partners, thus reaping many of the benefits that bypassed us earlier.

How do we become attached, and what is secure attachment?

Attachment begins in the first relationship of life, the relationship with Mother. This relationship begins early, even before birth, but is certainly shaped by the first hours, weeks, and months of life. It can be heavily influenced by the circumstances of birth, including the parents' readiness and desire for the baby, the mother's mental and emotional state around birth, and birth procedures. (Studies show that mothers who give birth by cesarean section take longer to attach to their babies.[1]) Even the levels of mothers' hormones have been found to have an effect, with higher levels of oxytocin supporting more attachment behaviors by mothers.[2] Many different ingredients contribute to the quality of attachment between mother and child.

Attachment is built through attunement and caring. In the infant-mother relationship, it is spun largely out of the infant's needs (expressed in what are called attachment behaviors) and the mother's responses to these needs. In fact the mother's responses, their consistency and quality, are the key ingredient.[3]

Research indicates that attachment is created not just from meeting the immediate physical needs of the infant but also from the *quality* of these interactions. The baby looks at Mother, who is, in turn, looking at baby, and something passes between them: a smile, a mirroring movement, a synchronized dance way below the level of consciousness.

The most important caretaker behaviors associated with secure attachment are these:

- Responding to the child's physical and emotional needs promptly, consistently, and in an attuned way.

- Responding to the child's attempts at closeness in a welcoming way. The mother must meet the child who is reaching for her, not turn away or provide only a cool reception. She must show that she wants closeness, too.

- Tuning in to the child's emotional states and demonstrating empathy.

- Looking at the child with love. One researcher reports that this is the most critical element in developing the part of the brain responsible for social behaviors.[4]

When we know that we can go to Mother and our needs will be met and our feelings will be understood and welcomed, we feel *secure* in that relationship. I have stated this as an older child might experience it, but the pattern is largely set in the first year of life, when our knowing is at a much more primitive level. Mother is either there or not there when we cry; she takes care of our needs, or she does not. In the developmental model of psychologist Erik Erikson, this relates to the basic sense of trust or mistrust that we develop in the first year of life. When the world (generally in the person of Mother) meets our needs consistently, we develop trust that we will have what we need and the world is perceived to be a safe place. This is what many today call *secure attachment*.

There is a significant amount of evidence that if a secure attachment is created in these early months and is not interrupted (by loss, by separations that are too much for the child, or by a loss of attunement), it will tend to be consistent throughout childhood.

Why is attachment so important?

The attachment bond, which is the glue between the child and an attachment figure, is critical for many areas of development.

First, it very naturally affects self-esteem. "Secure individuals learn to perceive themselves as strong and competent, valuable, lovable, and special—thanks to being valued, loved, and viewed as special by caring attachment figures."[5] They score higher on every measure of self-esteem.[6]

Second, secure attachment gives us what is called a secure base, which means exactly what you might guess: the security needed to go into the world and explore it. When we don't feel this security, we're less ready to leave the nest or even to look inside ourselves, and thus are hampered in our development.

Author and therapist Susan Anderson describes how secure attachment allows for eventual independence:

As a young child, you needed to connect in order to move forward. As an infant, you depended on your mother to give the nurturance you needed, and your attention focused almost exclusively on that relationship. When you were a toddler, she became a background object as you began to develop and function more independently. . . . If something interfered with that development—if Mommy had to go to the hospital for a long stay—your ability to function independently may have been delayed.[7]

Anderson goes on to explain that when your need for attachment is thwarted, it becomes primary; when satisfied, it blends into the background. Both children and adults with secure attachment aren't hung up on getting other people to see or support them and can focus on meeting other needs.

In addition to providing a secure base from which to explore the world and attend to other things, attachment correlates with a number of long-term effects. Studies show that securely attached children have enhanced emotional flexibility, social functioning, and cognitive abilities.[8] They are better at initiating.[9] As middle school children, they handle frustration and challenge better, and when they start falling behind, they try harder rather than collapse as insecure children do.[10] Secure children become well-adjusted adults with the ability to form secure attachments and regulate their emotions, and they hold a positive outlook on the world.[11]

In contrast, a number of studies suggest that the various forms of insecure attachment can be associated with emotional rigidity, difficulty in social relationships, impairments in attention, difficulty in understanding the minds of others, and risk in the face of stressful situations.[12]

The latter is because the stress response is less healthy in those with insecure attachment. Stress response plays a role in our susceptibility to many mental and physical illnesses. The stress response is mediated by the hormone cortisol, and insecurely attached children are disadvantaged by having too much of it circulating. High levels of cortisol have been associated with depression, anxiety, suicidal tendencies, eating disorders, and alcoholism. Too much cortisol can damage parts of the brain responsible for retrieving information and thinking clearly.[13] High cortisol is also believed to contribute to insomnia.

Researchers have studied how the interactions that are the basis of secure attachment affect brain development and functioning.[14] The area of the brain most involved in complex social behaviors (so much so that it is sometimes referred to as the social brain) is particularly sensitive to these early interactions. It will sound like an oversimplification, but these caring, attuned interactions actually grow this part of our brains, which is responsible for important social abilities and social intelligence.[15]

So considering everything from the growth of neurons to one's sense of self-esteem, the security of our attachment is very important. Some consider this the most critical of all childhood needs.

How can you know if you were securely attached to your mother?

You won't know precisely what your relationship with your mother was in your earliest years, but here are some important clues:

- moments from your early relationship that were captured in memories

- your current feelings about your early relationship with your mother

- your patterns in relationships throughout your life and specifically your ability to form strong bonds with others

Since this last item is complex, it will take some time to get a clear picture of it. First, let's explore your early relationship with your mother:

- Do you have memories of close moments, her holding you lovingly, smiling and expressing affection? If so, do they seem like moments that were the exception or the rule?

- Do you have memories of going to your mother in times of need? What kinds of need? Is this representative of typical childhood needs? How did your mother respond?

- As far as you can remember or checking in with your feeling response, were your attempts at closeness welcomed?

- What descriptions have you heard about yourself as a baby and small child?

You may not be able to remember much about your early relationships, yet your feelings and impulses are often clues, leftovers from interactions you can't consciously recall. They have something to teach you. Listen, if you can.

What if you weren't securely attached? How would that look?

If you weren't securely attached, you've got a fair amount of company. Research indicates that about one third of children experience insecure attachment, which tends to be transmitted from one generation to the next.[16] This number climbs to half in children whose mothers are depressed.[17]

A number of "styles" of insecure attachment have been described. Since various writers in the field use different terms to describe these styles, it sometimes gets confusing. For each style, I have chosen the term that seems most memorable and descriptive and included the equivalent terms that the better-known researchers have used.

SELF-SUFFICIENT STYLE

The largest of the insecure categories is a style that has been called by several names—*compulsively self-sufficient* (Bowlby), *avoidant* (Ainsworth), and *dismissive* (Main, referring to this style in adults).

When the mother is consistently rejecting or nonresponsive and emotionally unavailable, the child gives up, learns it is futile or dangerous in relationships to need, and consequently turns off his or her needs and attachment feelings. This, in essence, is what this style is all about.

More specifically, mothers of avoidant children have been found to:

- reject the infant's needs for attachment and the behaviors the infant uses to try to get attachment

- be uncomfortable or hostile toward signs of dependency

- dislike affectionate, face-to-face contact

- be more aversive to cuddly contact and physical contact

- show less emotion[18]

When mothers don't show enjoyment when holding their babies, babies eventually seem to turn off their more natural desire to be cuddled. When held, they tend to go limp like a sack of potatoes.

These children have "turned off wanting." Of course you can't fully turn off wanting; you just disconnect from your awareness of it. Your wanting gets relegated to the unconscious, where it remains in very primitive form and has a sense of great urgency attached to it.

Children in this situation perceive that their parents don't want to deal with their needs and feelings and learn to conceal their emotions. The same child who goes limp like a sack of potatoes as an infant is the school-aged child with one-word responses when Mother asks about his day and who keeps Mother at arm's length. This child will not go to Mother for help. Even if she wanted to connect more with him later on, the child is now on guard, hidden behind a wall.

Cutting off feelings has costs. Without the caregiver noticing and responding to feelings, children—and later adults—will have a harder time noticing their own feelings and putting them into words. They also won't be good at having a nuanced understanding of other people's feelings.[19] As you can imagine, the lack of feeling awareness and feeling talk will hamper them in later intimate relationships, where they will appear more cloaked and cut off. Just as with wanting, their feelings won't go away but rather lurk beneath consciousness.

People who predominantly have this attachment style have turned off their attachment needs and, as one researcher suggests, become deaf to attachment-related signals.[20] Better to be as self-sufficient as possible. A person with this style is more armored in relationships and tends to not allow much closeness. Letting others close enough to develop real feelings of attachment even much later in life feels scary; it is too close to the unbearable pain of feeling rejected as an infant when one was so utterly dependent.

PREOCCUPIED STYLE

A different expression of insecure attachment consists of what we more traditionally think of as insecure behaviors, such as clinging, needing reassurance, and always wanting more closeness. The chief fear in this pattern is of the attachment figure leaving, what we might call a fear of abandonment. Of course the self-sufficient type fears abandonment, too, but protects herself by not letting the relationship feel as important as it is to her.

This second style has been called *anxious attachment* (Bowlby), *compulsive care seeking, ambivalent* (Ainsworth), *dependent,* and *preoccupied.* All of these names reflect some important quality in the pattern. The dependence and care seeking are obvious; the ambivalence, slightly more complex. Children with this style show both a heightened need for closeness *and* an angry, rejecting quality. In the Strange Situation, a much-used research design, one-year-old children are extremely distressed at being left by Mother but have a difficult time accepting her ministrations when she tries to patch things up. They go back and forth between being very demanding and clingy and being hostile. I've chosen the term *preoccupied* because through both sets of behaviors, these children (and later adults) are so anxiously tied up with how available others are that it dominates their lives.

This style of attachment has been correlated with mothers who are less consistently rejecting than the self-sufficient children had, but not consistently responsive enough to create secure attachment. Sometimes they're there; sometimes they're not. Sometimes they are experienced as loving; other times, as inexplicably rejecting. The preoccupied child (and later adult) doesn't know what to expect.

Insecure attachment styles are actually strategies for managing the uncomfortable emotions aroused by Mother's inconsistency, according to author Diana Fosha. "Their coping style—watching Mother like a hawk and clinging to her to reassure themselves she won't disappear again—is their way of managing their fear and pain associated with the inconsistency."[21]

Unfortunately the strategies used to secure the desired attachment often drive people away. By the time we reach adulthood, these include:

- heightened needs for closeness
- hypervigilance about attachment signals

- always questioning and testing the other's commitment

- emphasizing need and helplessness in order to get others to stay

- punishing others for not providing what is desired

- anger when attachment needs are not met

Being alone, especially during times of distress, is upsetting for those with anxious attachment, and they don't do well when their attachment figures go away. In later relationships, they are likely to feel insecure when their romantic partner goes away, and more likely to be jealous. Those with an anxious attachment style are always looking for love.[22]

Children with this style appear too caught up in attachment concerns to explore their world, and there is some evidence that adults with this style are so preoccupied with relationships that they turn into underachievers.[23]

Sometimes people show elements of both of these patterns: for example, alternating between cutting off feelings and plunging into them headlong, or acting detached and self-sufficient and then collapsing into a dependent pattern. What is common to all forms of insecure attachment is a lack of confidence that others will be emotionally available and can be counted on to provide support.

CARETAKER STYLE

Another pattern identified in attachment theory is called *compulsive caregiving*. In this pattern you deny your own needs and focus on the other person's.[24] You help other people (whether they want it or not) as a way to be close to them. It is associated with mothers who were not able to provide for their children but welcomed their children's caretaking of them.[25]

Most modern attachment theorists don't include this style, and there is some evidence pairing a caretaker style in adulthood with a preoccupied style as a child,[26] which makes intuitive sense, since caretaking is one way to maintain connection.

DISORGANIZED STYLE

Some children fit a pattern that is called *disorganized* or *disoriented* attachment. Here, there isn't a consistent pattern. These children show behaviors characteristic of one or more other attachment styles alternating with moments of confusion and fear. This is the pattern found in the majority of children who are abused.

Of course abusive parents aren't only abusive; sometimes they provide needed care. So they are both a source of fear and a source of reassurance, and this is understandably confusing.[27]

The behavior of the child is likewise inconsistent. Such a child may appear confused or apprehensive in the presence of that parent and even dazed at times. How can you know whether it's safe to go to Mommy if sometimes she comforts you and other times she seems to spiral out of control and hits you? And why is she sometimes so spaced out? (Neglectful and abusive parents are often untreated trauma victims.)

Disorganized attachment is also often found in children whose parents abuse alcohol or drugs, or are chronically depressed.[28]

These children are often found to take on caretaking roles with their parents, in essence abandoning the child role altogether. It's a pretty smart response, if you think about it. Children in these situations often see that adults can't really be trusted or aren't very competent, so taking a provider role is probably safer.

Some of the effects associated with disorganized attachment include:

- marked impairments in emotional, social, and cognitive functioning[29]

- not being able to soothe yourself[30]

- feeling that you are to blame for what was done to you and that you are of no value[31]

- feeling alienated from the world around you

- being vigilant and distrustful, avoiding intimacy[32]

- use of dissociation, distraction, and/or aggression or withdrawal as coping mechanisms[33]

- smaller brain size and damage to fibers connecting the two sides of the brain[34]

While disorganized attachment is the most insecure of the attachment styles that have been identified, it is not the same as an *attachment disorder*, a term that refers to a condition of nonattachment and most often refers to *reactive attachment disorder* (RAD). With RAD, a child does not develop an attachment relationship with primary caregivers or easily develop relationships with anyone. It is associated with severe early neglect, abuse, abrupt separation from caregivers before three years of age, and frequent change of caregivers.

What is attachment-related trauma?

A number of events related to attachment figures are traumatic for a child. For a young child, being left alone is traumatic.[35] A separation that is more than the child can handle is traumatic. Significant disruptions in the attachment relationship or loss of an attachment figure is traumatic. Physical or sexual abuse by an attachment figure is traumatic.

Being abandoned as a child in times of urgent need is also traumatic and leads to attachment injuries. An example is telling a parent that another parent is abusing you, and having the parent you tell not believe you or either ignore or minimize what you've said and not protect you. Remember, your relationships with attachment figures are where you're supposed to learn that the world is safe. Secure attachment grows from your needs being met. Not being protected or being overlooked in a state of emergency will be felt as abandonment and perhaps a violation.

Trauma at any age is devastating (see my book *Healing from Trauma*), but when you combine it with an attachment figure its mark is nearly indelible.

Maybe you weren't securely attached to your mother, but is it really fair to hold her responsible?

Although children come into the world with significant differences, there is considerable support for the notion that the caretaker's behavior is critical in forming secure attachment. Particularly telling is the fact that an infant may be securely attached to one parent and insecurely attached to another. When this is the case, the infant clearly has the capacity to attach, given proper responsiveness.

There is evidence that coaching mothers and helping them become more responsive to their child can alter the attachment pattern. In a short time, improvements in a mother's attuned responsiveness lead to increasingly secure attachment in their children.[36]

Holding Mother responsible for our insecure attachment is not saying that she is somehow bad or even uncaring. There are many things that may be going on. For one, she may love her baby but feel frightened or repulsed by being needed. Unfortunately this often leads to a vicious cycle, because the more she withdraws or withholds her care, the more the baby signals his need, and it is this signaling of need and the urgency behind it that may frighten the mother. Other contributors include being unskilled at reading a baby's signals; being preoccupied, overwhelmed, or depressed; being insecure and overly sensitive to rejection; or having been undermothered herself. If her mother was not able to graciously give to her or attune to her needs, if her mother was too busy or too cold, then this is the pattern branded into her, which she unwittingly repeats. Often people find it elicits deep hurt and is hard to tolerate when others receive what was so painfully missing for them, and mothers are subject to this, too.

We'll talk later about coming to a more objective understanding of what was going on with your mother, but for now it's better to give the responsibility for your early relationship and attachment style to her than to somehow wonder what you did wrong. Even when you were part of the dance, as in the complicated situation where both mother and child mirror each other's turning away, it is the mother, as the adult, who has the greater responsibility to become aware and change the pattern.

Can you still develop secure attachments if you've only partially done so in the past? How would this help you?

Even if you have never had a secure attachment, it's never too late to develop one. There are many benefits to secure attachment. They include:

- giving you an anchor in the world, a place where you are connected

- supporting a more positive picture of people and more optimistic sense about your life

- helping to build a sense of security that you keep with you

- offering you a place to rest, where you are not alone but rather held by another

- providing a platform of good feelings that strengthens self-esteem and confidence

- making it more likely that you can reach out to others in the future with your needs

- strengthening favorable neural pathways and stimulating brain development

- improving your capacity to self-regulate (p. 28)

Developing secure attachments with trustworthy others is important in healing the deficits left by undermothering.

Identifying attachment figures

Often as adults our attachment figures are intimate partners, but they may also include therapists or other helpers, mother substitutes, and best friends. Some children have imaginary friends who perhaps fill some of these needs, and many people— adults as well as children—rely on pets for a sense of comfort and connection.

If you are unsure who might be serving as an attachment figure for you or potentially could, here are some questions to ask yourself:

- Who do I feel comfortable going to when I am most upset? Who can I go to in times of need?

- Who do I trust really cares about how I'm doing? Who cares about me for *me* (and not what I give them)?

- If I were in a state of almost complete dependency (say, after a major accident or illness), who would I want to be with?

- Who can I trust to be consistently there for me?

What is your attachment style?

If you haven't already identified yourself with a particular attachment style, you might find it interesting to read the following descriptions and see which is more like you. Note that these are oriented toward adults and close relationships rather than the infant-mother relationship.[37] I've also limited them to three items each. Research scales have been developed that are quite long, but this small sample can give you a taste.

Style A:

- I often worry that romantic partners don't really love me or won't want to stay with me. I can get obsessed and act quite jealous at times, even in friendships.
- Sometimes my desire for closeness scares other people away.
- I don't understand when others appear to not see my needs. If they cared about me, they would not let me hurt like this.

Style B:

- I don't like to have to depend on others. It feels like a setup for being hurt.
- I would rather not show my vulnerability to others. In fact, I would rather not *feel* vulnerable!
- I am nervous when someone gets too close to me.

Style C:

- I am comfortable depending on others and having them depend on me.
- I find it relatively easy to get close to people.
- I trust that others will be there (most of the time) when I need them.

Style D:

- I get close to others by meeting their needs.

- I think that if I meet enough of their needs, they won't leave me.

- There doesn't seem to be room for both of our needs.

If it wasn't already clear, A is the preoccupied style, B is self-sufficient, C represents secure attachment, and D is compulsive caregiving. Since disorganized attachment is the absence of a clear style, it is much harder to self-identify using an instrument such as this. If you still don't identify with these attachment styles, there are much longer attachment style quizzes online with a graded scale that will give you a clearer view of your attachment strategies.

There are many ways to dig deeper into your attachment style, and I'll mention a few other things that you may notice in your life now.

One interesting clue is how you respond to perceived abandonment. Some of the early research in attachment styles was done by having mothers leave their toddlers for a brief time and then reenter the room (the Strange Situation). The children with the more defended, detached style (self-sufficient) had the hardest time reconnecting when Mother came back. Often they ignored her. These children, in essence, communicated, "Oh, you. You're not important to me." Instead, they focused on what they were doing. The ambivalently attached, (preoccupied style) tended to fuss more when Mother left, yet showed resentment when she came back, with displays of either anger or helplessness.

Notice what your style has been in situations in which someone you are attached to has left. Does it feel too vulnerable to show loved ones that you miss them? Do you find it hard to warm up again when they return? Are you so focused on the loss that it's hard to let it go when the person returns (as is typical of preoccupied, ambivalent attachment)? Do you want to punish them for having been gone (as the preoccupied/ambivalent are more prone to do)? In the research described above, it was young children's response to reconnecting with their mothers more than how they responded to separations that was most indicative of their attachment style.

I believe our basic security or insecurity also gets reflected by our response to disappointment and hurt in important relationships. What happens for you when someone has disappointed you? Maybe you were expecting to receive an acknowledgment of an important event in your life and it was totally forgotten. Do you feel crushed, even if the oversight was minor? Do you pull your heart back a little? Do you want to punish the other in some small way? Do you try to make it unimportant to you and hide your disappointment, or can you show it? Secure attachments build more resilience and allow us to be more expressive. I would expect those with a more self-sufficient style to hide feelings of hurt and disappointment (as well as desire for closeness) and those with the preoccupied style to perhaps accentuate such feelings, using guilt if needed, in an effort to create a more secure relationship. (I am focusing on these two subtypes of insecurity, as they are the most researched and talked about.)

Can you have more than one style?

You can certainly have characteristics of more than one of these styles. Rather than focus too exclusively on these categories, it may be more helpful to look at various spectrums that can be associated with them, such as your comfort with dependency and showing vulnerability, your capacity for closeness, your ability to handle feelings, and your sense of security and being wanted—all matters we'll continue to address in later chapters.

It may also be helpful to think about these as qualities of particular relationships. Just as a child may show different attachment styles with each parent, we show an assortment of attachment-related qualities in our various adult relationships. The value of looking at styles is to illuminate these elements and discover patterns. It's also valuable to consider that these patterns were first established in our most significant early relationships.

Does your relationship with your mother really affect later relationships?

Whether you had no relationship with your mother, had a secure and happy one, or fall somewhere in between, it is impossible to escape the influence of this central relationship.

What happened to you as an infant and young child powerfully shapes how you see yourself and other people, what expectations you have for relationships, how you feel about yourself, and what defensive (and healthy!) habits you've learned.

For example, if you enjoyed secure attachment, you learned that showing your needs for closeness or comfort or expressing your needs in general was okay; in fact, it was the basis of forming relationships. If, however, your mother (or mothering figure) pretty consistently rejected these bids for affection, support, and protection, you learned not only to stop showing these needs but also to cut off your own awareness of them (self-sufficient style). If Mother was inconsistent, sometimes responding positively and sometimes not, you may have learned that the only way to make sure your attachment needs are met is to keep focused on them, keep close tabs on the people you are in relationships with, and continue highlighting your feelings and needs (preoccupied style).

Take a moment now to reflect on your own situation.

- From what you've learned so far, what can you see about your pattern of showing or not showing attachment needs? How does this relate to your experiences as an adolescent and adult?

- How does this relate to the attachment patterns you imagine you had as a child with your mother?

How difficult is it to change attachment patterns?

It is easiest to change insecure attachment patterns as a child. I've mentioned that coaching mothers to better attune to their infants can have very rapid, positive results. The longer a pattern is in place within a particular relationship, the harder it is to reverse.

Insecurely attached children are thought to be relatively amenable to change throughout their early years, although this is primarily tied to their ability to develop a secure attachment that helps offset (and provides an alternative to) their insecure attachment with their mother.[38] Research has shown that a secure attachment to the father (or to another secondary caregiver) is the most important factor in children compensating for or overcoming an insecure attachment to the mother.[39]

It's considered a bit tougher as an adult to change our fundamental pattern of attachment, but by then we have a new set of options. We're more able to do the therapeutic work involved in grieving old wounds, uncovering core beliefs, and establishing new ways of being. Having relationships that create new, healthier patterns can change our expectations and attitudes and give us a new foundation from which to work. We'll talk more about all of this in later chapters.

Remember, we are wired to form attachment relationships. It is how nature intended it.

4.

More Building Blocks

ATTACHMENT IS ONLY ONE of the many building blocks that make us who we are. In this chapter we'll do a quick review of the secure relationship and then proceed to other elements that help support a child's developing sense of self.

Feeling safe and secure

Safety and security are experienced somewhat differently for a child than for many adults—although, as some have noted, In times of emergency we all want contact (including touch) with the people most important to us. When the bombs are flying, we cling to those we hold most dear.

For the young child, safety is being enveloped in an attuned, caring environment. It's not about locks on the doors but the sense that "Mommy will watch out for me; Mommy will remember me. I'm precious to her, and she's not going to forget about me." If Mommy is preoccupied, distracted, or annoyed and doesn't provide this, the child feels less safe. When you are dependent, security is feeling that the person you rely on is dependable.

To appreciate the vulnerability of dependency, imagine that you are flying in a plane that has only one pilot—and you realize that the pilot is drunk. Or you're just going under for surgery, and it dawns on you that the surgeon doesn't know what she is doing. For the young child with an emotionally absent mother, it's like discovering the captain of the ship is just a mannequin and not really human.

The child's sense of safety is built from many things—feeling the mother's competence, sensing her attunement to the child, and feeling held. Writing from the perspective of a very young inner child, one woman recorded this in her journal:

I want to be held in a pink blanket with support all around me. I want to feel securely held, securely contained. Secure. That seems like a new feeling. Wrapped in a warm, safe place with lots of protection around me. . . . If I was securely contained, I wouldn't need to hold myself together.

This last phrase is interesting given the comment by pediatrician and psychoanalyst D. W. Winnicott, who said that the mother "holds the child's bits together." She is his glue, his container. When the mother is really there, lovingly holding the child, it gives the child something to hold on to. Ultimately, that is the mother's heart.

It's worth repeating that this sense of security provided by the relationship, this secure base, is what makes it safe for the child to explore the world. When we have a safe place to come back to, we can leave, just as when we are securely held, we don't need to cling. Research shows that secure babies explore when they feel safe and seek connection when they do not. This is our innate programming.

Not feeling safe, on the other hand, is the setup for anxiety to take hold. Anxiety, which is seen by many in the mental health fields as the basis of unhealthy defenses and the root of psychopathology, starts here. It comes from feeling alone and unsupported in situations we can't handle by ourselves and from being in relationships with unavailable or unresponsive caregivers.[1]

A happy home

For the child, the secure relationship with Mother is a first-level container for his growth, and a happy home is a larger, second container. It would be like a houseplant potted in good soil and then kept in a room with the right light and temperature.

A happy home is a place that feels good to be in. People feel friendly toward one another and at peace within themselves. Members recognize that the family is a cooperative unit in which everyone's needs and satisfaction are important, and, as a child, you feel that your needs are considered right at the top of the list. Knowing this gives you a place. It gives you support for having needs and for being yourself.

In a happy home, there aren't continuing crises you need to solve (or wonder how to endure when you're too young to solve anything). People aren't stuck in power struggles. There aren't silent or not-so-silent wars between family members. In a happy home you're not all holding your breath. You can relax and be yourself.

A happy home may have a second parent (not necessarily of the opposite sex), but it doesn't have to. It helps Mommy be happy if she has the support of other important adults. It certainly doesn't help her when there is ongoing friction in those relationships. In a happy home there may or may not be other children, may or may not be pets. In a home steeped in the feelings of strain and deprivation, more beings to take care of saps a mother, but in a happy home Mother seems to have enough to provide for everyone without resentment. She seems to enjoy giving! (This may be a shock for those whose experience has been quite different.)

Feeling that Mommy is happy is a great boon to a child. Imagine for a moment a snapshot of Mother smiling and laughing. She's happy to be here. She's happy with you and anyone else in the picture, and she doesn't need things to be any different than they are in that moment. She is relaxed! When Mommy is relaxed and smiling, we sense that her world is right. And when her world is right, then our world is right.

But when Mommy is distracted or worried or depressed, we don't have the same kind of support, and it's harder for us to relax and be fully present. It doesn't feel quite right to be expansive and expressive when Mommy is withdrawn or frazzled. There isn't really a place to be happy, unless we're putting on a happy face trying to cheer Mother up. Mother's happiness relieves us of these burdens, and we can simply express ourselves as we are.

When things go wrong, they can be fixed!

A happy, healthy home is not without problems, but these problems can be fixed rather than swept under the rug where they gather into huge mounds. Conflicts are resolved, and there are competent adults who can problem-solve a variety of needs.

This is critically important in the arena of relationships. A child needs to know that there can be angry feelings and times of falling-out, but these ruptures can be repaired. In chapter 1, I described how the good-enough mother is frequently off the mark and that repairing ruptures in relationships again and again is part of securing the bond and creating a sense of resilience. This is true whether we're talking about the mother-child bond, a therapist-client relationship, a relationship with a partner, or any other significant relationship. We need to know that the other can manage the upsetting feelings that come with such ruptures and won't go away, and that together we can fix it.

We don't know this without experience. I remember how shocked I was when in a therapy session with my therapist, my frustration and anger finally burst out against her—and my next thought was that I could now kiss our relationship goodbye. I apparently held a belief that if I expressed my anger, I would destroy our bond forever. The relationship was not ruined; in fact, it was strengthened. But I had no reference, no previous experience to tell me this could be so. I had never dared express my anger at my family and had a marked lack of experience in this process of rupture and repair.

Knowing that ruptures can be repaired is another aspect of secure attachment and contributes to a child's sense of resilience.

A sense of belonging

Many factors go into creating a sense of belonging for a child. There are obvious external things, like sharing the same name, having the same home, and perceiving a likeness with family members—sharing the same look of the eyes or nose or mouth.

Secure attachment creates a deep sense of belonging, because it anchors you, giving you a place in the web of life. That place is bigger than any one relationship, but Mother as our first relationship sets the stage. Later, we may find belonging by knowing that we are part of a team, a tribe, a neighborhood, a club, a community, a nation, or a social movement—or by having our own children and partner. When we have a sense of belonging at several of these levels, we feel embedded, part of something.

Feeling valued and known are also part of this belonging. If a family claims you as their own but you don't really feel that they know you or see you for who you are, you'll feel like an outsider within your own family.

The budding self

A baby's emerging self is highly impressionable, and a good mother knows that. She treats it with utmost care and respect, just as she treats the growing bond between them. Their interactions are like passing a shuttle of yarn back and forth, weaving a connection between their hearts.

These interactions are critical in shaping the sense of self. The baby's sense of self does not yet take the form of a separate individual but is steeped in the feelings of the relationship with an Other—in this case, with Mother.

Mother is the facilitator of the child's developing self, and her support and encouragement of the child's emerging qualities are essential. For the child's "true self" to have a chance to take hold, it needs to be seen. The only way the child knows that she is seen is by other people mirroring back her feelings and experiences, acknowledging and celebrating them. If the child's unique qualities are not mirrored or supported, they are not available for her as a foundation. Instead of becoming grounded in her own nature, she adapts to what she thinks she is supposed to be, taking on a false self. For some people, this false self (which we all have to some degree) so obscures everything else that it's all they know.

A place to grow

If we are to have any chance at becoming our true self, we need an environment in which we can grow into ourselves, one that provides the ingredients we need in order to develop fully. Just as insufficient minerals in the soil will dwarf a plant's growth and change its character, insufficient nutrients in the early environment stunt our development.

These nutrients include unconditional acceptance ("I accept you just as you are"), respect, and value, in addition to the mirroring and attuned responsiveness already discussed. You need to be valued for who you are and also valued simply because of the fact *that* you are. If you don't get this, you feel out of place and like you don't belong. This makes it hard to embrace life.

What is respected and valued in a particular family is what gets reinforced. Here is an exercise to explore this.

- Look at the following list and note which of these your family valued.
  - intelligence
  - mastery and achievement
  - sweetness

- innocence
- delicacy
- sensitivity
- hardiness
- humor and silliness
- being tough
- being affectionate
- needing others
- being confident and, on occasion, "full of yourself"
- being in your body in a sensual way, enjoying your contact with the world
- being attractive
- helping behaviors
- expression of feelings
- imagination and creativity

• Note which of these same qualities were disregarded, almost as if they didn't exist. Which were mocked or belittled? What can you see about this? What happened to those qualities that were not valued when you were growing up?

We can give ourselves a new experience by working deeply with imagination. To do this, select a quality that was not supported, and then imagine someone important to you recognizing this quality in you and really celebrating it. Imagine this person saying that it is one of the things he or she likes most about you. Notice what you feel in response. Take that feeling all the way in, experiencing it in your body.

Often we need to work through our own rejection of the qualities that were not valued and fight for the right to have these qualities or behave in these ways.

Support for being a child

Think about the characteristics that are simply part of being a very young child. These include the following:

- being dependent
- having needs
- having limited tolerance for frustration, needing things to be just right for us
- being innocent and naive
- being undeveloped and without mastery
- expressing emotions quite immediately and authentically
- seeking closeness and affection
- being delicate and sweet

Aren't these characteristics universally found in children of all cultures and conditions if they are not censured?

Now the more telling question: Aren't these the very qualities that are often ignored or rejected in our families? To the extent this is so, we are valued not for being a child, but for growing out of it.

Of course we need our parents to cheer us on and value our growing independence and mastery, but too often for the undermothered there has been more support for this side of development than for the innate characteristics of being a child. There is often more interest in our outgrowing early childhood needs than there is in meeting these needs.

There may be numerous reasons that parents reject these softer qualities. In their own development, they often had to skip over this same stage as quickly as possible. A woman whose sweetness got no support as a little girl, for example, will find it difficult to embrace her child's sweetness. It rubs up against her own wound. This is true for dependency, sensitivity, and the other softer qualities. Maybe a mother's innocence was torn away from her by early hardship or abuse and she blamed herself for being open and undefended. She will see this condition as dangerous and feel uncomfortable when her child seems vulnerable.

There may be times when undue stress and hardship interfere with a mother's ability to nurture these softer qualities, but often the culprit lies in her own childhood experience. Also, if she was expected to grow up fast and quickly leave childhood needs and limitations behind, she often will have an unrealistic expectation of what her child is capable of. It is these mothers who often become angry and abusive.

- Looking again at the innate characteristics of a young child, which of these do you think your parents supported?

- What, if anything, do you think made it difficult for your mother to embrace these softer qualities?

To develop naturally, we need to grow at our own pace. In fact, forced growth, pressured growth, is often distorted growth. To eventually grow beyond childhood, we first need support for being a child.

Touch

Nurturing, caring touch is an important building block in developing not only a sense of self but also a self that has value. It is such an essential need that babies deprived of touch often die.

You perhaps have heard of failure to thrive (FTT) syndrome, which was discovered years ago in orphanages. The babies whose bassinets were at the end of the line withered and died at a much higher rate than those near the front of the line, even though all were being fed. This syndrome was drastically reduced when researchers realized that the difference was that those at the far end were not being picked up and were not receiving the attention the others were, and they then worked to remedy this.

Nurturing touch has all sorts of physiological benefits, including promoting the growth of the nervous system, stimulating the immune system, and decreasing stress hormones, but let's focus on the emotional and psychological value. It is through nurturing touch that we feel loved, soothed, and protected.

Appropriate touch also helps us locate ourselves in our bodies. The untouched child may be alienated from his or her own body and experience feelings of unreality.[2] The sense of reality comes from being grounded in the body, and touch is part of what accomplishes this. A lack of touch or abusive touch may also encourage dissociation, a psychic separation from the body.

Paradoxically, a lack of touch can also lead to a sense of imprisonment within the body. In *Touching: The Human Significance of the Skin*, Ashley Montagu writes, "It is in large part the stimulation of his skin by touch which enables the child to emerge from his own skin." Montagu explains how a child who has not been sufficiently touched becomes locked inside his own skin and then experiences normal touch as threatening.[3] This is called *tactile defensiveness*. Such defensiveness can manifest as insensitivity or hypersensitivity to being touched or in being touch-avoidant.

Children who do not receive enough positive touch will often (unconsciously) feel untouchable, as if there must be something terribly wrong with them. Negative touch often occurs as rough disciplinary touch or hostility, neither of which communicates any sense of valuing the child. Young children don't have the cognitive development to understand that parental misbehavior and failings have nothing to do with them. In general, the earlier the touch deprivation, the more devastating it is.

There are many reasons that mothers may be uncomfortable touching their children. If they haven't received enough nurturing touch themselves, they may have become tactilely defensive and may not be very present in their body. Nurturing touch may feel unfamiliar to them, not part of their repertoire. Because of abuse or other factors they may be uncomfortable with their own body and with other bodies, including those of their children. A mother who feels shame about her body will often pass that down to her offspring.

Here are some questions to help you explore this:

- What touch was available to you as a child? (You may want to think of yourself at different ages.)

- If your mother didn't seem comfortable with touch, why do you think that is?

- If you feel you have not had sufficient touch, how has this affected you? Do you crave contact and sometimes do not-so-safe things to get it? Are you comfortable receiving touch of various kinds?

- If you weren't touched much, what did you make of this experience? Do you resonate with the feeling of being untouchable?

Love is the medium, love is the message

We could say that touch is the medium and love is the message, but love is also a medium in the sense that it is the best soil for a child's growth. Every heart is nurtured by love and opens as it accepts love. Being loved makes one more loving. It also helps create resilience.

Love is communicated not just through touch, but also by tone of voice, facial expression, responsiveness, words, and quality of care. A child can feel how much (or how little) love is there.

When present, love informs other kinds of mothering behaviors like protection, encouragement, support, and guidance, and they are better received. The absence of love causes each of these to be experienced in a way that can make them a detriment rather than a help. For example, when love is absent, protective limits may be experienced as restrictive and unfair. When limits are set without love, a child may perceive such limits as a power trip. When encouragement is given but the child doesn't feel love, it may feel like pushing rather than supporting; the child may even feel that the parents want his or her success for their own glorification. Thus, without love, nothing works well, and with love even the clumsiest parenting can be forgiven.

Now that we've talked about the building blocks and the many essential functions that a good mother provides, let's turn to the question of what happens when these are missing.

PART II

When Mothering
Goes Wrong

5.

Mommy, Where Were You?

YOUNG CHILDREN DO NOT have the perspective to understand all the external factors that influence people's behavior. They mistakenly believe that when others hurt or abandon them, it must be because of something they did. They conclude that they must be bad or unlovable. The feeling at fault isn't always conscious, but it's usually there on some level. We see it at the end of the poem that opened this book, "Mommy, Where Were You?" when the child asks, "Was it because of me?"

The hole where Mother was supposed to be

To feel that you aren't important to your mother leaves a hole. Most often it is felt as a hole in the heart. It's the hole where Mother was supposed to be.

On close examination, there are three layers to this. The first layer is the outer one related to the external lack. Here the absence of mother may be evident in unsupervised, undernurtured, undersocialized children. It shows up in children whose development is a bit slower than it needs to be because they haven't gotten the individual attention and support for their growth of language, motor skills, and earliest academic skills.

The second layer is the hole in the sense of self that results from being undermothered. If we want to be precise, we can view this as a family of holes. There is the hole left by feeling unloved, the hole left when you're not mirrored and consequently don't feel fully real, the hole in your confidence that results from a lack of encouragement and praise, the sense of not belonging anywhere, and the hole of feeling homeless, among others.

One undermothered adult described to me the severe love hunger she was left with. "When there's a hole in your heart, you can't get enough," she told me. Since she was premature at birth, she had been put in an incubator and missed out on the contact she would have normally had. This left her with a craving for loving touch and any kind of positive attention. Throughout her youth and young adulthood, she felt an intense need for affection and developed crushes on anyone who seemed to see her at all.

Often this hole results in extreme loneliness. One woman remembers at age four feeling a wave of loneliness and thinking, *It's the I-don't-have-a-mother feeling.* The rational part of her then countered that she did have a mother, so it was confusing. This hole is written about by others as a feeling of emptiness, aloneness, and "emotional loneliness."

The third layer comes into view when we look at how we mother ourselves and find the same deficits that were present in our actual mothers. We see that we don't know how to support or encourage ourselves, don't know how to be patient and tender, don't know how to take into account our needs and limitations. Here, there is a hole in our inner mother.

This book is concerned with all three layers of this hole. By explaining what a good mother provides and asking how this compares with your experience, you can see which capacities were lost or underdeveloped. The healing chapters (9 to 14) are about filling these holes.

Our memories of Mother being there or not being there begin very early. One woman's first memory is of lying on a blanket, reaching up with her arms until eventually she drops them because no one comes. When something feels utterly futile, we give up, collapsing on multiple levels.

An exercise sometimes used in workshops is to lie on the floor, reach up, and call for help. If as a child you experienced the futility just described, or any kind of rejecting or punishing response, you might not now be able to reach and call. A very telling finding is that even those without major wounding in their history cannot continue reaching if the mother figure in the exercise fails to respond even a small number of times.

Over the years I have heard these early memories many times. It is not unusual to feel rage at this mother who will not come, and to have initially expressed that rage, perhaps by banging on the crib and screaming. Seldom do I hear my clients describe their efforts as successful. Usually their screams go unheeded and they give up. Yet this rage seems to live on, perhaps under the surface, and is easily reignited in adulthood when, for example, a boss is equally unresponsive.

Rita was middle-aged and working through childhood wounds left by extreme maternal deprivation when she suddenly had a vision in which she saw herself as a baby sitting on the lap of a woman who didn't exist above the waist. In her mind she was railing, *How could you do this to a baby?* This is a potent image. This is how the emotionally absent mother feels to a child: like someone who doesn't really exist. It is a shock, a threat to survival, and therefore a trauma to the child's nervous system.

The need for Mother's physical presence

Infants and young children absolutely require the physical presence of a caretaker. Without a caretaker, a baby can't survive. Absences that are too early or too long or too frequent will leave deep scars.

I am not one to argue that women must be stay-at-home moms. Many mothers don't have a choice about working if they are going to feed their families, and others are enriched and fulfilled in important ways that enhance their capacities as mothers. Studies have shown that a mother's satisfaction is a key variable in determining how well her children do. A mother who stays home because she is "supposed to," even though it makes her depressed and cranky, is not an asset.[1] There are also findings suggesting that for toddlers and older children, high-quality child care may support their development.[2] The greatest concern is with leaving children for long stretches during their first year when they are least able to tolerate separation. The length of the workday is also a factor. It's hard for moms to be sensitive and attuned when they are gone ten or twelve hours a day.

Apart from whatever level of physical availability is needed (which varies by the child), it becomes more a matter of quality than of quantity. I have seen cases where even extraordinary levels of physical absence can be forgiven when the child is bonded to the parent and feels loved. This isn't to say there isn't a price to pay with significant physical absence, but it appears to be a lower price than that paid by many who had mothers at home most of the time. The permanent absence by death is another subject altogether and has many different impacts.

Of course a child's age is a significant factor. Older children have more resources to help them tolerate Mother's absence. If they have been well cared for early, they have had more of a chance to internalize an image of a loving mother and are further along in developing a sturdy sense of self.

Children should be involved in discussions related to a planned absence of mother, even into their teen years. These kids still have needs, and it is appropriate for a departing mother to problem solve with them around these needs. The mothers who leave kids for weeks or months at a time (with other adults) without such discussions are the very mothers who were not in tune with their children's emotional needs earlier. Emotionally negligent mothers often see their children as more independent than they are.

What happens when Mother is not emotionally present?

Daniel Stern, MD, author of several books on the mother-infant relationship, notes that a baby is very tuned in to the energetic presence or absence of the mother. The mother is the center of the baby's world, and the baby is intensely tuned in to her feeling world.

It is extremely distressing when a baby cannot feel his mother being emotionally present. Stern describes how the baby senses his mother "mentally hovering somewhere else. Somewhere he does not want to go. In identifying with her, he feels her emotional dullness creeping into himself."[3] In essence, a baby of a dissociated woman may follow her into the state of dissociation, sometimes taking on the mother's sense of woodenness and numbing.

A pattern of dissociation may be the result of either imprinting Mother's dissociative states or our own response to abandonment. As one insightful adult reported from the perspective of her childhood self, "Mommy's presence props me up. When she goes away, I go away and lose contact with myself."

Understandably, it is more difficult for a child to stay present without the anchor of Mother. Often the child blames herself for Mother's "going away" and concludes, "I am too much."

Researchers have identified two response patterns in infants whose mothers are emotionally absent. One is to turn away from the mother, avoiding contact with her in order to maintain a more pleasant state. Not surprisingly, children with mothers who show little emotional expression more often develop a self-sufficient attachment style.[4] It's just too painful to attach to someone who is not really there with you. The other pattern, as Stern describes, is "to make extraordinary efforts to charm his mother, to pull her along—to act as an antidepressant to her."[5] Hardly a job for a baby!

So the options seem to be to follow Mommy into the black hole of no feeling, to sever some of the connection in order to avoid the hole, or to become Mommy's rescuer. Take a moment to consider which, if any of these, you might have done if your mother was emotionally absent. (You may have done all three at different times.)

This distress in the face of Mother's emotional blankness is evidenced by the "still-face" experiment, which investigated how babies respond to their mothers' inexpressiveness. In the experiment young mothers were instructed to suddenly adopt a totally blank face, showing no expression or movement while looking at their baby. The experiment lasted only three minutes, but "the consistent pattern of infant behavior in the still-face situation is a repeated attempt to elicit Mother's response, followed by somber expression, orientation away from Mother, and finally withdrawal. All this takes place in less than three minutes."[6] The researchers describe the babies collapsing into a self-protective state in which they later resort to techniques for self-comforting. The same pattern has been noticed in hospitalized infants. Infants depend on the stimulation they get from Mother's energetic and emotional presence to connect with the world.

In the still-face experiments, the previously secure babies warmed up again to their mothers and returned to their former intimate relational dance once Mother became animated again, but what happens when Mother is frequently remote, dazed, and inexpressive or the child is not securely attached? What if Mother herself is at times frightening? Or if the child has experienced other trauma—say, medical trauma, or physical or sexual abuse? Will it be so easy to reengage then?

Citing research, author Sue Gerhardt concludes, "For a baby, the most painful experience of all seems to be not being able to get Mother's attention."[7] This seems even more unbearable than maltreatment. Mother, after all, is the baby's link to the world and the best hope for getting needs met, assuming Mother is the primary caretaker.

One common type of emotionally absent mother is the woman who is depressed. Depressed mothers are found to be less interactive with their children, and their babies show fewer positive feelings, become insecurely attached as toddlers, and do less well on cognitive tasks.[8] (Remember that the brain is largely turned on and built through social interaction.) The stress will also lead to a more sensitive gastrointestinal and autonomic nervous systems and inability or unwillingness to interact socially with an adult trying to establish contact.[9] Such children often grow into adults who are not used to warm, nourishing contact, and still need to learn how to establish what they should have had as babies.

The depressed mother's face is too like the still-face experiment. An absence of nonverbal signals deprives the child of support and direction. Even something as simple as a smile has tremendous power to cheer on the toddler taking his first steps, to communicate safety and acceptance, and engage the child in relationship. How else does the young child know that Mommy is okay? In a similar way, a look of surprise or disapproval helps a child orient to his environment. Mother's responses are an important help in navigating the world.

The emotionally absent mother is not present to provide many of the functions of the Good Mother, but perhaps most important is that her heart is not available to the child. She doesn't create an emotional bond with her child. While other types of mothers may do a poor job of providing some of the Good Mother functions such as guidance, encouragement, and protection, some do create a bond. The needy mother, for example, creates a connection heavily influenced by her needs, rather than the child's. The overcontrolling mother is often both bonded to and overidentified with her child.

Why was Mother so emotionally absent?

Here are some common reasons:

- She was grieving for a prolonged period.

- She had too many children to attend to.

- She was mentally unstable or depressed.

- You were separated by circumstance (war, natural disaster, economic calamity, prison . . .).

- You started off on a bad foot and didn't bond well. Mothering felt like work to her, and this brought up internal conflict and/or shame.

- She had narcissistic wounds and was too busy attending to her own needs.

- She didn't know how to mother and avoided contact out of guilt and inadequacy.

- She was busy taking care of someone else (an ill parent, spouse . . .).

- She was overwhelmed with practical tasks, like moving the household time and time again.

- She was addicted to alcohol or drugs.

- She was working two or more jobs to keep a roof over your head.

- She was a "career woman," and this took all of her energy.

- She was going to school (which took forever!).

- She was too busy with her romantic and sexual liaisons.

- She was just a child herself.

- She was worn out, exhausted, or physically ill.

- She didn't want to be there. Maybe she didn't even want to have a child.

- She never bonded with her mother, and had no reference point for being an attentive, involved parent.

- She was afraid to show her love, afraid to bond with anyone.

- She thought you had what you needed, and she was told by others to not do too much for fear of spoiling you.

- She spent all her energy trying to protect herself from a raging or abusive partner.

- She was emotionally numb from medication.

- She cut off emotionally to protect herself from the unresolved pain of her own childhood.

How a child interprets Mommy's absence

If we boil these reasons down to three basic messages, what the undermothered child hears is one or more of the following:

- I don't have it to give.

- You ask/take too much. Your needs are too much.

- I don't really care about you.

When children perceive that Mother simply doesn't have it to give, somewhere in their souls, they are often compassionate. Farah, for example, told me, "I could feel that my mother was suffering and unhappy, so I tried to not ask for very much." Knowing her mother was overstressed, Farah minimized her needs as much as possible. Curiously, her mother much later commented that Farah had separated from her prematurely. How do you stay connected to someone who is rarely there? Farah said the message she received from her mother was "Don't lean on me." She was simply complying.

While in some ways the situation may seem easier when a child perceives that Mother simply doesn't have love and attention to give, it is extremely difficult for a child to not personalize this and much harder if Mommy seems to have it to give to someone else. How can a child understand this, except as a rejection?

There is also a felt difference for a child between the mother who is working two jobs and coming home exhausted and the mother who is busy talking on the phone, laughing with her friends. Then it becomes, "I'm too busy *for you.*" When Mother really could do more but just isn't motivated to we will end up believing that she doesn't really care about us. If she then acts burdened when responding to us, we'll feel like something about us is too much.

It might be useful to spend some time reflecting on how you felt as a child about your mother's unavailability. If you have cultivated a relationship with an inner child (as we'll cover in chapter 11), listen carefully and see if you can understand how this child felt. If you can't go there, just stay where you are and let yourself muse about how you may have interpreted your mother's unavailability. I suggest you write it down and come back after you've read the next several chapters, or even much later and ask yourself what your more objective assessment of it is now.

When Mother is the only one there

Unfortunately, there are times when a not-so-adequate mother is the only caretaker in or consistently in the home. The absence of a father (or a second mother figure) makes it even harder on an undermothered child. There is no one else to go to for care, and maintaining the fragile bond with Mother becomes even more essential.

It is commonly believed that part of a father's role is to help a child separate from Mother. Whereas Mother represents the nest and the early merged relationship in which the child does not yet know himself as separate from Mom, Father represents the world beyond Mother and is a bridge into that larger world. Whether the relationship with Mother is satisfying or not satisfying, it's harder for a child to move beyond Mother's orbit when she is the only parent there.

While being an only child may not be much of a disadvantage with a capable, attuned mother, an only child will often suffer greatly in the care of a parent who is disturbed.

Why some children suffer more

There are many reasons that children raised by the same parents may have very different experiences. Each is born at a different moment in their mother's life, each child may hit critical periods when different things are going on in the family and surrounding world, and each has a different makeup. Research has confirmed what every attentive parent knows, that some children are hardier and more easygoing than others. Children born with a more sensitive temperament lurch at bumps in the road that less sensitive siblings hardly notice. So, one reason children raised by the same parents have such different experiences is that each child has a unique physiology, bonding experience, and set of life circumstances.

Another reason is that parents do not treat their children equally. While our first impulse may be to champion equal treatment, it's a little more nuanced than that. Yes, parents should not make it more difficult for one child than another, and should not show favoritism, but they do need to show that they notice their children's different needs and capacities, and respond accordingly. When siblings are dressed alike, signed up for the same activities, or given the exact same toys, for example, their individuality gets quashed or never has a chance to develop.

We could say that good parents don't treat children equally for good reasons—they are sensitive to their children's differences—while bad parents don't treat children equally because of their own biases. They may favor children who are easiest, or are a gender they prefer, or who they can show off (the child being their proxy). Narcissistic parents may favor the child who will not outshine them.

There are reasons for a mother's unequal treatment that we will never know. Sometimes a mother can show up for a less demanding, less sensitive child, but not for a sensitive one where she lacks confidence that she can get it right. Or the child is similar to her and she projects her own self-rejection or shadow onto the child. Or a given child reminds her of someone she has a troubled relationship with—perhaps her own mother.

In some cases, Mommy simply runs out of gas. She is often most engaged with her first child, but with three or more children, she may be just going through the motions, coping as best as she can by the time her last child comes along. Now imagine nine or ten! In large families, older children often take on parenting responsibilities for the younger ones and serve as surrogate mothers. Of course the baby in this situation doesn't know that Mother is exhausted; all he knows is that Mother isn't there.

Other times the first child is most rejected; I see that most in cases where the pregnancy was unwanted, and the mother resented being drawn into parenthood and tied to a partner she would have left or to a partner who left her once a child was involved. Children know when they are not wanted. I am convinced that many know this in utero.

Unfortunately, scapegoating can be taken up by siblings as well as parents. When there is abuse by a sibling, it generally signals that 1) the offending child has not been well parented, and that 2) the parents are failing in their responsibility to see that kids are treated respectfully and are safe from harm. Being a target of sibling mistreatment in addition to parental makes for a heavier load.

Mutual standoff

I have not seen a case in which a child (often now an adult) has turned away from a mother who is consistently turned toward the child.[10] Attachment research indicates that when a child defies the instinctive urge to want to attach to his or her mother, it is because the mother has been perceived in some important way as unavailable. My basic thesis is that children turn away from Mother out of disappointment and hurt and in self-defense. They turn away because it hurts too much to turn toward another and not be met.

Mothers, being the imperfect humans that they are, can react to perceptions and fears of being unwanted or rejected by a child. They turn away out of their own wounding. Mother and child can get into a state of mirroring each other in which both are rejecting the other, building walls in response to the other's walls or unavailability.

For a year my local newspaper followed the story of a teenage girl who, with her boyfriend, planned the murder of the girl's mother, which the boyfriend then carried out. Both showed signs of being seriously sociopathic, without remorse or feeling. It was uncomfortable for me to contemplate a child being so coldhearted toward her own mother, although I am certainly aware of the rage many, if not most, of the undermothered feel. A psychologist testified that the girl had turned off her feelings as a way of coping with the severe neglect, verbal abuse, and occasional physical abuse she had experienced over a period of many years with her raging, alcoholic mother. She had the maturity of an eight-year-old, evaluators said. The same girl had reportedly "blossomed" earlier when living in a supportive family environment with an aunt. The story is a tragic example of the deep damage that can occur in a toxic parent-child relationship when the more normal feelings of mutual affection get distorted into a mirroring of the mutual defenses of numbing and out-of-control acting out.

Most of the time, thank heaven, it doesn't get to such extremes, but the mirroring is still evident. For example, mothers who cared for their children out of obligation are later cared for in their elderly years by their adult children out of a similar obligation. Both need to change in order to break the mutual standoff. One will need to offer something new, and the other to respond positively in return. We'll look at this complex issue of changing the dance in the final chapter of the book. Let's go next to what it is like living with an emotionally absent mother.

6.

Living with an Emotionally Absent Mother

ON A MORE COLLECTIVE level, we have images of what it is like to live with a "good, caring mother and with a "bad," witchy mother. What has not been recognized is the mother who looks quite adequate on the outside but is emotionally absent. This mother generally provides for the physical needs of her children, but is missing many of the outlined functions of the Good Mother. That is the task we take on now.

Who was that masked woman?

Those of us of a certain age remember *The Lone Ranger* show on television. There was always somebody at the end of the show asking, "Who was that masked man?" The hero of the show was a one-dimensional character never seen without his mask.

Likewise for many of the undermothered, their mothers are never fully seen. Sometimes they hide out in their bedrooms. Sometimes they hide behind a still, expressionless face. Sometimes they "put on their face" and go out. In more extreme cases they are cardboard figures to their children.

Part of the healing process is taking the mask off Mother, seeing her life story and the forces that shaped her. (The first two exercises in chapter 14 can help with this.)

Sometimes these masked women are further shielded by their husbands. I think of a mother of six, where the father always warned the children, "Don't upset your mother." When I inquired into this, there wasn't a lot of evidence that Mother needed all that extra protection, but it gave her cover for not really showing up in an active parental role. In such cases, Mother becomes more like a doll in a china cabinet than someone you can touch and smell and interact with.

Cultural context also plays a part. Particularly before the 1970s, most women didn't perceive that it was an option to not be a mother. It was the expected life course for a woman to marry and have a family, whether this was her natural inclination or not. The result of this (then and now) is that women become mothers who are not really suited to the job. They are, as one woman put it, "reluctant mothers." They would have been more comfortable doing something else, perhaps being a career woman or a social dilettante. Caring for children simply is not "their thing."

Men could get away with this. When I was growing up, we didn't expect very much of fathers beyond financially providing for the family. If they weren't naturally suited to parenting, it was much less visible, because they were a small part of the picture. With the greatly expanded involvement of fathers in recent years, many of today's children will remember their fathers providing basic care and nurturance, along with many of the other functions of the Good Mother I described in chapter 2. This gives younger people a chance to know more dimensions of their fathers, and they are less likely in later years to ask, "Who was that masked man?" Good parenting by a father has always helped make up for the holes left by an emotionally absent mother.

Slim pickin's from Mom

Looking at my list of mothering functions, many of those I interviewed (as well as readers and clients) told me their mothers fulfilled none of them. It seems that when Mother goes missing, she is nowhere to be found. In this chapter I'm presenting what I have found both in my research phase and my clinical practice. Here is an overview.

Occasionally Mother provides so little of the basic structure that when her kids grow up they know nothing about setting up a home or having daily rhythms. A living room should have furniture for sitting? A family might sit together at a table to eat dinner? Kids have a bedtime? All news. The basic structure for daily life is missing.

The interactions that form the scaffolding for developing a healthy sense of self are also missing or less than optimal, leading to the host of problems we'll see in the next chapter. A key piece to a child's developing self is provided by mirroring (See Mother as Mirror, p. 32); unfortunately this is rarely available from emotionally absent mothers.

These mothers are unschooled in dealing with emotion and generally have no tolerance for it. They don't know how to deal with their children's tears, sometimes even saying aggressive things like "Stop crying or I'll give you something to cry about!" Other times children are not directly shamed for showing their feelings, but their emotions are ignored, and they get approval for holding in any sad or "weak" feelings.

When praise and encouragement are present, it is usually qualified. These children are praised for what the mothers value (most often school achievement) but seldom celebrated and praised for themselves. The immature or narcissistic mother often doesn't notice and appreciate what is different from her. Such mothers reward their children when they mirror her or conform to her idea of how her children should be, but they don't actively support the child's unique self.

These remote mothers are frequently remembered as most attentive during times the child was sick, although many have no memory of being tenderly touched or held at such times, while others remember cold, functional touch. For some, Mother was simply a worried face at the door.

Compared with our picture of ideal mothering, there was little that the undermothered received. Like looking at empty cupboards, it was slim pickin's.

Lack of mentoring

Another key role almost entirely missing for the undermothered is guidance. One of the jobs of the Good Mother is to teach a child how to negotiate tasks that are challenging and somewhat beyond the child's current abilities. The Good Mother helps the child assess what he or she can handle, what is maybe a little too much, and how to back off from that. She calibrates the task to the child's abilities. When we don't get this (and haven't since learned it by other means), we're often left not knowing how to navigate life. One response is to collapse in the face of a challenging task and not try. Another is to plunge into something without the preparation or respect for our limits that would be more self-caring.

Imagine how a skilled mother helps her children plan what to pack for summer camp or how many courses at school to take without overburdening themselves. The Good Mother teaches the child how to modulate difficulty, taking into account needs and limitations (such as tiredness, stress, and hunger). When we bite off more than we can chew, the Good Mother says, "That's too much, honey. Let's make it a little easier."

What I am describing is really a combination of the roles of Mother as Mentor (providing calibrated help) and Mother as Modulator (ensuring the child doesn't get overwhelmed). When we get enough of this as a child or we learn to mother ourselves, we ask, "How big a step is the right size for me? What's too big?" We recognize what we need in order to be able to take a bigger step.

One woman reported that her mother had shown her a few things like how to make salads and wash the dishes, but had taught her nothing about how to "do life"—how to have a conversation or relate to other people, how to manage her emotions, or anything important. Such mothers seem to have vacated the mentor role, or at the least to feel quite insecure in it.

Another described how it seemed his mother didn't mind being a sounding board on occasion, but she seemed reticent to get involved otherwise, perhaps afraid to pry. She never put out a welcome mat, inviting her children to come to her with problems or needs. It is the mother's responsibility to build the foundation for this. Children can't be expected to intuit when it's okay to ask Mother for help.

Missed connections

One of the questions I asked in my interviews was, "If you could give your mother one quality that was missing, what would it be?" Most often the answer had something to do with the ability to make an emotional connection. Generally it was connection to them as a child that felt missing, but some acknowledged that their mothers didn't seem to make emotional connections with anybody.

More often than not, adults who are undermothered have no memories of close times with their mothers as children. No memories of being held, being looked at with loving eyes, or being emotionally met during important moments. To be emotionally met is to have others touch your experience in such a way that you know they get it. They know what you've been through and what it means to you. Generally how we know this is through responses that demonstrate empathy or mirroring. It's not possible for others to know our experience precisely, but we want them to at least try. We want them to care about our experience. When we're brushed off or discounted or told that we feel something other than we actually do feel, it leaves us feeling isolated and alone.

Carol described an incident that happened when she was six. Her life was actually endangered for a few moments, and she successfully negotiated this. When Carol told her mother about it, her mother dismissed the danger and acted as if the account was implausible, thereby missing a very important moment in Carol's life. It was a moment when she could so easily have given a Good Mother message like, "You were so smart and so brave, and I'm so glad you're here." It could have been a moment when Carol felt cherished and knew she was loved. Instead, it left her with the feeling that she couldn't trust her mother to be there for her.

These nonconnecting mothers are not good communicators. Not only do they miss opportunities like the one just cited, but they fail to respond to overtures made. One woman put a self-disclosing letter under her mother's pillow as a teen, hoping to open up some level of communication, but her mother never mentioned it.

For those who feel well loved, it may be astounding to hear that people can go through their entire childhoods and not have a single memory of closeness and connection, yet I have seen this a frightening number of times. What makes it so hard to imagine is that it flies right in the face of our collective image of what a mother is supposed to be.

The mechanical mom

The picture we get of mothers who are emotionally absent is one of a woman who seems not quite fully human. One man said his parents were like statues to him; they didn't feel like real human beings. Others have spoken of not being able to find a human heart in there and feeling as if Mother was "not real."

Alma told me she remembers her mother as a person, remembers that her mother was there, but has absolutely no memory of interacting with her. Alma felt like a nonperson to her mother, as if she didn't exist. She felt more at home in the tree house in the backyard than with her mother. I suggest this is the result of a mother who brought no sense of realness to their interactions.

Many of these mothers were quite checked out, living in their own world. This condition was not always ongoing, but might be present for a period of years. I suspect this coincides with unresolved trauma, grief, and depression.

Certainly if a mother is emotionally absent, it will be impossible for her to attune to her child's needs. I am speaking here both of a particular child's needs and of children's needs in general. I have previously listed some of the aspects inherent in being a child—being undeveloped and without mastery, having limited capacities, being dependent, needing lots of affection and holding, and needing protection, guidance, and mentoring, among others. I found that the experiential world of the child was totally lost to these "mechanical moms." These parents (and it was usually both) seemed more comfortable seeing their children as little adults than responding to them as children. Children were not allowed to be loud, exuberant, or messy, and their bids for closeness were pretty consistently rejected.

Sometimes Mother is obviously out of commission. More insidious are the cases where she looks like the desirable mother, does many of the outward things that she believes constitute the central role of the mother, but is experienced by her children as not really there and not attuned. Some of these mothers may even think of themselves as happily settled into mothering. It's just that they define it so differently! Their focus is on making sure the children are clothed and educated and that family conflicts stay out of sight.

In many homes there is pressure to maintain the illusion of a happy family. In one case, the father repeatedly told the children what a wonderful mother they had. The mother, incidentally, spent most of her time in her bedroom, forcing herself out to participate in important holiday celebrations, times when it was most important to prop up such a picture.

Children of such mothers often grow up intellectually believing they were loved but not *feeling* loved. Especially if mothers make an effort to do some child-oriented things like go to parent-teacher conferences and throw a birthday party once in a while, it can be confusing. Because children have nowhere else to go and are dependent on their parents, they will often push out of consciousness any feelings of not being loved. The feelings erupt later when the adult is in therapy or struggling with self-esteem or relationship issues.

A few of these mothers learned to connect later in life, although most did not. One mother first told her daughter (now middle-aged) "I love you" after reading in a Dear Abby column that this is something mothers should say to their children.

As might be expected, these emotionally distant mothers did not touch their children much, leading to a strong touch hunger or the opposite, touch aversion. Often with these touch-avoidant mothers, touch enters the relationship when the mothers are aged and the now-healed children initiate more warmth. Sometimes the mothers start reaching out when they are widowed, lonely, and need more support themselves. It is often in their advanced years that the mechanical mom finally becomes human.

Is anyone watching? Does anyone care?

The picture that emerges of many of these parents is one of extreme disengagement. Both mother and father are missing in action.

One of the ways this shows up is in a marked lack of supervision. I've heard of children wandering on their own outside the home as young as two and often by three or four. They are walking home alone from school or from the corner store and often sent to do things on their own at an age that most today would consider totally inappropriate or dangerous. When the dentist of an eight-year-old called the child's mother, the mother thought the child must have misbehaved. She couldn't imagine that sending a child that age to a dentist alone could be overwhelming to the child.

Some disengaged parents don't seem to care or want to know what their children are doing. When one adolescent boy told his mother where he was going or what he was going to do, she would reply, "I don't care."

Children may, especially by adolescence, like the freedom of not having anyone to answer to, but this comes with a price. Children and adolescents often have not yet developed the judgment that leads to wise choices, and not having parameters on their behavior feels like no one really cares. When Bobby fell off his bicycle and had to have stitches, his mother grounded Bobby for a short while, limiting him to the backyard. He noticed that he actually felt happy about this, because for the first time it felt that his mother was watching out for him.

In many of these households there is virtually no conversation in the family. There is a minimal amount of functional communication, but no discussion of the child's activities or friends. Contrast this with parents who talk with their children about essentially every part of their kids' lives, who know their children's ups and downs, hopes and fears, and who support them where they lack confidence and celebrate even their smallest successes.

The lack of involvement described in this section is neglect. It's not the physical neglect of children going without food or shelter; it is emotional neglect. The scars caused by this lack of involvement and emotional nurturance are significant. Homes without toys, children never related to as children, children who are strangers to their parents—these are serious failings.

Living with a disengaged mother, especially if coupled with a disengaged or absent father, is like living on your own as a child.

- In what areas of your life was your mother engaged, and where was she disengaged?

- If you had a father in the home, did he mirror this or have a different pattern?

Clueless

I found these emotionally absent mothers singularly unreflective, clueless about any role they may have played in their children's early or later problems.

When a middle-aged woman recently shared with her mother how difficult her childhood had been for her, the mother responded, "If we'd known how unhappy you were as a child, we could have put you on medication." While this might show a small sense of advocacy and caring and does reflect our dominant culture's orientation toward mental health problems, it totally misses the fact that perhaps what was needed was more demonstration of love (or any of the other Good Mother roles). I think such mothers miss this fact because in their own minds they do love their children. They just don't know how to show it in a way that children really get it.

No place to go for help

We all know that bad things sometimes happen in the world, so for the world to feel like a place we want to be, we also need to believe that there are places we can go for help.

In "Mother as Home Base" (p. 41), I described Mother as the place where we can always go for shelter, help, and comfort. This is clearly not the case for the undermothered. None of the people I interviewed could recall a time when they went to their mother for help and received a satisfying response. Most learned early not to ask. One man recalled how anytime he went to his mother with a request as a child, she would counter with, "What do you need that for?" Children of such mothers often feel that asking for help will get them in trouble. The feeling is that their mothers don't want to be bothered.

I noticed a disturbing pattern of mothers being unable to respond to direct pleas for assistance even when their children were grown. A notable number of the undermothered whom I interviewed reached a point in their early adult years where their mental health failed and they needed help. Naomi was visiting at her mother's when her psychiatrist phoned her. When Naomi finished the call and told her mother, "I'm very depressed. I need help!" her mother replied, "You don't need help. All you need is a hot bath." Another mother, confronted by her twenty-two-year-old son sharing that he was seeing a psychiatrist, walked out of the room without a word.

Margaret asked her parents if she could live with them when her young husband was hospitalized and their situation was terribly unstable and stressful. Her parents refused her request, which led to years of strained distance between them and to Margaret's decision to never go to them for help again.

Another woman asked her very outwardly capable mother if she could count on her if she really, really needed her. Her mother's response: "I'd have to think about it." Of course this mother never came back after that with any reassurance. This was in contrast with the woman's in-laws whose response to any kind of need was an unconditional, "We'll be there."

So, unfortunately, we see mothers minimizing their children's problems, mothers denying significant problems happening right under their noses, mothers shaming and blaming their children for having problems, and mothers acting with callous indifference. To further complicate the picture, we even find mothers expressing indignant anger when children *don't* come to them with a problem, as we'll see next.

When Sharon's mother discovered that Sharon had undergone an abortion and not told her about it, she confronted her fifteen-year-old daughter. Perhaps she felt hurt, perhaps insulted; her behavior was angry. What she failed to communicate was caring about Sharon. She didn't ask how and why this had happened or why Sharon didn't feel comfortable sharing it with her, although she was obviously upset with the fact that Sharon hadn't come to her. Rather than being a time when Sharon could at last feel some support, she simply felt in trouble with her mom.

The foundation for children knowing they can come to their mothers with needs and problems is established early—as is the sense that mothers either don't want to know, don't have time and energy to deal, or aren't much help. By the time a child becomes an adolescent, trying to reach him or her during periods of significant stress is often a case of too little, too late.

- Did you go to your mother for help in times of significant need? How did she respond? How did this affect your relationship?

- Would you go to her for help now (if she's still alive)? If not, why not?

A mother's failure to provide a home base, a place to return to, a place that's safe, sets a person up for feeling like a motherless child.

Feeling like a motherless child

The undermothered often feel as if they don't really have a mother—although they do, which complicates the picture. The feeling is of being motherless, but the actuality is that someone is there, whom the world recognizes as one's mother. How to reconcile the feeling of being motherless with the actuality is part of the challenge of the undermothered adult child. To dismiss the feeling is to continue to abandon the child. Much of healing is learning to respond to that feeling.

A term sometimes used to describe this is *orphan complex* or *orphan archetype*. It is the feeling of being without parents and without love, of feeling alone in the world. This feeling is often deeply repressed because it is so painful; to be without these things threatens a child's survival. One adult described opening up to her long-repressed feeling, *I could die for want of love.*

In writing about the orphan archetype, Jungian analyst Rose-Emily Rothenberg notes a pervasive feeling of unworthiness and a felt need for support. "He [the orphan] feels that he is the 'injured one' and needs all the care he can possibly get."[1] She describes a pattern of dependency and clinging to whatever and whoever represents the protection and security of the mother.

One way this shows up is in a kind of love hunger that causes people to stay in relationships that are abusive or unsatisfying, because the feeling of need is so desperate that the individual can't leave. Not having an internal reference point for being well loved, they often feel, *This is better than nothing.* Others find it easier (and more familiar) to go without love than to go near that wound.

This need for nurturing goes beyond partnership and can be as subtle as finding it difficult to turn away from anyone offering any kind of positive attention. For years I found that if someone did something nice for me, I felt bound to them. Slowly, I realized that emotional nurturance is not such a rare thing and that I can decide in each relationship when I want to turn elsewhere. One act of kindness isn't a life contract.

Others who are emotionally starved fixate on food, attempting to use physical nourishment to stand in for emotional nourishment. Perhaps because it never does and never can, the satisfaction is never complete. One woman who knows that she goes to food to feed her emotional hunger or when she is stressed suggested that emotional starvation is behind our obesity epidemic. Many of the undermothered have histories of eating disorders and binge eating.

Here are some questions to help you explore this.

- Have you ever felt "like a motherless child"?

- How does your love hunger show up?

- How might you cover up your hunger for love, support, and protection?

No anchor

The sense of being connected somewhere is an important anchor in our lives. Without it, we can feel disconnected, lost, and ungrounded in the world. This is sometimes reflected in images of floating in a dark space, like an astronaut whose connecting cord is broken. Others describe it as drifting at sea, like a piece of flotsam. This feeling is often carried throughout life unless efforts are made to change the situation.

Without a welcoming mother as anchor, we may not even come fully into this dimension (which is known as the schizoid defense in psychological circles). Likely we will not fully occupy our body and may feel a bit more alien than human. We may continue to drift through life, never part of any community and never solidly connected to anyone.

When a baby is nursed by a mother who isn't really present, the child has nothing to anchor to and loses her connection with her own body as well. (Recall the child following Mother into dissociative states described earlier.) If you are not tuned in to your body, you don't know when you're hungry and when you're full. You don't know what your body wants or needs because you're not really there. This contributes to eating disorders as well as to accidents and illnesses.

No mother, no self

When I was brainstorming titles for this book, I considered a play on words on the title of a well-known book by Nancy Friday called *My Mother, My Self*. On the most basic level, it is simple: *No Mother, No Self*.

Our relationship with our mothers has a big impact on how we experience our selves as children. A child with an abusive parent often internalizes the rejection and criticism and is riddled with self-doubt, inadequacy, and shame. Usually there's a sense of self, but it's a damaged self. With a neglectful parent, an emotionally flat or absent parent—especially from early in a child's life—there may not be enough feedback for a child's fragile self to cohere, leaving one feeling as if there is no *me*.

Blank begets blank, absence begets absence. No mother, no self.

Perhaps the positive side of this is that unlike those who are identified with Mother and fail to individuate from her, thus shadowing her their entire lives, those without this connection—if they do the psychological work necessary—are freer to fashion a self that is more of their own making.

We'll look at the impacts of emotionally absent mothers in the next chapter, both in terms of those who are unintentionally neglectful, as described above, and those who are more menacing.

7.

Childhood Emotional Neglect and Abuse

IN THE LAST CHAPTER we looked at living with an emotionally absent mother. Here, we go a step further to investigate when emotional neglect becomes emotional abuse, and what exactly the relationship is between neglect and abuse.

What is emotional neglect?

Emotional neglect is the failure to provide what a child reasonably needs for emotional development and a healthy sense of self. Everything in the last chapter, "Living with an Emotionally Absent Mother," describes this kind of neglect.

In the first edition of this book I distinguished between "sins of omission" and "sins of commission," with neglect fitting into the former category. Psychologist Jonice Webb, who also works in this area, uses the same terms and says simply, "Emotional abuse is something a parent does to a child—it is an action. Emotional neglect is the opposite—it is a lack of action. It is a parent overlooking a child versus a parent mistreating a child."[1]

This is a clean and simple contrast, often sufficient to make the distinction. Yet, life isn't always this black and white. For example, if Mother doesn't feed you, it is a sin of omission, but it could also be seen as an active withholding and as a punishment that can only be judged a sin of commission. Might this also be true on an emotional level? If Mother refuses to acknowledge you when you are lying outside her bedroom door crying hysterically, is her lack of response something she is doing or failing to do? For these situations we need a second criterion. We need to understand the *why* of an action or lack of action. Is the suffering caused intentional or unintentional?

Let me add a qualifier: *Unintentional neglect* is the failure to provide care out of ignorance or oversight. We can neglect our health, our finances, our homes, and yes, our children. Unintentional neglect does not have malicious intent, although it can have devastating outcomes. It might be that Mother actually didn't know that children need to be shown affection and listened to.

Is there neglect that is not intentionally harmful but also not really to be forgiven as accidental? What if Mother just feels too tired to get up and attend to the crying baby? Or she is too busy with her social planning to stop and listen to you, even if you just experienced the first major loss in your life when your best friend died? Where is she slacking on what should be her priorities?

It is difficult to entirely separate childhood emotional neglect from abuse. The line shades into gray and becomes difficult to find.

How is emotional abuse different? Can both be present?

Abuse is not accidental or an oversight. It is doing something (or even not doing something) with the knowledge that it will cause emotional pain.

Emotional abuse often takes the form of ridiculing, scolding, blaming, and humiliating. It doesn't only happen when Mother is angry, but can be said in everyday conversational tones, even in a lighthearted way in front of your or her friends.

Although it often takes the form of cruel and critical words, emotional abuse can be nonverbal as well. Refusing to talk with a child (that slippery slope again of action or inaction), hateful looks, behaviors that undermine a child's sense of self, self-efficacy, or self-respect, or sabotaging a child's success—all of these would qualify as emotional abuse.

The word *emotional* simply confirms that we're not talking about physical harm but emotional harm, even though the means might include the material world. For example, I've heard of pubescent girls undergoing tremendous shame when forced to wear dirty, torn, ill-fitting, inappropriate clothes. Emotional abuse may involve degrading the child's gender or purposefully exposing the child to terrifying or overwhelming situations.

Threatening abandonment is emotional abuse. Comments such as "I'll take you to the orphanage" or "I'll leave if you keep doing that" communicate that Mom's presence can't be counted on. Such threats elicit terror in the young child for whom Mother equals survival. Older children will also be controlled by such threats (which is their purpose), reinforcing an insecure attachment and insecurity in general. The threat of physical abandonment is emotional abandonment. It is saying, "You can't count on me." Because it is a deliberate action and it is traumatizing, it is abuse.

A mother who is cruel knows where you're most vulnerable and sometimes goes after that weakness. She knows how to ignite your shame. Shame is one of the most painful emotions anyone can feel. It is the sense of being fundamentally flawed, wrong, or bad. To shame someone is to make them feel wrong or bad (not just guilty for a behavior), and is a kind of emotional abuse.

My observation is that when there is childhood emotional abuse, there is also emotional neglect, although not always vice versa. Emotionally absent mothers of the more checked-out variety don't have the meanness that emotionally abusive mothers have and don't intend to hurt their children. They are emotionally neglectful but not abusive. What allows emotionally abusive mothers to be cruel is partly a lack of connection and empathy with their children, and this disconnect also means they will be emotionally neglectful. In both cases these mothers lack emotional attunement to their child or awareness of what makes good parenting.

It is easier (though never easy) to recognize the monster mother as missing something than it is to find the flaw in the pleasant but clueless one.

How bad are they?

Both emotional neglect and emotional abuse are severely damaging. Short of outright denial, there is no way to say they are not that bad. They are that bad, even though it usually takes some time to fully face that.

Not infrequently, survivors of childhood emotional neglect or emotional abuse minimize what they've gone through by saying something along the lines of, "At least I wasn't beaten. I don't have that much to complain about." But a study reported by the American Psychological Association found that "Children who are emotionally abused and neglected face similar and sometimes worse mental health problems as children who are physically or sexually abused."[2] They discovered that children who had been psychologically abused suffered from anxiety, depression, low self esteem, symptoms of post-traumatic stress, and were suicidal at the same or a greater rate than children who were physically or sexually abused.

Extreme early neglect can be life threatening. An infant deprived of early interactions doesn't have the scaffolding or the brain stimulation to fully enter the human world. Whereas extreme neglect can leave a child floating above life, disconnected from her body and wondering if she even exists, emotional abuse is soul-crushing in a different way. The feeling of being scorned by the one you depend on, being hated even, is hard to fathom. If your mother falls into the witch category, you may have felt as though your life could be snuffed out at any time. The extreme end of both emotional neglect and emotional abuse completely undermines any foundation for a healthy life. (This doesn't make a healthy life out of reach, but you'll have to build a new foundation.)

How damaging these are depends on a number of mitigating factors. In "Why some children suffer more" (p. 87) I discuss individual differences that make people more vulnerable or more resilient, so this is one factor in explaining why we may suffer more or less from early injuries of this type.

Another important factor is the amount of emotional abuse or neglect. The more consistently a child is treated a given way, the more deeply it seeps into him. Although something like occasional abuse certainly robs a child of his safety, ongoing abuse allows no time to establish stability before being knocked down again. Likewise with neglect, the mother who is emotionally absent for a period of time, say in a child's later life or during a hospitalization, is less damaging than one who was consistently absent for the entirety of her child's early life.

A third mitigating factor is what else is in the environment: Are there others present who help offset Mother's harmful behaviors? Is there another parent figure, and are they a buffer, a support, or no help at all? Often I hear of rageful mothers married to collapsed men who are not themselves abusive but are neglectful in that they don't protect their children from Mother's mistreatment. Does Mother, perhaps out of jealousy, interfere with her children's forming of affectionate bonds with other adults? Insecure mothers do this often.

Are there siblings? Sometimes a sibling shares with you the unique world you live in and is a port in the storm (even though you're both vulnerable and disempowered); other times the sibling is part of the abuse. When a sibling is perpetrating violence it is always a red flag of serious problems in the family system. Unequal treatment of children and unfair roles may make it difficult for siblings to form an alliance of equals. Sometimes siblings are pitted against one another by Mother. Other times, for their own survival, siblings find a way to stay out of harm's way, either by hiding out in their bedrooms or by escaping from the house. Occasionally you hear of a child who has learned to shut it all out by getting absorbed in something like a book or a game right in the middle of his family's chaos. When siblings disappear like this, it can lead to a feeling of even more aloneness and abandonment.

Now that you see how unique each person's situation is, let's look at common impacts of both emotional neglect and emotional abuse.

Effects of childhood emotional neglect

Let's start with neglect and look at its long-term effects. The problems experienced by the undermothered come as no surprise; they relate quite clearly to the missing functions of the Good Mother. Here are fifteen common problems:

1. HOLES IN YOUR SENSE OF VALUE AND SELF-ESTEEM

The undermothered do not feel valued and especially do not feel seen. They are not mirrored and receive very little support or encouragement. Almost always, they do not feel loved (even if intellectually they believe their mothers loved them).

The most common explanation for all of this in a child's mind is "I don't matter" or "Something must be wrong with me." The central pillar around which a healthy sense of self develops is missing.

2. FEELING AS IF YOU DON'T HAVE ENOUGH SUPPORT

Not having received much support as children leaves the undermothered with a less confident sense of self and less inner support because there wasn't a Good Mother to internalize. This lack of felt support often shows up as insecurity and difficulty moving ahead. When things get hard you may find yourself collapsing. Even being at the front end of a normal learning curve may be overwhelming and bring up feelings of not being up to the challenge.

Those who have become particularly self-sufficient sometimes don't feel this lack because they've learned to soldier through on their own; yet with the right push, the defense breaks down and the need for support is exposed.

3. DIFFICULTY ACCEPTING AND ADVOCATING FOR YOUR NEEDS

In general, *need* is a dirty word for the undermothered, because needs are associated with the painful memory of having needs that were not met or the perception of Mother turning away from you because of your needs. Needs often are a source of shame and something to hide. There may be a not-so-conscious belief that *my needs are a burden*.

You can't advocate for your needs unless you feel some right to have them and some expectation that others will be responsive. With a history of mother not being emotionally present for their needs, some find it almost impossible to ask for help.

4. FEELING UNDERNOURISHED AND EMOTIONALLY STARVED

Many of the undermothered feel like they are still trying to make up for the affection they missed as children. (See "Feeling like a motherless child," p. 102). As an adult, you may experience the more preoccupied attachment style of still reaching for emotional attachment. This is unlike adults who may have tried to disown their need for love and have cut off the hope of having emotional intimacy. Sometimes there is an oscillation between feeling little or no need for closeness and feeling starved for love, which, in attachment language, relates to the disorganized style of attachment that you may now experience (see p. 53).

5. DIFFICULTY TAKING IN LOVE AND MAINTAINING INTIMATE RELATIONSHIPS

Although the undermothered often feel starved for love, this doesn't make it easy to take love in, as there is often heightened tension and protective armoring blocking the way. Being intimate requires being vulnerable and showing your needs and feelings. Those with a more self-sufficient, avoidant attachment style have particular difficulty with this.

The undermothered also have limited reference points for close relationships and less expectation of having their needs met. It's hard to trust that someone will really be there for you when this wasn't the case in that first, most formative relationship. Many also feel undeserving (sometimes unconsciously), believing that if they were deserving, Mother would have been there for them.

Those with a more dependent style may not only scare people away with their clinging behaviors, but may also become angry when their partners do not provide the perfect love they still seek. Their anger pushes others away, recreating the pattern of their original loss.

6. LONELINESS AND FEELINGS OF NOT BELONGING

There's a sort of outsider complex that comes from not feeling like a treasured part of a family. It can leave you longing to be part of something—some group or community—yet deeply ambivalent and uncomfortable putting yourself in that situation again. Many wonder if there is a place for them in this world. Feeling unloved as a child sets the stage for chronic loneliness.

7. NOT KNOWING HOW TO PROCESS FEELINGS

When a range of emotions are not freely expressed in the childhood home (or only by an out-of-control parent), and when Mother has not helped her child learn how to regulate or to communicate feelings, it creates a hole in an important part of life. For many, learning to identify feelings rather than act out through addictive behaviors has been a major therapeutic task. Those who have kept feelings at bay need to learn how to let an emotion rise and cycle through.

8. A PERVASIVE SENSE OF SCARCITY

Not all of the undermothered suffer from a sense of scarcity, but a number of them do. Deprivation can be so deeply branded into your consciousness that it becomes a lens through which you experience life. You may feel as if there's never enough money, never enough love, and never enough joy.

Often this is complicated by discomfort around receiving. If your mother was scrooge-like in her psychology and didn't give generously, often a part of your psyche has this same filter and doesn't give or receive in a gracious way. You then continue the legacy of scarcity.

9. SENSE OF STRUGGLE

For many of the undermothered, life feels hard. There are struggles around livelihood, around relationships, and to simply feel okay. This struggling is a different octave of the failure-to-thrive syndrome identified in orphanages.

10. DEPRESSION

A very common entry point for therapy is seeking help for depression. Depression has a lot to do with loss, deprivation, needs not being met, not having received enough love, battered self-esteem, undigested pain and disappointment, grief, and lack of support. Depression is also a clue of significant parenting deficits, especially when it begins in childhood or when more than one child in the family is depressed or suicidal at some point in their lives.

11. ADDICTIVE BEHAVIORS

Addiction is a common response to pain that has not been metabolized. It is related to not being able to self-soothe and regulate your emotions or to when your body becomes revved up and reactive to some cue under the surface. Unable to process these uncomfortable emotions and sensations, you learn to push them away through addictive behavior, usually a behavior that provides some kind of soothing or narcotization.

Food-related addictions are especially common to those who were emotionally undernourished. Food has also often been associated with Mother's love, so it's easy to understand why eating may be used to self-soothe and cover up the hole of emptiness left by poor mothering. Eating to satisfy unmet emotional needs of course easily leads to overeating and obesity.

12. FEELING DISEMPOWERED

Not feeling empowered is the natural result of a number of items on this list, especially the first three. Without a positive sense of self-esteem, strong internal support, or healthy entitlement around needs, it's hard to feel empowered. In addition, if Mother didn't champion you during your preschool years, didn't guide and praise your growing competence, your sense of efficacy may be seriously compromised.

Yet, it starts even before this. Your first task as a baby is to get Mother to come. When Mother is not responsive to your cries, it creates a very deep sense of futility. An under-responsive mother can then deeply hamper your sense of being able to affect your environment.

13. NOT FEELING SAFE

The undermothered often had to fend for themselves, many times in situations that were not safe for children. When Mother isn't there to protect you as a child, your nervous system may take up a pattern of hypervigilance to make up for it. Turning off this hypervigilance is not easy.

Insecure attachment will also lead to feeling less safe since attachment is the primary vehicle for providing safety to a young child. Without having internalized the warm, comforting presence of the Good Mother, there isn't a reservoir of feelings of safety or security.

14. PERFECTIONISM AND SELF-CRITICISM

When Mother doesn't give love or praise easily, children often go to great lengths to conform to what they think Mother wants. They monitor themselves carefully and create high standards they hold themselves to. *If only I can be good enough, I'll finally earn Mother's love*, they think, clinging to this hope well into adulthood.

This push toward winning love and respect by being good enough leads to the overachieving we might expect but also to underachieving. People who need to do everything well don't have permission to fail or to try new things that require a learning curve, so they often stop themselves before they begin.

15. DIFFICULTY FINDING YOUR AUTHENTIC VOICE AND FOLLOWING YOUR PASSION

Without a champion or a cheerleader, without mirroring, and without unconditional acceptance, it's much harder to find your authentic self-expression. Neglect can be a setup for a lost self and lost life.

Additional effects of emotional abuse

Emotionally abusive parents are rarely attuned to their children and responsive to their needs, so the effects of emotional neglect will most often be present in those whose mothers can be labeled emotionally abusive. Depression and addiction are even more likely here, and of course one's sense of safety requires a great deal of repair. In addition to the challenges listed above, those who experience emotional abuse are likely to face further challenges.

16. HIGH LEVELS OF ANXIETY

Anxiety is the feeling that something is not quite right, often with a foreboding that something bad is about to happen. It is easy to see why those who suffered emotional attacks as a child might carry a lot of anxiety. In my experience, holding a lot of unprocessed emotions is also correlated with anxiety. What we don't work through gets jammed up inside, creating this same unease.

Anxiety shows up in many ways. Sometimes it spills out as a panic attack. Or it takes the form of phobias or obsessive-compulsive patterns. Often anxiety interferes with sleep. I have clients who are afraid to fall asleep or afraid they will die in their sleep. Anxiety can also be involved in nervous behaviors such as pulling hair, worrying excessively or becoming overly cautious, or being irritable and restless. Feeling anxious and on your guard makes it hard to relax, and the body is then deprived of much that it needs to maintain good health.

17. DEEPLY ENGRAINED AVOIDANCE

If you don't have good skills for regulating your emotions, as is the case for so many who were emotionally neglected or abused, you've got a very big stake in avoiding setting off emotions. That can lead you to not venture out into life and also to avoid going inside. It leaves you with a small emotional range, perhaps living primarily in your head. The need to avoid can also feed addictions.

18. ALIENATION FROM THE BODY

There has often been so much body shaming and such serious physical neglect of emotionally abused children that they experience even more distance from their body than do unintentionally neglected children. More numbing and shame and unprocessed trauma in the body make it even harder to occupy the body. The result of all these internalized attitudes and cutoff is that the body may then not seem real, but more like a collection of inanimate parts. You may feel as if you're not fully human.

19. DEGRADATION OF HEALTH

Not occupying the body fully makes it harder for the body to thrive. The body is separated from the energetic matrix it takes instruction from. On a more practical level, if we're not present in our bodies, we won't be responsive to our bodies' needs—for rest, hydration, food, movement, and so on.

High levels of stress also make for a compromised physical system. Adverse events in childhood are highly correlated with more disease in adulthood as found in the large-scale Adverse Childhood Experiences (ACE) Study.[3] Your immune and nervous systems, along with all the others, were burdened when they were developing and needed to be supported. They cannot function as efficiently as systems blessed with uninterrupted development.

Those in the somatic wing of the trauma field understand that "the body bears the burden" of trauma. (There is even a book by the title *The Body Bears the Burden* by Robert Scaer.) What I've suggested so far is the body bears the burden when we are not fully occupying and attuned to it and when it faces disruptions in its early development, thus compromising important systems. There is an additional way the body bears while simultaneously trying to reveal the burden, which is when it expresses through physical symptoms what has not been worked out psychologically. So, for example, heartache that is not worked through results in heart pain, or a vocal disorder expresses holding back a secret that must not be revealed or a "voice" (individual expression) that has been denied. Sometimes there are notable physiological disease processes supporting these complaints, and sometimes we don't see the physiological underpinnings, yet nonetheless the symptom is there, causing real dysfunction of some kind (technically called *somatic symptom disorder*).

For all of these reasons, health suffers when we carry the burden of unresolved early life trauma.

20. DIFFICULTY TRUSTING

If emotionally abused as a child, you may carry an expectation as an adult that you will be hurt, used, manipulated, and dumped on. You may feel too vulnerable to let down the walls you've erected to protect you. It feels foreign when people act genuinely interested in you, and it's hard to trust that any interest will last or not have an ulterior motive. There is also a fear that if you rely on someone then they will leave. To those with abuse in their histories, too often relationship means pain.

There are different ways you may try to protect yourself from this pain. One is to not let others in. Another is to constantly scan for danger, sometimes using your judgments of others to keep a distance. You may pull out your laundry list of criticisms of your partner when you start to feel vulnerable and you fear becoming too dependent, for example.

It can be a long road to learning trust.

21. USED AND UNHAPPY IN RELATIONSHIPS

Of course being mistreated in your first relationship with a parent makes you more vulnerable to getting involved with others who act in a similar way or make you feel a similar way. You may have learned to be compliant to minimize the other's aggression, even becoming somewhat numb to it. Those who stay in abusive relationships often have a history of childhood abuse.

Another likely pattern is that of caretaking—becoming a doormat and giving too much to people who are "takers," or enabling people to become takers by giving them everything and expecting nothing in return. You inconvenience yourself to meet others' unreasonable demands and always put your own needs last. This happens because you've learned to expect only crumbs. Because you desperately want a relationship and don't expect more parity, you may end up propping up people who need an audience.

22. INTERNAL CEILINGS

Oftentimes we perpetuate the deprivation we experienced in our childhood. One form I see this take is the sense that "I'm not allowed" to feel certain emotions, make decisions, or succeed. I had one woman tell me she was not allowed to feel joy. (We'd expect not allowed to show anger, but joy!) Another said she had "no right" to make her home environment the way she wanted. Very competent adults can be paralyzed by feeling they cannot do what their parents would disapprove of. Another woman said she was not allowed to have children in her twenties or early thirties, and it subsequently took years and many surgeries before she could get pregnant, which she ties to this feeling of "not supposed to."

Many learn early on that they are not allowed to succeed or to surpass Mother. One woman told me she had to hide her successes at school and work, or Mother would smash them. How sad that rather than be celebrated, successes had to be hidden. In this case, her Mother gave very clear messages of "You'll never be good enough." Rather than the highly educated professor that the daughter became, she was repeatedly told by her mother to be a secretary.

Even when you push past barriers to achieve success, other residues remain. One is the feeling of not being good enough, even being a fraud; another is a tendency to take away your own wins, just as Mother did. Perhaps you do it in a different way, like making it invisible or through subtle self-sabotage. Many survivors of this kind of childhood track their failures much more than their successes, and deprive themselves of a more empowered self-image.

23. INTERNAL PERPETRATORS

While we all have an inner critic who pops up at times, those who were cruelly criticized while growing up often have an inner critic that is unnecessarily brutal. While it is sometimes believed that the inner critic is motivated by a positive intention of somehow protecting us (though in a very unskilled way), those with a history of abuse either have a critic gone wild or another part that is an inner perpetrator and who actually intends harm. This inner perpetrator often holds the same judgments as your abusive mother: *You are no-good, fat, lazy, stupid, and should be exposed.*

Living with an internal perpetrator or even an out-of-control critic is hell. You are never safe from attack.

24. A COLLAPSED SELF

When you are rejected as a child, you tend to internalize the rejection, consequently living at odds with yourself, not feeling worthy, and perhaps not trying very hard. You may not know that you have a right to be treated with respect, a right to be well cared for and to take good care of yourself, and a right to thrive.

Some who've been treated with aversion end up feeling untouchable, poisonous to others. If you feel that your being is somehow rotten and repellent, you're certainly not going to step up and ask for anything. A life shaped by rejection is often a life that is very collapsed and with the self-harming described in the next item.

Further, if parents were controlling and made all the decisions, you may feel that you have no right to make decisions for yourself. I think of a middle-aged woman for whom it was radical to think that she could decide how she wanted to wear her hair. She had not fully stepped into adulthood.

This collapse is an extension of the disempowerment that many who had been neglected now feel.

25. SELF-HARMING

Self-harming behaviors can range from subtle self-sabotage and lack of good self-care, to forms of self-injury such as cutting or burning your body, to suicide. Self-harming can be understood several ways:

- as a continuation of the abuse of a perpetrator, now internalized

- as a result of blaming oneself for the abusive behavior received

- as a distorted attempt by a controlling part of you to make you behave well

- as both an expression of shame and an attempt to manage it

- as an expression of self-hatred that comes from either the hatred you absorbed from the outside or the hatred created by your repressed rage and turned against the self

- as a desperate attempt to feel something or, alternately, to go numb

If you experience self-harming, I recommend that you work with a professional to protect yourself and turn that behavior around.

26. FREQUENT OR ONGOING DISSOCIATION

Dissociation, as I wrote in *Healing from Trauma*, is when you are *not all here*. It is most often a disconnection from your body, your feelings, or your environment. We all have small experiences of dissociation, like when we zone out and do something on autopilot, withdrawing our conscious attention and presence. For those with trauma in their backgrounds, this dissociation is both more frequent and more disconcerting.

Dissociation often comes on suddenly. It is a circuit breaker for a nervous system that has become overwhelmed. Dissociation is an emergency response that is only partially successful in managing the feelings of being overwhelmed, since the state of dissociation itself feels compromised—you feel like you've just lost your brain. In a severely dissociated state, you feel so disoriented and unable to focus that you don't realize you must put the milk in the refrigerator for storage.

Dissociation is a learned response to stress and to threatening situations. There's no vote or conscious decision but an involuntary *I'm outta here!* Dissociation may last a few minutes or a few days, but some people spend most of their life in a severely dissociated state where they are numb to significant aspects of their life—most commonly their feelings, their body, or their environment.

Parts of your psyche can get dissociated and disconnected from other parts to a degree that constitutes a dissociative disorder. (See p. 137 for more on dissociative disorders.) This happens when fragments of self carry certain parts of experience but function as if encased, with a separating barrier that does not allow them to share in the experience of other parts. See more on this in the chapter on parts work (p. 178).

One woman described to me feelings from infancy of waiting for Mother: *Where is she?* This was followed by a sense of splitting off and leaving, and of never quite feeling her current self was real. She sobbed when I said, "It's time to move in." (i.e., to come back into her body and this life). "But that unbearable pain will be here," she protested. "It was unbearable then, but it can be different now," I assured her. "I'm here helping you hold it."

27. AMNESIA

Having no memory of significant events or chunks of your childhood is common with psychological trauma. Not the same as amnesia caused by head injuries or other physiological factors, dissociative amnesia is forgetting what is too painful to remember. A defense structure in the psyche says this is too hot to handle and it is "disappeared." This is the defense mechanism called *repression*.

We're perhaps most familiar with this phenomenon in cases of childhood sexual abuse, especially within the home; however, it can occur with any memory that is too difficult to emotionally hold. Awful things said to you or ways you were threatened can make it feel impossible to go on with daily life, so it's a matter of survival to put them out of your mind.

28. NOT SURE WHAT IS REAL

Feeling that you can distinguish what is true and what is false is an important element in trusting your experience. If you were the victim of repeated emotional abuse at a young age (especially if this mistreatment was either denied or blamed on you), and you had no safe place to go but had to retreat to an inner world, it can leave you with a sense that you're not quite sure what is real. You may wonder, *Did that really happen, or did I just imagine or dream it?* Especially if Mother denied much of your experience and perhaps constantly rewrote her own, your sense of reality may be shaky.

This can also happen with the fragmentation I described above. In fact the same woman in that example had not really understood that she exists on her own. She had always felt that she needs checking in on, someone watching her progress, someone seeing her, or she "doesn't exist" (isn't real).

When there has been ongoing dissociation, it's hard work to be *here and now* with all of you present. Becoming "real" may be a major therapeutic goal.

29. WHY AM I SO SENSITIVE?

A childhood that did not feel safe, and in which parents were emotionally abusive, leaves its victims hypersensitive to criticism, rejection, and abandonment, and always scanning for danger. This hypervigilance, along with self-boundaries that are weak (because they were never fully developed or were shattered by invasion), can contribute to a situation where you can feel other people's emotions and motivations. When this is an unconscious, involuntary, frequent occurrence, we often say this person is an *empath*. You might think of it as an excess of empathy. Part of the problem it causes is that empaths often confuse these experiences as their own. They are left wondering why they are so angry or depressed or have that back pain rather than seeing this is something they picked up from another person due to their porous self-boundary.

A large portion of my clients are empaths, and I think this is no accident. I've described it in psychological terms here, but there may be other factors involved, like starting out with a more sensitive nervous system and physiology (being a "highly sensitive person" or HSP).

Trauma survivors show many of the same characteristics as HSPs. Those with attentional disorders also have many of the characteristics of trauma survivors, as do those with some on the high end of the autism spectrum and with brain injuries. We don't always know why something happens. Different models posit different causes. It's not necessarily that you have each of these conditions, but that characteristics overlap.

Let's wade further into this ambiguous territory as we turn to the question *What's wrong with Mother?*

8.

What's Wrong with Mother?

WE MOVE NOW FROM that awful, gnawing question of *What is wrong with me?* (that mother doesn't value me) to a new question: *What is wrong with Mother?* I'm glad you finally asked! It's true: A mother who is emotionally absent, even if otherwise perfectly pleasant, is missing something, and a mother who is emotionally abusive is lacking in an even greater way. In this chapter we'll look at both. We'll start with common reasons Mother is missing in action and move on to factors more often involved in abusive mothering.

She doesn't know better

The first and perhaps most common reason a mother provides so little in her parenting role is that she really doesn't know better. She grew up with mothering that was little different from what she is providing. This is the intergenerational legacy that those of you reading this book are involved in changing.

I've seen this frequently in mothers from large families, where there was simply not enough to go around. Or their mothers were busy surviving, perhaps as new immigrants. Our views of parenting have changed in recent generations, yet the stories of the undermothered are generally of parents who hold old worldviews, where a parent's job is simply to provide for a child's physical needs. They know nothing about the many faces of the Good Mother as I describe them in this book.

An emotionally absent mother may have been undermothered for any of the other reasons included in this book and may not have understood what her children needed. Or perhaps she lost her mother when she was just a child or her mother was sick and she had no reference point for an involved, capable, giving mother.

She is emotionally shut down

Mother can be emotionally closed off for a number of reasons. Two of the most common reasons are depression and unresolved trauma, although any number of reasons (like having emotionally unavailable or aggressive parents) can make her guarded and unavailable. Being emotionally shut down is common in American culture and exacerbated by a lack of work-life balance.

Collectively we are saturated with untreated trauma. War, disaster, sexual assault, and abuse are just a few on the list. When interviewing people for this book, I learned that many people's mothers were untreated trauma survivors or the children of trauma survivors. Some bore scars of the Holocaust. Many experienced the tragic loss of a family member, which they never got over. The not-getting-over is the critical factor here. Research indicates that a woman's ability to form a secure attachment with her child is related more to her capacity to deal with painful emotional events than it is to her actual history of trauma and loss.[1]

Another reason Mother may be emotionally shut down is that she was depressed. Chances are that such depression was undiagnosed and untreated, a tragedy for all it affects. There are many physical contributors to depression, including certain medical conditions, nutritional deficiencies, and even the medications created to treat depression or other conditions. In this book, we've seen depression is a common result of not getting what you needed to create a strong foundation in life and of being under- or poorly parented. I ascribe to a rather old understanding of depression as putting a lid on (literally depressing or pushing down) feelings that we aren't willing to or don't know how to deal with. The result is the flattening that usually marks depression. When depressed, it is difficult to feel motivated, to care, or to experience any satisfaction or joy.

We stumble here on the paradox that many depressed people live in a fog and cannot feel their emotions clearly, while others are drowning in painful feelings and are crying much of the time. Depression is not simple. There are many contributing factors, many kinds of depression, and many different ideas about what causes it.

Regardless of what's behind it, depressed mothers tend to have retreated. They don't have the energy or emotional strength—or even the clarity of mind—to actively and sensitively parent. Many a depressed Mother spends much of her life in her bedroom, disengaged from family life.

She never grew up

Descriptions of many of the more dysfunctional mothers reveal stunted emotional, social, and even cognitive development. Such a woman may have learned to be gregarious and charming, but beneath that interaction, she functions at the level of an adolescent or even a young child. Sometimes these mothers were treated as little princesses in their own families and as a result never learned to take responsibility. More likely they were raised by emotionally immature parents themselves, and just never grew up.

Immature mothers are sometimes taken care of by their husbands, who put them on allowances and take over household and parenting chores. Or the chores of mothering are handed off to older children. Kids as young as three and four are tasked with putting younger siblings to bed, bathing and feeding them, washing dishes, all before they are tall enough to stand at the kitchen sink!

Immature mothers are often described as superficial, vain, petty, easily offended, manipulative, and prone to playing victim. This emotional immaturity may become even more accentuated with aged mothers now needing more care. They may play victim and throw tantrums with family members helping to care for them or in any assisted living situations they are in.

In *Adult Children of Emotionally Immature Parents*, author and psychotherapist Lindsay Gibson spends considerable time describing approximately thirty characteristics that constitute emotional immaturity.[2] They very much coincide with what you as a child of an emotionally neglectful and abusive parent have likely experienced—parents who can't handle their own feelings or anyone else's, who act out their emotions with little conscious awareness, who blame others and never take responsibility, who don't respond empathetically but expect their children to attend to their needs and feelings, who are preoccupied with themselves, who are closed-minded and don't respect differences, who are inconsistent, and who don't repair ruptures in relationships but expect you to leap over a problem and just go back to normal. Sound familiar?

Why Mother can't give

In my therapy practice working with underparented adults, I hear heartbreaking stories of parents who can't give. I hear of the young girl sitting in a cold, dark car while her parents drink at the local bar; the woman whose parents cannot acknowledge her success; the birthday gift that is so paltry, pathetic, and misattuned that in receiving it you feel more like someone has just taken something from you.

How can Mother be such a grinch? There are many possibilities.

- She may carry resentment, even if this resentment is unconscious. (I've seen this dynamic a number of times when a child was unwanted.)

- Her own narcissistic needs feel threatened by someone else's need and she can't leave her own needs long enough to really be generous.

- She may have grown up severely underparented or desperately poor and now muzzles her grief by not giving her child what she didn't have.

- A few mothers are so deeply insecure that they fear being rejected and so do not extend themselves in any meaningful way.

It can be confusing to the point of crazy making when a withholding mother acts out of character. One of my clients brought in a letter from her mother gushing about how much she loved her daughter. Yet the daughter, except for this confusing letter, has no memory of this love ever being demonstrated and no evidence of it. What she had mostly experienced was her mother's resentment. Was the letter showing real love that had been walled off out of insecurity? Was it a compensatory fantasy of a mother who couldn't own or manage her negative feelings? Was it manipulation or image management? It's not what people say so much as what they do over time that reveals who they are.

Does she have a mental illness?

PSYCHOLOGY'S LEXICON
We can talk about what is wrong with mother using common terms like *insensitive, emotionally shut down, self-absorbed, mean*, and *crazy* or by using the language of psychopathology: *narcissistic personality, borderline personality*, and so on.

It can be informative to identify your mother (or any other person) with a bonafide disorder, but also important to understand that disorders are constellations of symptoms, and that these same symptoms are found in more than one disorder.

These symptoms have to be found in a certain quantity and degree to qualify as a disorder, but are also found in subclinical forms. So you may see the basic flavor of a disorder, yet it doesn't meet the criteria to be diagnosed as such. To make matters more complicated, people can have more than one "disorder." Let's also remember that the codification of mental illnesses is a work in progress. Our views change, the political process turns a certain way, and presto, we have a new disease—or one disappears.

If using psychology's lexicon gives more validation to what you're going through or helps you understand your mother better, that's useful. But let's not discount that we may be talking about the same very real phenomena with simpler words like *mean*, *childish*, or *emotionally absent*. There can be a lot of suffering and distortion in the psyche without it fitting into one of these discrete patterns.

A few psychiatric disturbances show up consistently in mothers who are the most unloving. These are borderline personality disorder and narcissism. Understanding these will help us as we continue through common problems in more everyday language.

NARCISSISM

Many do not realize that narcissism is a normal stage of human development because narcissism is usually discussed in the context of pathological behavior. This section is about this pathological, "extreme" narcissism.

Narcissism arises from a wound to a person's sense of value that leaves one feeling so unworthy that she constructs a cover-up image of exaggerated value. Defending such a wobbly self-image leads to many extreme defensive behaviors, often going on all-out attack to discredit anyone who threatens that image. The vindictive narcissist will do anything to destroy you if you've managed to activate their underlying shame.

Here are some common characteristics of extreme narcissists:

- It's always about them.
- They crave admiration and attention.
- They are never wrong (in their eyes). (Don't let them see it in yours!)
- They are superior or superlative in every way.
- They are emotionally shallow and without empathy.

Since a narcissistic mother makes it all about herself, she takes credit for her child's successes—anything that in her eyes makes her look good. But since she must defend her self-image at all costs, she blames anything that goes wrong squarely on others. She may also offload her underlying shame onto one of her children, which is then sufficient cause for treating them poorly.

The basic feeling left by a narcissistic mother is *I must not be good enough*, which results from her criticism and her need to always outshine you. How can you really flourish and succeed if you know Mother will punish you for it or try to take it away from you, often in a passive-aggressive way?

A narcissistic mother can have some of the emotional volatility of other types, going into what's been called a "narcissistic rage" when most threatened. She may scream vile epithets and make wild accusations. Or she may crumple into victimhood if nothing else is working. With an extremely narcissistic parent you learn to accept their (unfair) blame, suck up your needs, and become a good "admiring mirror."

Narcissistic mothers are confusing, because unlike the most emotionally shut-down mothers, they can be caring and supportive when they're not threatened and especially when children are young. Narcissistic mothers often become competitive as their daughters grow older, and can be obnoxious in criticizing their daughters' appearance, flirting with their boy-friends, or chumming up with their friends.

When someone denies your reality, it is very destabilizing—and narcissistic, borderline, and dissociative mothers can all respond with "that didn't happen." They may even lie. Unless you are confident in your own perceptions, you can begin to doubt your own reality, which deeply undermines your sense of self.

BORDERLINE PERSONALITY DISORDER

Like the narcissist, borderline mothers easily feel betrayed and attacked when others do not validate their feelings and perceptions. They then reject, punish, and vilify the person who has, in their eyes, failed them.[3]

The central features of those with borderline personality disorder include:

- intense, irrational anger

- emotional volatility

- impulsivity, often in areas that are potentially self-damaging, such as overspending, promiscuity, eating disorders and substance abuse, reckless driving, and even self-mutilation

- chronic feelings of emptiness and unstable identity

- desperate fear of abandonment

- trouble maintaining relationships, often alternating between idealizing and devaluing the Other

Borderline mothers are prone to overreact and can be unpredictable, sometimes behaving in a caring way and other times lashing out in uncontrolled fits of rage. A particularly difficult dynamic most often found with borderline mothers is their tendency to make one child the golden child, who can do nothing wrong, and another child all bad, who in their eyes can do nothing right. The scapegoated child carries the mother's offloaded self-hatred and shame.

Christine Ann Lawson, in her book *Understanding The Borderline Mother*, describes how borderline mothers don't respect boundaries, use fear and guilt to control their children, manipulate their children ("If you loved me, you would . . ."), demand that their children side with them, and often punish their children for expressing their own views or feelings.[4]

Lawson outlines four types of borderline mothers, based on a predominant emotional tone. These include the Waif, a victim who constantly refuses help and has pervasive low self-esteem; the Hermit, who is essentially a frightened child hiding from the world; the Queen, who is "mirror hungry" (i.e., narcissistic), entitled, and demanding; and the Witch, who is rageful and sadistic (taking pleasure in another's suffering) and demands absolute power. If any of these descriptions sound familiar, I highly recommend Lawson's book.

The feeling of living with someone with borderline personality disorder is that of having to walk on eggshells. You never know when the other will explode in rage, take unintended offense, or collapse in self-pity. This leaves you with no sense of normalcy or safety.

Watch out for Mother's anger!

Even the most saintly mother gets mad at times, but when mother's anger is eviscerating or leads to physical abuse, something is wrong. Several types of mental illness can leave a person unable to titrate anger, so it's never just a little angry, but all-out rage. We saw both the narcissist and the borderline mother are quick to anger because their sense of self is not securely anchored and thus wobbly.

Borderline personality and narcissistic disorders are not the only ones associated with extreme anger. Mothers with bipolar disorder can also explode in rage. Diane Dweller in her memoir,

Mom, Mania, and Me, describes a mother who would go off the rails, spending recklessly, driving dangerously, and being a terror to Diane, including being verbally and physically abusive.[5] Bipolar disorder used to be called manic depression. Depressed episodes alternate with episodes of getting sped up, thoughts sometimes racing ahead of one's ability to express them coherently, hyperactivity, inability to sleep, or in Diane's example, her mother's fast driving and impulsive spending. When not in a manic episode, bipolar mothers can look and act more normal. The impulsiveness and abusiveness Diane describes can also be found in borderline mothers. Of course it is common for someone to have multiple conditions; for example, one may have post-traumatic stress disorder (PTSD), borderline personality disorder, and depression or attention deficit disorder.

Anyone who cannot regulate emotions is likely to have a hard time keeping anger within more reasonable bounds. Mothers with unresolved trauma, such as PTSD, are also in this camp. One young mother with PTSD I am working with found that facing her trauma (repressed sexual abuse) immediately led to less volatility and anger with her children. Mothers with schizophrenia and dissociative disorders (both covered below) can also act out in unpredictably rageful ways.

The mean mother

Meanness also crosses the line into emotional abuse. Through her words and actions, a mother who is mean purposefully acts to hurt you, tear you down, and take away any good feelings you may have. Mean mothers are routinely critical and rarely complimentary. Such a mother's remarks are not just insensitive but consistently cruel.

How does someone end up a mean mother? While there are occasionally physiological factors (a brain tumor, bipolar), more often than not her meanness comes from her own psychological wounds. She may be envious and in competition with you (especially her daughters) or she may be offloading her negative feelings about herself. She may also be acting out her own misery. The mean mother is an unhealthy mother and has a good chance of suffering from either borderline personality or narcissism.

Mothers who are "crazy"

People have long used the term *crazy* to refer to behaviors that make no sense. It is, of course, a word that is used too broadly and usually in a demeaning way. Translating it into our psychological lexicon, *crazy* is having a disorder so severe as to be classified as a psychosis. When someone is actively psychotic they are no longer operating in consensual reality.

When psychotic, people may see things that aren't there, feel under the influence of inanimate objects or punishing voices (more than just an inner critic), are often paranoid, and may believe things that fly in the face of the facts.

People with severe depression can become psychotic. People can become psychotic while on medications or drugs that don't agree with them, secondary to a medical problem, or even by lack of sleep. The disorder most often associated with psychosis is schizophrenia.

Schizophrenia is a debilitating condition. It's as if your wiring is off and you can't organize thoughts, follow through with intentions, connect the dots of life, articulate your ideas or experience, or sustain relationships. Mothers with schizophrenia, more than other types of dysfunctional mothers (perhaps with major depression as an exception) tend to have been hospitalized for the condition, often several times. They are generally unable to hold a job and are therefore dependent on their partners financially and for any kind of stability. If they don't have a partner or someone watching out for them, they may not be able to keep a roof over their head.

Schizophrenic mothers may be actively psychotic only a small fraction of the time, but their relationship with reality is so shaky that they are generally low functioning, and it is fair to say they have never really thrived. They cannot provide stability for their children, and their shifting moods and unfounded reactions likely scare their children.

Having a mother who is so low functioning and so invalidating deeply wounds a child's sense of confidence and normalcy. Not having grown up with normal routines, they often struggle in adulthood to find the right amount of structure for daily living, falling at either end of the continuum—living without any routine or discipline, or clinging to structure and rules, trying to find a way to live.

Mother's changing face

Children need consistency. The sense that your caretaker can suddenly turn on you causes your nervous system to always be on high alert, with ongoing hypervigilance and anxiety as a result.

You can see from the description of the borderline mother that this mother wears a changing face, sometimes sweet and sometimes monstrous. This can also be true of the bipolar mother and of those with dissociative disorders, which I will describe here.

We all have parts of self, but with a dissociative disorder these parts are more encapsulated and out of touch with each other. In the form of dissociative identity disorder (DID), formerly multiple personality disorder, many of the parts don't know that other parts exist, and communication and coordination between parts take quite a bit of effort to establish. A "different personality" can sometimes appear, as depicted in the many movies about this subject. What is less known is that the different parts aren't usually as obvious as Hollywood makes them. In fact, it often takes years for therapists to identify those with DID. For children, it's even more difficult to understand why Mother sometimes has no memory of an important conversation or event or can act radically different at different times! Mother's changing face in these circumstances creates a very unstable world, and the child may end up fragmenting in a similar way to cope with it.

Unlike those suffering from schizophrenia, which is often confused with dissociative disorders, many who have dissociative disorders are high functioning, with a disproportionate number holding advanced degrees. So Mother being a doctor or a judge doesn't necessarily mean that she has it together in terms of her own personality.

Of course we all show different sides of us at times and experience memory lapses, so it's important to not quickly pathologize someone. But when there is a Jekyll-and-Hyde type of radical change, you're looking at someone who is not very integrated, to say the least, and who, for a vulnerable child, will be frightening and disorienting.

Mothers who are relationally blind

Sometimes Mother is not just misattuned to you, but is misattuned in most relationships because she can't read people. Occasionally this may come from a background with little socialization, while other times it is wired in.

Asperger's syndrome is the high-functioning end of the autism spectrum, which in 2013 was eliminated as a separate diagnosis but is still a useful way to talk about a particular complex. People with Asperger's have at least average intelligence and verbal skills (and may even be brilliant in their own way), but are handicapped in a number of capacities that help others be relationally tuned in and socially intelligent.

Here are some of the common traits of Asperger's, which you might notice in an emotionally absent mother:

- lack of eye contact and two-way conversation

- limited ability to read nonverbal signals, such as gestures and facial expressions; may therefore misinterpret or be confused about what others feel and want

- can't follow conversation when it leaves the realm of fact and is more metaphoric or nonliteral; missing humor and the intent behind teasing or irony

- difficulty understanding other people's perspective or why they are doing what they are doing

- doesn't understand why their own behavior is inappropriate in a given situation, because they don't really grasp the larger relational field

You can see how easily this pattern can appear selfish or insensitive to others. It may be helpful in understanding Mother to notice if she has this whole syndrome.

What Mother can't let herself see

There is one other rather unique situation in which Mother may be emotionally turned off to her child—when she can't let herself see that her child is being abused by someone close to her. Most often this happens when her husband or partner is sexually abusing her child.

There are several very potent reasons Mother would not want to see this. An obvious one is the protection of her primary relationship. Who would want to believe that her partner is abusing her child? She may feel dependent and unable to survive without her partner and therefore be unable to see what is unacceptable. To allow herself to become aware of the abuse, she has to care more about the child than the partner, and this, unfortunately, is not always the case.

Very often the non-abusing spouse also has a history of her own that she is protecting herself from. Mothers who marry abusive men were often themselves abused as children, and many times this abuse is wholly repressed and unknown to them. Sexual abuse once again happening in her home is something that Mother does not want to see. In an effort to keep this further away, she may harden herself to any child who is placed in the position of the unhealed child inside of her.

Although we hate to consider it, on a rare occasion there are mothers who allow a child to be the target of some kind of abuse by another (sometimes a sibling) because that child represents her own self-hate.

It's painful to look at how deeply Mother may be disturbed, but seeing Mother clearly is a step in healing. You do not have to diagnose her with a psychiatric disorder, but you do need to see the ways she is broken so that you can stop interpreting her behavior so personally. This is an important step of healing, where we will go next.

PART III

Healing Mother Wounds

9.

The Process of Healing

AS WE TURN TO the task of healing, let's begin with an overview. In this chapter, we look at how we protect ourselves from our deepest hurts and how we need to uncover them in order to drain away the stored emotions and begin the process of recovery. We'll also talk about journaling as a place to do some of this feeling work, and will look at anger and grief, two of the primary emotions we need to confront on our healing journey.

The cover-up

It is probably apparent to you that you or someone you care about has a "mother wound." You may be surprised that some adults who suffer significantly from mother wounds are unaware and deny them completely. Therapists recognize that many times those with the most wounding have created the biggest cover-ups to hide the damage from view. Clients may go so far as to idealize their parents, as if to create a monument that cannot be questioned.

Unfortunately, that's what it is—a monument, a bigger-than-life story. But denial is never foolproof, and there will often be clues that something was amiss in the mother-child relationship. In addition to the problems described so far, other indicators include the following:

- When you see a tender mother-child interaction, you are emotionally triggered. You may feel choked up and teary or push away the pain by becoming critical and dismissive. (It hurts to see what you didn't have.)

- You would just as soon not look deeply into your relationship with your mother. Better to "let sleeping dogs lie."

- When you visit your mother, you find yourself numbing or going into a trance state in which you are not fully present. Visits are always upsetting, and you find yourself back in painful childhood feelings.

- When asked to come up with examples of how wonderful Mother was or times you felt well-loved, you can't come up with many examples, although you've just proclaimed that everything was great.

- You crave true closeness yet feel uncomfortable and afraid of it. It is unfamiliar to you.

- You avoid having children of your own, feeling somehow not quite like "parent material."

Discovering the wound

Creating some kind of protection is natural for the places where we hurt, and it may take some time to uncover what is beneath it.

Sometimes life circumstances brings the wound to the forefront. One of the most powerful of these is being left by a partner as an adult. It brings up the hole of someone not being there to love and support you, and you may experience a sense of abandonment similar to what you felt as a child. This can happen whether the partner chose to leave or died.

Unresolved feelings about your mother may also be prompted by situations that have to do with mothering, such as having a child yourself or the loss that comes when your last child leaves home. Other times Mother growing old and wanting your help may be the prompt.

You may begin with noting that your relationship with your mother doesn't feel simple to you. If you are still merged with her on some level, the relationship will feel sticky and have in it the feelings that you associate with your mother. If she seemed heavy and depressed, for example, you may feel some of that when thinking about the relationship and find it difficult to see her objectively. Her feelings have become your feelings, her views (especially of you), your views.

This relates to what is commonly referred to as *codependency*: a situation in which you're not really free to live your own life because you are so inside someone else's head. If you have been making up for Mother's shortcomings or caretaking for her, or if she has imprinted you with a sense that loyalty to family or specifically to her is all important, disentangling yourself from this sticky web will not be easy.

Often it will take quite a bit of time in therapy for someone with significant mother wounds to really begin to tell the truth about their childhood. There's a considerable distance between the story that one tells at first and the lived experience; and it is the lived experience, stored in the unconscious, that takes time to get to. As this is unearthed, the story that was constructed to protect the wound slowly crumbles.

Even for those who are quite aware that their relationships with their mothers somehow fall short, opening to the full depth of what was missing is likely to be resisted and happens only slowly over time. Because the wound is so painful, we naturally shy away from it. We become less sensitized only as some of the pain is carefully drained away and we have grown stronger.

Reframing "defects" as deficits

Although the undermothered often have some sense that there was something they missed and that this "something" affects them yet today, we seldom see the correlations in a direct way.

It is my hope that the early chapters in this book have helped you make connections between what was missing in your early environment and the difficulties you struggle with now. One of the benefits readers most appreciated in my book *Healing from Trauma* was that in knowing how their symptoms related to trauma, they could stop blaming themselves. In a similar way, knowing how dissatisfactions and limitations in your life relate to mother wounds can help you realize that your struggles are the natural result of certain conditions. Just as a plant grown in soil depleted of minerals will show certain weaknesses, a person who has not had enough nurturance, support, mirroring, and other essential nutrients will be underdeveloped in certain ways. In the language of John Bradshaw, your *defects* can then be recognized as *deficits*—things you missed.

Working through your feelings

There are many ways we stay out of contact with our deeper feelings: We may keep ourselves busy, with no time to drop into feelings; stay caught in thinking (obsessions can be very useful); tense our bodies, blocking the physiological counterparts of emotions; and breathe shallowly to minimize and contain experience.

Most fields of psychotherapy and programs like the twelve-step recovery movement hold to the notion that you can't heal what you can't feel. Numbing and cover-ups protect the wound but prevent the healing.

When we finally break through our self-protections and connect with the lived experience of our childhood, it hurts. There is a well of grief that we haven't wanted to touch. This well contains both the feelings that were too painful to experience at the time and have been stored in "encapsulated form" somewhere in our systems and the grief we feel now when we recognize what we went through and how very much we missed. Those tears we shed when we watched the movie of the child with the loving mother are grief spilling out about what might—and should—have been.

Bradshaw calls this *original pain work*. "Original pain work involves actually experiencing the original repressed feelings. I call it the uncovery process. It is the only thing that will bring about 'second-order change,' the kind of deep change that truly resolves feelings."[1]

Original pain work involves a large number of feelings to work through, including shock, anger, loneliness, fear, shame, confusion, and raw, undifferentiated pain. It also involves grief, but grief is only part of the story.

We need support and tools for this leg of the journey. We usually scoot away from our pain when we can, so we may need the presence of caring or facilitating others to provide the support necessary to do this work. I think individual psychotherapy is probably the best container for it, but it is not the only one. Group therapy, support groups and forums, workshops, and loving relationships may all help. Revealing this pain to another and having it touch another (unlike one's mother, whose heart too often could not be touched) is very healing.

Because of the nature of the injuries we're talking about, you may have intense feelings and not be able to connect them to any content. This is not a reason to dismiss them. We can have emotions separated from content because they are part of pre-verbal memories that occurred before our mind could delineate and hold them. If you look, you might identify feeling very young at these moments. A similar separation of feelings from content happens in our most traumatic moments, when experience shatters into different tracks, like a movie where the picture and sound get disconnected. At these times you are likely to also feel discombobulated and not all of one piece. That's why in recovering traumatic memories you may have the "facts" but no feeling, or you may have body memory but no visuals, and so on.

Although it may feel like the pain could go on forever, it won't. Not if you can stay present with it. When emotions of any kind are contacted (felt) in a genuine way, they change. It helps if you can take a half step back, disengaging enough that you notice the process and are not just glued to the feelings. This takes you out of identification with content and into a part of yourself that is aware but not involved, often called the "witness." This provides you with some emotional distance to help in exploring difficult feelings. I sometimes call this "getting bigger than the feelings" because part of you is seated outside of them.

Modern spiritual authors have gotten quite involved in helping people find ways to work with difficult emotions. Michael Singer, in *The Untethered Soul*, invites his readers to "fall behind the energy" when they start to get drawn into big feelings. Relax your shoulders and your heart, he instructs, and let it all pass through you like the wind.

Another method to not drown in your emotions is to oscillate back and forth between the intense feeling and any other sensory channel (sight, hearing, or touch, for example), often by focusing on something in your immediate physical environment. You can move to the thinking channel, which will often happen without trying, but can also be used intentionally. If you can fasten your mind to something outside your distress long enough, your system will calm down. Or you can stay in your emotional channel but oscillate to a positive memory. Oscillating helps you to not get stuck.

Yet another helpful strategy is to bring in a caring Other, either in person or through a dialogue in your journal. I almost always use this latter technique when working with painful feelings on my own, as it helps provide an anchor in a turbulent sea.

There is an art to skillfully working with painful feelings, and while various recipes have been offered in recent years, not every method may work well for you. I encourage you to experiment. The good news is that you get stronger with practice.

Journaling

Journaling is a safe place for your feelings while going through original pain work. You don't want to wear out your friends, and your therapist (if you have one) is not always available. Researchers have recognized that expressing feelings on paper (like expressing them verbally) is helpful, whereas holding in feelings is correlated with higher stress levels and disease. The journal can serve as confidant, mirror, and guide. In your journal, you are safe from judgment and criticism, and with advanced techniques like dialogues, you can learn to comfort and support yourself.

Since your journal is your confidant and a place to heal old wounds, it is an appropriate place to express your pain. It may be the pain of grief, disappointment, loss, victimization, betrayal—anything that hurts you. You honor the journal by sharing your pain, and your journal honors you by accepting it.

Writing your feelings may bring tears, and this is fine. You can make a short, parenthetical note in the journal that you are crying as you write a particular passage, which later helps you identify what exactly seems to elicit the most feeling. Obviously you want to be in a safe place to do this work, and it is helpful to have tissues and perhaps some comfort objects around you.

I find that often the tears mark a turning point. The tears show me that I have hit "pay dirt," and continuing to write through them helps open my heart, which is then there as a resource for me. The open heart, with its compassion, is per-haps the most important resource we have for working with our pain.

Although we may feel like we could cry forever, it's usually a fairly limited time as measured by the clock. And in terms of intensity, we generally can handle a lot more pain than we give ourselves credit for. Avoiding pain seems so reflexive that we rarely test our capacities.

Know that you can take a break when you need to. You can lay down your journal and do something else for a while. You might choose to think about a pleasant memory (for example, a memory of someone who really cares about you). What we often call distraction may be the mind's natural way of trying to give us a breather.

You can dialogue in the journal between two parts of yourself—for example, between a part of you that is feeling the pain and an inner representation of someone who is receiving your pain (such as your therapist, if you have one) or with a wisdom figure who is outside that pain. In writing dialogues, you simply go back and forth expressing different aspects of something, usually starting on a new line each time you switch voices.

When you are writing in your journal, you're no longer alone with your emotions. You are much more alone when you are holding your feelings inside.

The healing power of anger

John Bradshaw says, "It's okay to be angry, even if what was done to you was unintentional. In fact, you *have* to be angry if you want to heal your wounded inner child."[2]

It can feel hard to be angry at your mother, the woman who gave you birth and bandaged your scraped knees. It's especially hard to feel angry when you believe that she *tried* or that she did love you—even if she was not able to show it in a way that you could feel. It's important to remember that anger isn't the goal or where you will necessarily stay forever; it's simply part of the healing process.

If you're still trying to get something from your mother (love, respect, validation, connection . . .) and need to avoid upsetting her, your anger may feel too dangerous to even admit to yourself. If you have to maintain a certain self-image that excludes anger, you'll also need to keep this emotion at bay. But if you want to champion your wounded inner child, if you want to create room to feel what was too threatening to feel earlier, if you want to release the feeling (rather than stay unconsciously stuck in it), you need to give yourself permission to feel angry.

The origin of your anger toward Mother is likely very early, as is the habit of turning off anger. The attachment theory pioneer John Bowlby said that anger is a natural response to a child's attachment needs not being met. When a child feels that anger will only lead to more distancing on Mom's part, the child learns to turn it off. Here again the two primary insecure attachment styles come into play. Those with an avoidant, self-sufficient style are most likely to repress or hide their anger and to believe it can only hurt a relationship, whereas those with the more ambivalent, preoccupied style have learned to use their anger to get another's attention.

Beginning in childhood but continuing into adulthood, we may use anger to help us push off and separate from another. Anger therefore has a positive developmental role to play. It is part of coming to your own experience, which sometimes differs from the family myth. Now as an adult, anger comes when you say, "This was my experience, and what I got was not enough."

It's important that you know you have a right to be angry and that feeling angry doesn't mean you're a bad person or even a generally angry person. Anger is a message that something is not right. It's a healthy response to violation that is wired into us, if we haven't suppressed it.

We have to move from anger-phobic to realizing that it is not the anger that is dangerous, but an unhealthy relationship with it that is. When we can't soberly contain our anger but have it spill out indiscriminately, our anger controls us. When a person who has suppressed their anger for years hits a breaking point and violently acts out, anger can become an ingredient in tragedy. Anger is dangerous in these situations. There is also a *clean anger* that positively serves our relationships by bringing more honesty to them in a way that is not demeaning but still conveys respect.

An example of healthy anger is when something happens that is disrespectful or violating in some way, and anger comes up to say, "This is not okay." This is what anger is designed for—to create boundaries that are needed.

It is also important to liberate anger that has been locked in your body, anger that may have been suppressed even before it was felt. This may even include rage you felt as an infant or toddler. It is my belief that this anger can be metabolized and released by skillfully feeling or expressing it. Sometimes, however, releasing anger becomes a self-reinforcing loop, which is what we want to avoid. It's safest to do this release work with a skilled therapist.

Anger comes in all stripes, so here is another important distinction. There is a kind of *victim anger* that feels whiny and impotent and an empowered anger that feels like standing up for yourself. What I'm talking about is getting to the *empowered anger*, even though you might start out with the other.

Some people find anger easy to do and use it as their all-purpose emotion to stand in for disappointment, sadness, fear—all kinds of things. Others hold their anger in for all they're worth out of a subconscious fear that letting themselves feel it will mean opening floodgates that can't be shut. Healing emotional wounds of any kind involves becoming emotionally fluent, able to experience and distinguish among a vast array of emotions without being slave to any of them.

The journal is a great place for anger, especially since so many people are uncomfortable with anger, and we may have fewer friends willing to provide support for anger than for a softer emotion such as sadness. Anger is hard, and sometimes it is hateful. These are not pretty feelings that you readily display to people, yet the journal holds them without judgment.

Working with anger is so much about permission. Many of us have learned to swallow anger, and it generally takes a long time to unlearn this. If we practice journal writing consistently and honestly, it will help undo this habit of self-censorship.

If anger is one of the emotions that you cannot contain and that you act out in harmful ways, you may need to take special precautions. It's important that you be able to calibrate anger, to have it run along a continuum rather than being something that is either "off" or "on." You need to recognize anger when it first arises and have tools for titrating it, being able to control how much is coming through at any given moment, using distraction, breathing, or time-outs to interrupt unwanted escalation. You might consider an anger management class or working with a therapist if you either feel no control over your anger or don't dare to even touch it.

Exploring your anger (an exercise)

In this exercise we'll work with what in journaling is called a sentence stem. The first part of the sentence is provided, and you are to complete it with whatever comes to mind, working quickly so that you don't censor yourself. I encourage you to complete this sentence ten times or more (the longer the list, the more effective the exercise), and target your thoughts on your mother:

I am angry that . . .

After you are finished, read all of your answers and notice how you feel. If you want to do some freestyle writing, this is a good time. I also encourage you to reflect on a further issue:

Beneath the anger, I feel . . .

Complete this sentence stem at least ten times as well. You might also make a list of the things you haven't forgiven your mother for.

Grieving

In addition to doing our anger work, healing from mother wounds also involves deep grieving. We grieve what was missing, grieve for the anguish suffered by that child that we were, and grieve how small or distorted our life became because of it. It may seem like an endless stream of tears.

You've likely heard of Dr. Elisabeth Kübler-Ross's work outlining stages of grief, although we tend to think of it more linearly than was her intention. But the elements of denial, anger, bargaining, depression, and acceptance are relevant here. To get through grief, we have to let go of unrealistic hopes (denial of what is most fundamentally true) and the *if-only*'s that constitute bargaining. In the case with Mother, the *if-only*'s started very early: If only I could be good and not disturb Mother; if only I would not cry; if only I could comfort her; if only I could make her proud . . . . These are sincere but desperate attempts to pull out of this woman the Good Mother that we need.

What must, in the end, be given up is the fantasy of this hoped-for mother. Author and psychotherapist Lindsay Gibson nails it when she writes, "Not realizing the magnitude of their parents' developmental limitations, many children of emotionally immature people think there must be a genuine, fully developed person hiding inside the parent, a real self they could connect to if only the parent would let them."[3]

Oh, how we want that intact, warm, available, responsible, attuned person to exist! And there may be just enough moments of responsiveness to keep the fantasy going despite the vast majority of our experience to the contrary. But ultimately, grieving is coming to terms with what is, even if it at first seems something we can't survive. This is why depression, our affective response to this loss, usually comes before acceptance. We feel our heartbreak, and if that is held with compassion and we have support, we eventually come to peace.

If only (an exercise)

Let's explore three sets of *if-only*'s.

The first *if-only*'s relate to Mom and her well-being. You may have held these earlier or be aware that you still hold them. Here are some examples:

- If only she could get on the right meds

- If only she could get on top of her depression

- If only she'd go to therapy

- If only she could have a stable marriage

In your hope to have more of the Good Mother to respond to, what *if-only*'s do you hold onto? Make a list.

Our second exploration is what *if-only*'s you held as a child. I gave examples of these above. Some of these you may infer from your behavior.

Lastly, what are the *if-only*'s you hold for the relationship now? The first part of the construction, *if only X were the case*, is followed by an assumption related to the effect on the relationship or your own sense of self. See if you can identify that part as well.

- If only I could make her see how well I'm doing, she would be proud of me, and I'd feel loved.

- If only we had quality time together, she'd see what a great person I am and she'd want to be close to me.

These assume that you still want something from Mother. But that may either be hidden from view or have been destroyed long ago. If you feel primarily aversion, your *if-only* may be more like this:

- If only she were dead, I'd never have to think about her again and I could be happier.

- If only she stopped wanting something from me, I could be free.

Healing requires letting go of fantasies and *if-only*'s and accepting actual circumstances and limitations. This is an incredibly thorny issue I'll discuss again in the inner child chapter, in the section, "Unlatching from Mother" (p 186).

Leaving the past

Those who would rather not go into these inner recesses often use words like *wallowing* when talking about feelings or our relationship with what is unfinished in our past. They throw out words like this to hook our shame and give the message, "Just get over it!"

And to be sure, it is a question we ask ourselves: How long will this go on? My sense is that *we let go of the past when we're done with it*. When we're complete. It's that simple.

At some point other things become far more interesting and the pull of past emotions just can't compete anymore. We've worked the ground, taken out the big stones, and new things are growing—things that captivate and enrich our lives.

This is not to say we won't flinch if someone touches the center of that wound (though maybe we won't), but we will have completed our active grieving and moved on. Until then, try to counter those thoughts that you should be over the past by reminding yourself that although not everyone may need to do this, it's part of the territory for you. No, you didn't ask for it, and you wouldn't have chosen it. Yet because you have this particular legacy and don't want to pass it on (if you are in a parenting role) or because somewhere deep inside you have a connection with that undermothered child and want to make things right, you're doing the work—"fighting the good fight," so to speak. It's not the whole work, this grieving and original pain work, but it is part of it.

It is true that there is some danger of getting stuck there. We can make an identity out of any potent experience, especially one that happens early and leaves deep scars. Working through these mother wounds is not easy, and will take tremendous commitment and resourcefulness. One such potent resource is "Good Mother energy."

10.
Connecting with Good Mother Energy

IN ORDER TO HEAL, we need to not only acknowledge and grieve what was missing but also find ways to make up for it. In making up for a nurturing deficit and a mother who was not fully present, we need to connect with "Good Mother energy." Fortunately, there are many ways we can do this (besides therapy), and this chapter will focus on three of them: connecting with the Good Mother archetype, finding others who stand in for the Good Mother, and working through unresolved issues and unmet needs in primary relationships.

Opening to the Good Mother

If you repressed your needs and longing for a good mother, as so many of us have, it can feel pretty intense when this thaws out and the lost feelings emerge. The longing may feel unfamiliar, dangerous, and embarrassing, but it is vital to the healing process. The desire for mothering is natural; it was there when you were a child, even if you learned to turn it off as a strategy for survival. As one therapist reminds her clients, the yearning itself is healthy. It is part of being human to want to be nurtured and cared for.

Although this longing may have been frustrated in the past, it can bear fruits now. We can receive the nurture, care, guidance, protection, mirroring, and so on from others whom we now *choose* to put in these roles. Eventually we can develop a strong Good Mother within us, modeled on the best of what we've experienced or perhaps on our experiences with the archetypal Good Mother.

Regardless of which of these levels you're working on, the dynamic is really the same. The Good Mother can't give to you if you're stuck in a funk about how unmothered you feel. She can't tenderly stroke your face when you defiantly turn away. You must allow yourself to be vulnerable and let her draw near. Only then will you receive her gifts.

Archetypes

Archetypes are larger-than-life patterns that we, as humans, imperfectly embody. They are larger than life because they are broader than any one expression of them. For example, there is not just one way a person embodying the crone will appear; one wise elder may be more extroverted or idiosyncratic than another. Archetypes are like the basic roles filled by new actors in every play. Every culture, like every theater director, casts them a little differently, but we see the same basic character types again and again.

This is not simply a matter of convention, according to those who experience archetypes in the realm of subtle energies. The same archetypes show up again and again because they exist as energy patterns in the larger transpersonal realm. Many of these archetypes have been recognized since the beginning of human culture, although in earlier times these basic energies were associated more with the natural world. Long before Mother Mary embodied the mother archetype, there was Mother Earth. Goddess cultures related to the Earth as the source of nurture and supply and primary mother image. They each had their own name and own image of this archetype, but they all knew her.

When the Swiss psychiatrist Carl Jung brought archetypes into modern psychology early in the twentieth century, he described them as residues of ancestral memory preserved in the collective unconscious (greater mind) that we all share. From a Jungian view, we are born with an archetype of the Good Mother as a psychic structure. This archetype is like a blueprint that gets turned on or becomes operative when we meet mothering that is "good enough."[1]

When this doesn't happen in our families of origin, we might find someone else to activate this archetype, such as a therapist. The therapist then becomes the embodiment and the doorway to the deeper energies of the archetype, which may later be experienced in additional ways, as described later.

Working with imagery and symbols

We often experience the archetypes through powerful imagery. This may happen in dreams, guided imagery, and artwork. Some of the archetypal forces that may appear include the Good Mother, particular aspects of the mother such as those enumerated in chapter 2, the bad mother/witch, the abandoned child, and the starving, primitive instinctual self.

Carla, a woman in her forties, reported that she often met a protective mother-bear figure in all of these venues (meditations, dreams, and art creations). She found herself creating mother-infant pairs and drawing circles, which many would associate with a mother's breast and which she associated with the mother, the womb, and being contained in a safe space. For Carla, these expressed the longing for maternal aspects that had been missing in her life. She had not been protected and received little nurturing and almost no time alone with her mother.

Carla experienced her cutoff instinctual desire as a primitive creature-child so voracious that it could eat her alive. Remember that whatever is pushed into the unconscious gathers force.

We can't cut off our instinctual needs and float above them without having some kind of counterbalance periodically erupt out of our personal underworld.

Making a representation of the Good Mother is a good way to bring that archetype deeper into your consciousness, and I encourage you to take the time to do this. It can be a collage, a drawing, a sculpture—any number of things. The idea is to anchor the ideal mother and give her a form. You can then use that form to evoke her energy when doing inner work.

You might also make a list of Good Mother messages and of qualities associated with this archetype. I actually wrote my Good Mother messages on the collage I made.

Help from the Divine Mother

One of the classic images associated with the mother archetype is Mother Mary from the Christian tradition. The Madonna and Child is one of the most frequently painted images in existence. It is an image found well before the Christian era and seems to have universal appeal. *Mary* is one of many names beginning with the syllable *Ma*, meaning "mother." Mother Mary is often associated with the rose, which is linked with the same Divine Mother energy.

Many people have reported receiving comfort and guidance from Mary or from mother figures of other religious traditions, such as Kuan Yin (or Guan Yin), the bodhisattva of compassion. Most, if not all, traditions have images of the Divine Mother, and believers within these traditions often have experiences in which they feel loved and cared for by this maternal energy.

One woman described feeling like a cranky baby who was able to let go and relax when she felt held by a loving presence that felt to her like Mother Mary. Another experienced something akin to this when she imagined being wrapped in swaddling clothes by the Goddess Mother. A third woman, Ann, described doing some inner journey work and meeting a goddess figure who seemed to take away her burdens and absorb her pain. Ann discovered that she could call on this being in times of need. I would categorize all of these experiences as the equivalent of Mother as Modulator experienced internally.

Sometimes the answer is to be mothered, and sometimes it is to become the mother. This is true on the human level, but it can also happen on the spiritual level. Ariel, who was very undermothered, turned to the goddess tradition to provide a positive model of the mother and the deep feminine, finding it healing and transformative. She considers herself a priestess now, which is not a designation assigned by any religious authority but simply means being a channel for the divine feminine energy. Her job is to embody this energy. The Divine Mother is the matrix, the web of interconnectivity that holds us all.

Devotional practices to any of the Divine Mother figures help open the heart to the Good Mother archetype and can eventually help replace the image of a withholding mother with something more generous and warm. We need models for developing the Good Mother within, and those coming from spiritual traditions are potent for many.

Taking on the "good" of the Good Mother

Whether feeling a child of the Cosmic Mother or bonding with a person (of either gender) who assumes the role of Good Mother, there are definite benefits to a secure relationship.

Connecting with the Good Mother allows us to appropriate some of her qualities, whether her confidence, her graciousness, her generosity, or other desirable qualities. Just as securely attached children feel that the physical dwelling they live in with their family is very much theirs as well (a feeling not always shared by those with an orphan complex), those fully and securely attached to Mommy are free to partake of her nature and make themselves at home there. This may take the form of imitating external behaviors of Mother, the way she stands or tilts her head, but it can also occur on a deeper level where the child feels that she is part of Mommy's heart and that Mother's qualities feel like part of her, too.

The child who adores his mother also takes on some of the halo around this idealization. The securely attached child who feels "My mommy is really special" may also feel "and I'm special because I'm part of her." This is related to Mother as Source (p. 22).

A second chance at finding a Good Mother

Fortunately, we have a second chance as an adult to receive the mothering we missed earlier in our lives. We might even experience this in more than one relationship. We might find ourselves receiving love, nurturance, guidance, encouragement, mirroring, protection, and the other Good Mother functions in multiple places: from our partners, therapists, close friends, in-laws, spiritual teachers, mentors, and from the mother that we eventually develop within ourselves.

To have someone consistently there for us is a great blessing, if we can take it in. If we cling to an earlier lack of love and don't take it in, then it can't heal us. It may take sitting through discomfort, struggling through feelings of unworthiness and learning to trust, but receiving this nurturance is essential to healing mother wounds.

When we see that what is offered is given *out of love* rather than out of obligation, we feel deeply touched. (Children of emotionally absent mothers often feel that any caring from their mothers came out of obligation.) If we can take in this freely given love and care, eventually we will develop a healthy sense of entitlement, the sense that our needs matter and we have a right to be supported and nurtured. Slowly our stance will change to a sense of positive expectancy that our needs will be met.

For this to happen, our Good Mother substitutes need to be generous with us: generous with their attention, their affection, generous with praise, and generous in giving us the space we need to work things out. Since emotionally absent, nonexpressive, and neglectful mothers don't give much, this generosity is a key ingredient in healing. We are often surprised to learn that the generous mother finds pleasure in meeting our needs. This pleasure forms part of her development, too.

Obviously the people in these Good Mother roles must feel safe to you. What is happening is nothing less than a radical transformation, changing your self-image, how you are in relationships, and awakening the child states that have been frozen inside. If you developed a hardened defense structure and have taken on the critical voices of those around you, healing will require stepping out of this. You need to be soft and receptive, like a trusting child asleep in Mother's arms, so you must find people who elicit this in you and who are trustworthy.

Remember that it is a journey—a long journey. Children don't grow up overnight. And while the goal is to heal the wounded parts of your psyche and become a healthy and whole adult, this happens in stages. I find it most helpful to think of this in terms of the inner child being healed, but you can think of it as simply filling in deficits or strengthening your system so you can absorb those nutrients that were lacking earlier.

Meeting mothering needs with partners

Naturally, a place we look for our unmet needs to be fulfilled is in our relationships with romantic partners. This is both an excellent choice and a troublesome one. Love relationships can be a place we feel cared for, tenderly held, treasured. They're great for snuggling, for meeting touch needs, and for our undefended, sweet selves to show up. But they are also so much more. Often they are partnerships in terms of household and material life, and frequently include raising children. Relationships with partners are the primary place where our sexual needs are met. They are also where we have responsibility for nurturing and caring for another. The existence of so many simultaneous roles creates some special requirements for meeting unmet childhood needs here.

Here are some questions that may help you look at your current relationship if you are in one. If you are not with a partner, you could use the same questions to reflect on a past relationship:

- What psychological and material needs does your relationship fulfill? Does either of you take on Good Mother roles with the other? Which ones?

- Does one of you do more nurturing than the other, or do you take turns? Is there a parent-child component to the relationship?

It can cause trouble when we're trying to get earlier needs met yet have no conscious agreements about this. When we begin the dating or mating dance, we're usually not asking, "Will you be my mother?" Partners can feel resentful to find themselves enlisted in this role without their consent. Especially if they get no time off.

It works better when we give our partners choices and negotiate for specific needs to be met. We can ask for these in adult ways: "Can you hold me a while? I am feeling lonely and insecure." "The child inside me feels scared right now and wants to hear you say it's going to be all right." "I need you to mirror back my feelings right now, so I know that I'm heard." It's best when the "adult you" can do the negotiation. There are many good books and classes that can help you learn to ask for what you want. (If talking about the inner child or "child parts" feels totally foreign to you, you may want to skip ahead to that chapter on p. 174 and then come back.)

This doesn't mean the child parts of you can't also have a relationship with your partner. It might be helpful for the adult you to be protective enough of this child to assess what's reasonable within a particular relationship and to take the lead in negotiating that. Child parts can step forward and make requests, too, but it is best if they understand that the partner isn't the only adult around. You might decide that the bulk of your inner child work and re-parenting can better be done elsewhere, but that it's nice to also have your partner nurture your child on occasion.

In romantic relationships, we also need to be willing to exchange roles and to provide nurture, protection, and care to our partners. This can be done as an adult-to-adult exchange or a nurturing parent-to-child exchange where one partner is acting as a nurturing parent to the child in the other. There can also be exchanges between child states in each of the adult partners. When you're both wounded children, there can be much hurt and blame, but two children learning about resilience and trust can have some fun together.

It's important to remember that our adult partners don't owe us the selfless love that we wanted from our mothers. They have needs and limitations, and we are adults now, responsible for ourselves. That doesn't mean you can't have vulnerable feelings, even some needs that are rooted in infancy, but it does mean that your partner has a choice about responding to these needs, which ultimately are your responsibility. Having your partner meet these needs is only one of many options. If your partner fails to do so at any particular moment, there are other options. It's important that you not get so absorbed in your child feelings that you forget this.

An example of an infancy pattern that might get played out between partners is trying to remain within the oneness of the early merged state in which babies feel themselves as part of Mother. This is referred to as a "fused" relationship. When two people are fused, they don't know themselves as separate, distinct individuals. Part of what makes falling in love so intoxicating for many people is reexperiencing this sense of oneness. In time, enough differences naturally arise that the sense of oneness disappears and each partner feels him- or herself as separate. If you haven't had enough merging, you might resist this and try to hold on to the sense of oneness. This will cause trouble, because if you can't see your partner as separate from you, you can't really be attentive to your partner's needs.

When early needs are prominent in a relationship, we can become hostage to these needs. Some people find it difficult to leave relationships because they've projected onto the partner many basic parenting needs and are developmentally unprepared to walk away from Mother.

Repeating the past

Many therapists believe that adults unconsciously repeat unhealthy patterns from their early parent-child relationships—for example, picking partners who are unavailable in ways that are similar to how a parent was unavailable. In these cases healing is often a matter of becoming aware of the pattern, working through these childhood wounds in therapy or other places, and making new choices in terms of love relationships. Trying to extract from a partner who is like Mommy what you didn't get from Mommy is usually not successful.

It is, however, common. There are entire therapies that revolve around the idea that we are attracted to people who have the same deficits as our parents in an unconscious attempt to heal the original injury. In approaches like Imago Relationship Therapy, therapists help partners use the difficulties in the relationship to bring up earlier injuries and heal them. Emotionally Focused Couples Therapy is another approach that uses the couple relationship to repair attachment injuries. From this view it's not that partners made the wrong choice—they made the perfect choice for healing.

The following self-queries may help you examine your own patterns.

- Write a paragraph describing how you experienced your mother as a young child. It doesn't need to be full sentences; you could even make a list of adjectives. Then write a paragraph about how you experienced any significant romantic partners and look for similarities. (Note that significant partnerships are not necessarily long-lasting relationships but are very often emotionally charged ones.)

- What are the sources of conflict and upset in your relationship? Do these mirror any elements from early childhood?

- What indications of earlier unfinished business or of insecure attachment can you see in your current relationship?

- At this point in your life, can you be with someone whose heart is steady, patient, welcoming, with plenty of love, or do you tend to find people who are skittish and not fully there?

Some examples of unmet childhood needs that show up in adult life include the following:

- needing an inordinate amount of support and reassurance

- feeling insecure, jealous, and angry when your partner is not responsive to your needs right away

- being unable to tolerate your partner's absence

- maintaining a fused relationship—"joined at the hip," as we often say

- projecting onto your partner negative qualities of your mother

- elevating your partner to a one-up position and feeling that he or she is smarter, more capable, or somehow has more value than you

- tolerating an unusual amount of abandonment or unavailability of your partner or reacting to it in ways reminiscent of how you felt as a child

- not expecting emotional closeness from your partner (because you didn't get it from your mother and don't expect it from anyone)

The healing power of secure romantic attachments

Author Susan Anderson says in *The Journey from Abandonment to Healing* that in a secure relationship, a romantic partner serves a similar function as a mother does for a securely attached child. In both cases, the relationship provides a primary sense of belonging, security, and connectedness. Speaking of adults, she writes, "Many people function as well as they do precisely because they feel so secure in their primary relationships. They are self-confident, self-directed, and content because they know someone is there for them." Ruptures in such a relationship can seriously undermine this confidence and well-being.[2]

Indeed, partner relationships have often been found to be good for people, leading to benefits like better health and longer life spans. They can also be the cauldron in which insecurely attached adults finally become securely attached and reap its many benefits.

A chance to be held (an exercise)

Here is an exercise you can do with a partner or a friend. It is a chance to be held by a safe person and let yourself receive without in that moment needing to earn it or give anything back. It is perhaps most healing if you imagine your inner child receiving this. Think of how often we hear women complain they want to be cuddled, but that it's hard to get without their partner turning it into a sexual opportunity. Well, here is one chance to get some of those early needs met.

Find a partner for this exercise who can agree to the guidelines and intention of providing safe, nonsexual holding.

This is a reciprocal exercise in which each gets a chance to be held and to be the one who provides the holding, so decide which role you want to take first. It's helpful to agree on a set period of time for each partner to receive; twenty minutes is a good guideline.

The basic instruction is that the person who provides the holding does not stroke or comfort the other, but is there more as a simple, accepting presence. Often this exercise is done having both parties sit on the floor, with the "child" in front and the "good parent" leaning back against the wall for support. Pillows may be used to provide a soft backdrop and also to somewhat buffer the body contact. The child leans back against, perhaps resting on, the chest of the person in the good-parent role, and the "good parent" wraps her arms around the "child." The person being held can change position as desired. When in the receiving role, do your best to relax into and really take in this very primal form of support and nurture. Do not talk during this period.

After you've switched roles, allow a time to verbally discuss what the experience was like for you.

Acknowledge yourself for having the courage and commitment to try something experimental. If it went well and was satisfying for both, you can set a time to do it again!

One woman reported that during her first experience of this exercise, she kept anxiously checking every few minutes, preparing herself for her partner's abandonment. After about ten minutes of her partner's steady presence, she was able to let go and really take in that she was being held and that the container was safe enough that she could rest in it. It was a profound experience and a new feeling that she was "worth staying for." Think how many young children have not had this quality time and the sense of being important enough for Mother to give all of her attention to for more than the briefest moment Exercises such as this can help change this deep imprint.

Your portable Good Mother

Just as it is believed that a young child constructs a picture of his mother that he carries around inside and that helps in the process of eventually separating and differentiating from Mother, so building an internal sense of a Good Mother figure creates, in essence, a portable Good Mother that you carry around with you.

This might simply be a conglomeration of memories of who-ever has filled that Good Mother role, but it can be more than that, too. It can be an internalization of the person's love and support. One time I had an image of my therapist holding my heart between her hands and supporting me with great tender-ness and devotion. It felt like I could take this image into my heart where it became a layer of me. I also dialogue with my therapist in my journal frequently, where sometimes she says surprising things, though never out of keeping with the person I know her to be.

The process of taking in and internalizing Good Mother energy is not a purely mental or psychological process. To steep in any of these good feelings requires letting them saturate the body. Here is a short practice you can use to aid the process of internalizing any feeling or resource state you want to strengthen. You could use it to take in the nurturing of a person in your life, helping you connect with the Good Mother archetype, or even one of the Good Mother roles described in chapter 2.

Strengthening a resource state (an exercise)

Start with consciously choosing what it is that you want to feel more deeply and incorporate into yourself. As you begin with the simple intention of tuning in to this, notice how you first register your awareness of it. Does it come as a visual image, a particular feeling in your body, through another sensory channel or combination of channels?

Notice how it affects your breathing and your muscle tone. Does it bring warmth or coolness to your body? Any other sensation?

Can you bring this feeling all the way through your body and into your toes?

How does feeling this affect your posture? Does it open up or support specific places?

Notice any memories or images that come to mind.

What can you use to remind yourself of this experience? (This could be an image, a word, a memory of a feeling in your body.)

Naturally, the more often you use a practice like this, the more vivid and enduring the result will be.

When you internalize an attachment figure, or any wisdom figure, you can turn to this figure in times of need. Having this as part of you gives you more resilience. In the next chapter, we'll expand this to include the Good Mother you cultivate inside yourself.

11.

Inner Child Work

YOU MAY HAVE HEARD the phrase *the child is father to the man*,[1] which means the child is the foundation upon which adult life is built. The kind of foundation we have is critical. A resilient child serves as the foundation for a resilient adult.

Unfortunately, some of us never got to that level of resilience in childhood. The child parts carry too many wounds and thus are the foundation of a wounded adult. Even if these wounds are for the most part well managed and out of sight, they leak out at times and we act immaturely.

Fortunately, it's never too late to heal these childhood wounds and for a resilient child to emerge, serving as the foundation for a healthy, resilient adult.

An introduction to inner child work

All of this talk about wounded inner children creates a lot of discomfort for some, who have little patience for children, inner or otherwise. The notion of an inner child is met with the same irritation as has met all too many actual children.

Yet millions of people have found it helpful to work with the inner child, or what I prefer to call *child states*. I use this term because I find no support for the notion that there is only one inner child. When used this way, it is often confused with inner life in general, and more specifically feelings and impulses. I think this is an error. Every time you feel sad or angry, that's not necessarily your inner child.

We are very complex beings. Far from having one stable personality, we have many different parts, which come into play at different times. We have child states that hold different beliefs, feelings, and memories, sometimes clustering around a certain age. Some of these child states are wise, some are creative, and some carry specific experiences, such as trauma or the abandonment wound. If we really want to understand ourselves and be as whole as we can be, it will help to know these various inner child states. Because it is often awkward to use the plural, I revert at times to referring to the inner child in the singular. The primary methods used in inner child work have been the following:

- using guided meditation, imagery, or hypnotic trance to meet and interact with child states

- pulling out old photographs from childhood to help access memories and feelings from that time

- working with dolls, teddy bears, or similar props (who then represent a child state) to help access child feelings or give your adult part practice in a nurturing parent role

- using art as a medium, especially for young child states to express themselves

- writing letters to an inner child or from an inner child as a way of establishing contact

- dialoguing between adult and child states through journal writing, internal self-talk, or through techniques such as the Voice Dialogue Method

Inner child work is something you can do on your own, in workshops, or with a therapist. It's important enough that even if you are introduced to it by a teacher or therapist and even if you use therapy sessions to go deeper with it, you will want to have ways to also continue these relationships at home.

The book that I find offers the most practical and helpful guidance in this is *Recovery of Your Inner Child* by Lucia Capacchione. It has more than forty exercises that cover a range of activities. Capacchione has made great use of art and writing to communicate with inner child states and popularized the practice of switching hands to help distinguish between inner adult and child, turning to the nondominant hand to express the child.

John Bradshaw's bestselling book *Homecoming: Reclaiming and Championing Your Inner Child* makes considerable use of letter writing and the use of affirmations for supplying Good Parent messages that were missing earlier. He works through different developmental stages—a good idea—although I find his descriptions of these stages to be more Freudian than I'm comfortable with. I think you can become responsive to inner kids and their needs without the theoretical filter of things like the Oedipal complex.

Often we are unaware of these inner child states, yet we are blended with them, feeling the same kinds of emotions and needs that we experienced as a child. We may be caught in a teenage snit or a two-year-old tantrum, feel clingy or insecure, get fixated on self-soothing, or feel too young to be out in the world. It is helpful to differentiate and identify each of the states that are part of us. This allows us to form conscious relationships with them and be aware of where we're coming from.

Some believe that we never outgrow our inner children, and the goal is for them to be happy and healthy. Others see the process of working with inner child states as ideally leading to integration of these parts into the adult. I don't really have a preference: It's nice either way. It is great to have a sweet and spunky kid inside, and it's great to incorporate their positive qualities into your adult self.

Just as children grow up by having their needs met, meeting the previously unmet needs of inner children allows them to mature. Parts of self that revolve around such needs may then fade or dissolve. Other child states come bearing important gifts, qualities that were often cut off and lost in our own childhood which can now be reclaimed. Some of these are the qualities of the natural child described below.

The child as mother to the self

Just as we have the understanding that the child is father to the man, we could say the child is mother to the real self. As it is usually expressed, the child is the essence of this real self. This is how Carl Jung described the archetype of the child, which he viewed as a symbol of wholeness.

This archetype is also referred to as the *natural child* or the *divine child*. Some of the qualities of this child include:

- honesty and genuineness
- sweetness and generosity, a loving heart
- innocence and "beginner's mind"
- openness and trust
- imagination and intuitive knowing
- curiosity
- wonder, awe, and an attitude of play
- spontaneity and the ungroomed, natural behaviors we enjoy in young children
- vitality and aliveness

Most of those who advocate for inner child work do so with the hope not only of healing the wounded child but also of reclaiming these wonderful child qualities.

"Parts work"

Many inner child states have been identified: the natural child (above), the vulnerable child, the wounded child, the neglected/abandoned child, and the angry child, to name the most common. We also have various "adult" parts—for example, parts that are nurturing and others that are critical.

With an awareness of these many different aspects, it is natural to talk of "parts work." This is a common way that people think of it for themselves, and the language is being adopted by many therapists as well.

Often all it takes to begin an exploration of these inner parts is simply permission to think in these terms and a willingness to set aside skepticism and fear and start paying attention. By paying attention to your feelings, your behavioral patterns, your inner commentaries, and your body language, you can begin to tune in to various parts of yourself that are shaping your experience. These parts have their own needs, motivations, beliefs, memories, and particular flavor.

Some people find it unsettling to think of such distinctive and seemingly independent parts functioning within them like separate personalities. They think of what we used to call *multiple personality disorder* (now called *dissociative identity disorder* or DID) and get frightened. The difference is that the parts of a person with DID are more completely separated from consciousness and don't so easily relate and coexist. With DID, a person "loses time" and is stunned to find evidence of behaviors she knows nothing about. The switching from one part to another is involuntary, and the parts are generally born of trauma. As people with DID work with these parts, the parts can become more aware of each other and work more cooperatively, which is the aim of most of the parts work therapies that are applicable to all populations.

Some of the newer therapies emphasize that in all of us, these alternate selves are "like real people" with their own style and energetic fingerprint. We seem to be moving toward more understanding and acceptance of the natural multiplicity in all systems, including the human person. If you don't find strange clothes in your closet and people don't come up to you and call you by a different name, your multiplicity doesn't have to interfere with your life.

Who doesn't have a pouting child? An irritated critic? It's okay to have these parts, but it's preferable to get to know them, to "catch ourselves in the act," and to choose where we want to be operating out of.

I find it helpful to name the parts and associate them with an image of some kind. You can use art materials and incorporate photographs of yourself if this feels helpful. You can also use objects of various sorts (such as a stuffed animal). Often you'll start with a particular representation, which, like any image, is a snapshot of a moment in time, and it will change. You may have multiple representations that combine and evolve in all sorts of creative ways. The following is the story of my work with Maria.

Maria's story: From stone child to sweet child

Maria began seriously doing parts work when she recognized the hole left by an emotionally absent mother. She had also experienced physical abuse in the family, and when prompted in therapy to contact an inner child, the only child she could find was a "ghost child" who seemed flimsy and insubstantial. Maria had almost no happy memories from childhood to draw on in finding resilient child parts. She agreed to buy some art materials for future parts work.

Immediately after buying the art supplies, Maria was surprised when she heard an insistent inner voice instructing her to make a representation of it. With red construction paper, glitter, and pictures cut out of wrapping paper, she made an image of a child whose name was Strawberry. Maria recognized Strawberry as the resilient child who was born out of our several years of work together and her secure attachment to me, her therapist. Strawberry was full of spunk, unschooled wisdom, and affection. Many would say Strawberry was the natural child; Maria saw her as the child she would have been if she had received the nurturing that would have allowed her to blossom. Strawberry became a source of comfort and guidance to Maria and various wounded child parts.

Some of these wounded parts included the Abandoned Baby (with a red, oozing hole in her heart); the Stone Child, which represented a state of shock; and Holy Rage, the anger related to her abuse. Maria also made a representation and dialogued with a part she called Sweet Innocence, which represented her original unharmed nature.

In time, working both at home and in therapy, the Stone Child was dissolved. Holy Rage also receded and disappeared off the stage. Before doing this, Holy Rage asked to be acknowledged by all of the other parts.

The representation of the Abandoned Baby kept shifting over time, becoming brighter and more complex. Maria found an old photograph of herself and used it in a representation she referred to as the "original injured child." She pasted the photograph on a small box and put several images of the remaining wounded child parts in it.

This (now-composite) injured child had three primary resources: her adult self, which was learning to become a more nurturing inner parent figure; me (her therapist); and Strawberry. With the love of all three, the injured child became brighter and happier over time.

At a later point, Maria made a composite of the injured child (now called by her natural name) and Strawberry, indicating that the boundary between them had become more permeable. She also worked with representations of the adult self (which also evolved with time) and a core spiritual self, which she called The Ancient One.

As so often happens, Maria's parts work dropped into the background as the parts became more integrated. Her adult self took on more and more of the flavor of Sweet Innocence as Maria let go of her defenses. This was supported by my mirroring in therapy, by Strawberry, and by her ability to appropriately defend herself both in her inner and outer worlds. We could say Maria evolved from a stone child to a sweet child to a more loving adult. Parts work wasn't the only factor in Maria's healing, but it was an important one.

Gifts and burdens

Dissociated parts usually carry psychological burdens. It is as if they take some toxic emotional material and become the exclusive carrier of it, thus in essence containing it so the rest of the system doesn't have to deal with it. When these parts can unburden themselves by sharing what they've been carrying and processing the associated feelings, they change. They become lighter, freer, happier.

Parts evolve in fascinating ways. They can go from feeling like dormant or nonhuman entities to individuated selves evolving through time. As unmet needs of these parts are attended to and hidden feelings get acknowledged, the parts can let go of them. The roles and defining features of these parts can then change.

In our deepest work, we reach something that is larger than our personal history. What is accessed has a nature that is both the deepest essence of the person and beyond it, a transpersonal state that I describe in Sophia's story on p. 189. It might also be considered archetypal energy, and may be part of what Jung called the natural or divine child (see p. 177). In some traditions it is called the Self. Any of these more essential energies tend to be deeply grounding.

These are the gifts. It doesn't really matter if we say they are the wounded parts evolving or dipping below the parts to deeper dimensions. What is important is to claim the gifts, making them a permanent part of us.

When inner child work gets complicated

Internal Family Systems and Voice Dialogue are two of the better-known therapies centered around parts work. A therapy that applies much of what is potent in parts work to developmental injuries (early life deficits) is the Developmental Needs Meeting Strategy. It uses specific protocols to identify and heal unmet developmental needs, utilizing a Nurturing Adult Self, a Protective Adult Self, and a Spiritual Core Self as important resources for doing so. You may recognize the nurturing adult and protective adult as aspects of what I've called the Good Mother. Young parts always need the care of parts taking a parental attitude. The Spiritual Core Self is a version of the transpersonal Self I was just describing.

Many therapists, such as myself, find parts work valuable but don't subscribe to an established framework. It's rare that my therapy with undermothered adults does not include at least some work with child parts. Often it is a substantial aspect of the therapy.

Although inner child work can be presented in a rather simple form, often it is all but simple. I have found that the clients with the longest work in front of them are those who live in child states most of the time or who have very complex inner systems with little communication and much conflict. Let's look at both.

NOT ENOUGH ADULT ON BOARD

Children aren't meant to navigate the adult world, and they're not prepared to. Adults who spend most of their time in child states feel what insecure children do: They are often afraid of getting in trouble, feel inadequate, feel alone and unloved (and too often unlovable), fear rejection, are often emotionally dys-regulated, and are incredibly disempowered. Some will find it difficult to not act out impulses, being in "child time" where everything needs to happen now or it won't happen. Some inner children living in adult bodies are stuck in self-soothing, whether that be with food or drugs or doing only what they want to do. They often resist efforts at self-discipline. In Freud-ian terms, they are all id: I want what I want when I want it.

In psychodynamic terms, adults who are living from a child's perspective are lacking in ego development. In the framework I am using here, there is not enough adult on board. They need to learn to delay gratification; to stop "thinking with their feelings" and become more objective; to learn to take risks, knowing they can survive disappointment; and to take more responsi-bility for their own well-being. Often, if they are married, they have put their spouse in a parental role and may become angry with the spouse in the similar way that children become angry with parents.

Some may not have these adult skills at all, while others, interestingly, can perform adequately in some aspects of life, but not in others—even without these skills. I think of a man who generally does fine at work and parenting, but cannot take risks in his personal relationships because the inner child takes over and he is overwhelmed by feelings of being unworthy, unlovable, and not enough.

If someone has at least some of this adult capability, it can be called on to help their less-developed parts. I like psycho-therapist and author Arnie Mindells' phrases "leading edge" and "trailing edge." As we've seen with parts work, we are not all one thing. Our more capable functioning is our leading edge and our youngest parts are generally our trailing edge. It's this trailing edge that makes it hard to move forward in life.

Developing a Nurturing Parent voice—one that encourages, supports, and cares—helps these young parts feel the support needed to lessen their clinging. It helps turn off the fear response that keeps them frozen and unable to act. With support and the critical skill of "taking in," the child can continue her development. Practicing the parental role also strengthens the adult.

DISORGANIZED SYSTEMS

As Richard Schwartz's Internal Family Systems and work with disorders like DID have shown, the individual psyche can become amazingly complex. We're far beyond the simple child-adult-parent map found in Eric Bern's Transactional Analysis almost fifty years ago. We now recognize there may be a hundred parts at various levels of differentiation. In a disorganized system it can feel like bedlam inside with everybody screaming or trying to talk at once.

Working with a high level of disorganization is slow and challenging work. It's not enough for a more prominent, conscious part to learn something, but a new piece of information often needs to be learned again and again by other parts that aren't online. An example is a woman I work with whose mother died a year ago, yet we keep encountering parts that are shocked to discover her mother's death.

Add the complication of protector parts that think certain things need to be kept hidden and who control the communication pipeline, and you understand why a lot of the system is in the dark. Such systems would have to be described as *dissociated*, as the parts are not connected. Dissociation is a state of disconnection somewhere in the system: whether from environment, body, feelings, or, in this case, a lack of connection between parts.

Trouble now is from trouble then

Most often I find that when a person is in a real meltdown state it relates back to a previous painful experience. This is stating nothing new. Many would say it activates the same neuropathways or is linked to an old experience. A slightly different way of looking at it reveals that the events are linked by a common carrier—the part that experienced the first one and is reexperiencing it in some form now in the present.

A situation I've seen a couple times is when a part isn't happy with a person's choice of partner. It may be that most of the time the person is content with the partner, but at times an old view with previous feelings erupt, such as lack of safety and a need to get away. By identifying the part that is upset and bringing this part out of the past and into the present, this part can adapt to a new reality and not continue going back to those more distressed feelings and fears. Parts tend to get frozen in specific times. A person always has more capacities in the present than at a younger age, which is why bringing past parts into the present can help them take new information and capacities into account and respond from a more resourced place.

Another example is when someone has a disproportionate reaction, such as when an adult reacts to aloneness as an overwhelming threat. When I encounter an adult who is terrified of being alone, most of the time this comes from a child part. That child may have experienced trauma when physically alone, and the ensuing sense of danger has been imprinted on the condition of being alone. It's the fear and the associations with aloneness that are the problem, not the absence of other people. A child part terrified of aloneness may need to be rescued from the earlier situation or may need to be soothed now, which you can do if you've developed a nurturing parent voice inside. This nurturing parent can remind the child that there is no danger now.

Unlatching from Mother

One of the most difficult and pernicious dynamics is when one of these child parts absolutely refuses to let go of Mother. This child feels *But she is supposed to be here for me!* and will not, despite Mother's innumerable failures, let her off the hook. The young child thinks, *If I scream louder and longer, she must come.*

Unfortunately, it doesn't work that way. Mother usually does not respond well to the demand of an adult offspring wanting her to be attentive in the way the inner child wants, which leaves both parties in a state of frustration and conflict.

Here is a three-pronged solution:

1. Help the adult I am working with see that the demands are coming from a child part, are not necessarily appropriate now, and will not likely be met.

2. Meet the frustration and anger of the child and whatever hopelessness or helplessness is also there. There will also be grief to process when we accept that what we wanted isn't going to happen.

3. Help this child register the adult she lives within now. If there isn't already a nurturing part developed, this will need to be developed. Often it is already there (for example, the person may be a nurturing parent to their real-life children) but hasn't been connected to inner child parts. It may take time for the child parts to trust this adult, creating what is referred to as an internal secure attachment. In essence, we pry the inner child's grasp from the historical mother and instead let her attach to a more responsive mother whom we foster within.

Part of step one above may also involve helping the adult have a more objective picture of Mother (and it takes a more mature mind to do this). When we can see how Mother is wired, what she is capable of, and what she is not, we can stop personalizing her emotional neglect or abuse and take our needs where they can be met.

Sophia's story: Reuniting with a lost self

Sophia had done many different types of psychotherapy by the time she came to me. Our work together involved many methods, parts work being only one. We also used many of the classic tools: examining beliefs, processing feelings, identifying resources, visualizing, role-playing, coming up with new coping strategies, deciphering early life scripts, and renegotiating some past trauma.

As I have seen with the clients who make the most progress in therapy, Sophia did a tremendous amount of emotional processing between sessions, showing phenomenal commitment to her healing. I share a very abbreviated portion of her story (with her permission) as it relates to parts work to give you a further understanding of how deep and far this work can go.

When we began, Sophia was very excited to work with inner child parts. There was tremendous clarity in her experience of parts. Her descriptions of interactions sounded indistinguishable from outer interactions, but these occurred on an interior plane.

One of the first parts we worked with was a fetus in the womb, which would not look at her. It is important to know that when Sophia was in her mother's womb, the doctor advised her parents to abort her, due to a complication that might have led to birth defects. Not surprisingly, she had earlier struggled with a feeling of not wanting to live. Now we were working with the part that held this feeling.

Sophia placed a crib in a corner of one room and began to spend time there, talking and singing to the part we were welcoming. Since there had been some experience of blending with the feelings of this part, I reminded her about this and explained that if she started blending, she could ask this unborn one if she would "not lasso you with her feelings."

With this welcoming environment, within a matter of weeks the unborn one was born, although at first she did not seem fully human. She was more like a caricature, a black outline. Sophia could feel her reactions and that she carried a lot of fear, anger, and victimization. I suggested going very slow, giving time for each adjustment.

Within a few months, this not-quite-human form had turned into a child about seven or eight years old without a name, but who we called "the homeless one." Sophia told me that this child part sits with her back to her but likes being able to lean in, having Sophia talk to her. This homeless one sits on the edge of the bed while Sophia cuddles with two other inner child parts. She tries to give them all the love they missed and create a safe environment for them to grow. Over time, all of these parts continued to evolve, becoming lighter and happier as they unburdened themselves in this compassionate holding environment.

The healing work continued, oscillating between present-day issues and early childhood, working with her family role and how that had clipped her wings. Sophia had a very clear memory of being six years old or so and making a "pact" (on an inner level) that she would give herself up. She had been a very active, energetic child but felt called upon to become caretaker not only for her siblings, but also for her mother. After this she became much weaker physically, losing much of her life energy, and became subject to fainting.

In the fascinating way that our inner and external worlds braid together, Sophia went through some horrendously painful experiences in current time trying to help her mother. It seemed that this excruciating experience pushed her to give up this pact with its contract of caretaking her mother and siblings.

When she did this, the most wonderful thing happened: She reconnected with the true nature that she had as a child before giving herself up. Sophia felt great freedom and happiness (like many a young child), but it was not just a child's thoughts and feelings Sophia was experiencing. It was a transpersonal state (beyond our experience as an individual): She felt boundless, not limited to her body, without problems or needs, content, and with a mind that felt spacious and still. The happiness she felt was an unconditional happiness, dependent on nothing. I watched to see if this state was short-lived, but it was not. As a state, it would come and go, but she learned ways to navigate back to it.

It was clear to me this expansiveness was not a dissociated state. Sophia could still feel her body and her current hardships, but it was like the foreground and background shifted, so during these times she was living from this larger expanse.

This is where our deepest healing can go—far beyond "wallowing" in the past that psychotherapy is often criticized for. It can go beyond the past, beyond the conditioned self, beyond even the limitations of being a person in this time and place to a greater freedom that rests in what many call *being*.

Sophia emphasizes that this freedom came from working through her pain, not by bypassing it. Early in our work we had brought in certain resources. She had learned to express her pain rather than push it away. It's wet work, all "snot and tears," as some like to say. As Sophia peeled off each layer of her past, more energy was liberated, there was more expansion, and more peace. It was as though she had been living in a too-tight box all these intervening years and had finally found a way out of it.

As generally happens in deep work, we don't spiral up out of the darkness never to return but continue delving into new pains, often discovering new parts in the process. Sophia told me recently that she is happy these parts "have someone to go to." This is what every child needs—as well as every part of us. Those who had no one to rely on as a child generally still need a healthy adult to go to. As Sophia's story shows us, that healthy adult is right here, inside of us.

Becoming your own best mother

The renowned Jungian analyst and author Marion Woodman said, "Children who are not loved in their very beingness do not know how to love themselves. As adults, they have to learn to nourish, to mother their own lost child."[2]

This learning happens in stages. We, in essence, grow into the job. Just as a woman doesn't automatically know how to mother offspring but her instincts and her heart can be awakened, so it is with our own capacity to bond with and actively "mother" the child states inside us.

It may feel awkward at first, and there may be any number of obstacles. In addition to the obstructions that arise as we inch into this inner mothering, we may be stopped before we start by a discounting voice (a critical parent or protector most likely) saying, "This is ridiculous." Its tactic is to deny the need. "You're making a mountain out of a molehill." "It wasn't that bad. Just buck up." Here is where being aware of parts comes as an advantage. Only if we can recognize that this is a part speaking up—a part that has an agenda—will we have a choice to bracket these thoughts and move forward with our intention.

One of the next barriers we may face is a feeling of inadequacy. If you were not well mothered, you can easily feel that you haven't a clue how to do it. You're uncomfortable, you don't know what to say or do, and you feel phony trying what doesn't come naturally. This is enough to stop you right here.

If you succeed in making an authentic connection with the undermothered parts within yourself, you may be struck by a sense of guilt that you have inadvertently continued the abandonment by not showing up earlier. No one likes to feel the sharp pain of causing harm to another.

And just as I've mentioned earlier that a mother may unconsciously keep a distance from a child so as not to arouse her own hurt, you may feel that opening up the locked-away pain in your heart is too high a price to pay for reconnecting with child parts inside you.

In addition to the pain, we fear being taken over. When we've pushed any aspect of us into the unconscious, we often fear that if we open to it, it will be overwhelming. (This is true of repressed anger, sadness, sexuality, and so on.) In a similar manner, we may fear that the needs of our inner child may be more than we are equipped to deal with and will overwhelm us or take over.

To the extent that you are still unconsciously identified with the undermothered child (and usually we are for a long time), you won't experience yourself as an abundant source with much to give but rather as someone who's dry and depleted. You may think, *I don't have enough for myself. How can I nurture someone else?* I've identified a number of obstacles you may encounter in becoming your own best mother.

- Which do you recognize in yourself?
    - demeaning, discounting messages that interfere with taking on a nurturing role
    - feeling you don't know how to mother
    - guilt about not showing up earlier

      ○ self-protection, not wanting to feel your own hurt

      ○ fear of everything that has been repressed

      ○ feeling that you don't have enough to give

    • What might help you work through these?

The most important step in becoming your own best mother is to move beyond your inadequacies, fears, and defenses and let your heart soften. The heart that is open is a heart that can love.

Your inner child will help you. A child is like a "love bank": The more you put in, the more you get back. Children are innately loving, so as you extend even a trickle of love to the unloved child within you, usually that child will return your love. It may be a little bumpy in the beginning, however. Frequently, an inner child will initially respond with mistrust. Just as a child who has been hurt or abandoned too many times by Mother will not open his arms to her, the inner child may react similarly. If this is the case, persist in your efforts to reach out to this child the best you can, realizing that it takes time to build trust.

As you become more nurturing to yourself, it may kick up reactions inside that parallel something in your early environment. For example, if your father couldn't tolerate anyone being "coddled" or treated gently, then when you start to treat yourself in a really caring, gentle manner, you may hear some internal self-talk that sounds an awful lot like Dad. You'll need to be on the lookout and recognize when the feelings and reactions inside are not really your own. Learn to stand behind the Good Mother that is slowly developing inside you.

Many women who were undermothered and who choose to become biological mothers have struggled with these internal forces and made a commitment on a deep soul level not to abandon their children as they were abandoned. They go to great lengths to learn how to become good mothers, looking for models to follow, reading books, asking for help. They don't expect to automatically know how to do it.

In a similar way, in re-parenting ourselves, we can make a commitment to developing in ways that may not feel natural to us at first. We can look for models, read books, and ask for help. We can also call upon capacities already within us that we haven't used this way before. Many who have been under-mothered have paradoxically taken on the job of nurturing and caretaking others, such as a sibling or mate. In helping clients develop a nurturing parent inside themselves, one therapeutic approach, the Developmental Needs Meeting Strategy, has clients recall a time they were nurturing to another and use that as a basis for creating a nurturing parent within themselves. You can try this for yourself.

> Remember a time when you felt nurturing or protective of another or were actually involved in caregiving. Bring this feeling all the way through you. Intensify it. You may have muted your natural inclinations then, but give them an extra boost now. Feel yourself as a nurturing adult who can mother the undernurtured child within. How do you feel this in your body? Take an inner snapshot of you in this role, so you have an image to call upon later.

Learning to check in with the child may require effort at first, but it can become a more automatic and integral part of life. Be aware of the energy you initially bring to this. You don't want to repeat the feeling tone of a resentful mother here. Your child is a joy, not a burden.

Fortunately, becoming a good mother to your inner child(ren) is innately reinforcing. One woman reported that it boosted her self-esteem. It feels good to be attentive and loving, and once the relationship is well established, there's lots of love coming back from the child.

Creating a safe place for the child

Healing begins with finding the parts that we've lost contact with, which, within the context of this book, are child parts. Many of these are child parts that split off and dissociated because it wasn't safe for them. These vulnerable child parts need to know that they are safe with you now and that the situation is different.

Nancy Napier, who works with self-hypnotic states (which are simply states of deep relaxation and receptivity), writes in her book *Reclaiming Your Self,* "Bringing the child into the present is an important part of the process. In the timeless unconscious, the child continues to experience the original childhood environment as if it were the present. When current situations link back to that dysfunctional environment, the child doesn't realize that he or she lives with you, now, in a different place."[3]

You have to give extra attention to safety to keep the child anchored in the present. By establishing a strong, nurturing relationship between child states and a loving inner parent, the child can get unstuck from the past and have a happy home life. This happens as we listen respectfully and with empathy to the child parts and give them avenues for expressing themselves, such as through art or the use of dialogues.

You might set aside a time to dialogue with your inner child states about what they need to feel safe.

Time together

Once you bring the child out of a traumatic past (which may require the help of a therapist), you can create a more child-friendly environment now.

This may involve a mix of time simply dialoguing with this child aspect or being together in an easy relaxed way and doing things that you know this child enjoys. If the child in you likes being outdoors, make sure you get some time outside. Or maybe horseback riding or roller skating feel nurturing. Sometimes we blend with the child when we're doing these activities, but often you will also feel your adult self present. Having the adult around is good in terms of supervision and also in terms of building relationship and re-parenting.

Another way that is just as effective is to create time in your imagination to meet the child's needs. One woman spends time with each of her three inner kids daily, treating them much as she would actual children those ages. She bathes and holds the baby and takes the teenager shopping. Each of the inner children can be seen going through the normal developmental stages that would have occurred in a stable, loving home. They are healing under her good-mother care.

You can heal the neglect of your childhood by caring for your inner children now.

Working with Good Mother messages

In the first chapter, I offered a list of ten Good Mother messages, repeated below. These can help establish you as a caring mother to any child within you. I encourage you to find some way that helps you feel the child's presence (whether working with a doll or picture or representation) and say these statements aloud. Notice if any are more evocative than others for the child and which are most difficult for you. These are the ones you will want to concentrate on.

Often when something is new for us, we need to step into it slowly, and this is true when dealing with positive states that are unfamiliar. We need to get used to them and give them a chance to become threaded into us and absorbed, so give this exercise plenty of time and space. By feeling a positive experience fully, you in essence "install" it into your reservoir of resources. Tune in to your body and see how it responds to each message. You'll want to work in a relaxed state where you are more receptive and able to notice your reactions.

- I'm glad that you're here.
- I see you.
- You are special to me.
- I respect you.
- I love you.
- Your needs are important to me. You can turn to me for help.
- I am here for you. I'll make time for you.
- I'll keep you safe.
- You can rest in me.
- I delight in you.

Don't stop here. You can also create your own Good Mother messages. If you do this in conjunction with specific inner children, they will be even more on target. Ask these child states what they want to hear.

Another exercise is to create statements from the child's voice that are reassuring. Here are some examples:

- Mommy loves to give to me and to help me.
- Mommy is available, ready when I need something.
- Mommy is really proud of me.
- Mommy really likes me!

Please don't think of these as a onetime experience. The more frequently and deeply you work with them, the more they can take hold within you and become part of a new foundation.

A letter to your child (an exercise)

Set aside some uninterrupted time and create a soothing atmosphere to do some inner work. (This might involve finding the right background music, lighting a candle, turning off your phone, or going to a special place.) After a short, centering meditation, compose a letter to your inner child (if you haven't differentiated several child states) or to a particular inner child or your child at a particular age. Write either from your normal adult state or, if you can access it, from the place in you that can be a nurturing parent to this child. Tell this child how you feel about what she or he has been through. If it feels appropriate and genuine to include some of the Good Mother messages, do.

Healing the unloved child

For most who are undermothered, the major focus of re-parenting will be healing the unloved child. There are other needs, of course—for guidance, encouragement, protection, anchoring—and providing these can be part of healing the unloved child, but first and foremost it is a matter of offering a warm, caring connection. This child, like every child, needs to be loved.

One inner child told me she just needed to be held, with no agenda and no time limit. She needed the "envelope" of a Good Mommy. Some of the infant states are very fragile and delicate and need very gentle holding so they can develop and mature.

In expressing nurturance toward an inner child, it is helpful to have an outer representation that you can have physical contact with. You might use a doll or stuffed animal to represent a younger self. Soft objects are the nicest to hold and stroke, and they absorb your tears. Sometimes people sleep with a doll or carry it in a snuggly baby holder. Most will at least hold or talk to a representation of this kind.

Not infrequently people first meet an inner child who is somewhere in the three-to-six-year age range, yet at some point an infant will show up. Working with the infant self often brings up the most painful feelings. Even though you may be going backward in terms of age, working through these primal wounds is a sign of your strength.

Changing your mind

Giving Good Mother messages to your inner child, receiving Good Mother messages from others, and cultivating the Good Mother within yourself does more than just satisfy needs of your inner child. It quite literally changes your mind. It changes your structure, your beliefs about yourself and the world.

Over time, the Good Mother voice you have cultivated can replace the Critical Parent voice that is a major filter in most people's minds. If you are stuck in Critical Parent, then you will be that way (at least in your mind) with others. You'll be impatient and judgmental and not able to open your heart to them. Of course you'll also be this way with yourself—and you likely know what that is like. Wouldn't it be much nicer to have a loving filter rather than a jaundiced one that you see the world through?

This reparative work is time consuming but worth it. Changing the inner atmosphere of your mind is the biggest remodel job you can take on.

12.

Psychotherapy: Mother Issues and Mothering Needs

Certainly since the beginning of talk therapy, psychotherapists have been listening to clients agonize about their mothers. We've come a long way since then in the proliferation of thera peutic methods, but Mother still figures prominently in therapists' offices.

Most types of therapy have methods that may be useful— whether expressive therapies like art therapy or movement, somatic therapies that use your body as a source of information and learning, or protocol-driven therapies like EMDR (Eye Movement Desensitization and Reprocessing) and brainspot ting. It's also important to mention parts work therapies (also sometimes called ego states), as discussed in the last chapter.

Other therapies that are relevant include work targeted toward birth trauma and pre-birth experiences, attachment-oriented therapy with partners (any secure attachment will help make up for some of these deficits), and therapies where the therapist herself deliberately serves as an attachment figure and attempts to meet some of these earlier needs (see Remothering, p. 206)

These options are not exclusive, so, for example, you might be working with a therapist building your own inner mother at the same time you experience the therapist as a Good Mother figure. And please remember that although more space is given to our earliest attachment injuries in this chapter, the issues we deal with in therapy and our unmet developmental needs go far beyond the first few years of life.

Generally, brief therapies and cognitive-behavioral therapies cannot be expected to provide much to those dealing with early childhood wounds. Stated one way, such therapies may affect the neocortex, the thinking brain, but never reach the emotional brain. In most cases, the emotional brain will need to unload its traumas and release its defenses, and this happens most easily in a safe, nurturing relationship that develops over time. Also, according to psychiatrists Thomas Lewis, Fari Amini, and Richard Lannon, authors of *A General Theory of Love*, what allows the emotional brain (limbic brain) of a person to change is falling into limbic resonance with the therapist and being tuned by the therapist's emotional brain, just as the baby's brain was originally tuned by the mother's. This generally takes a number of years; there is no quick fix for reprogramming the emotional brain.

Among the hundreds of kinds of psychotherapy, there are strong disagreements about issues like touching clients and how far the therapist should go in meeting needs directly. Most of my discussion will stay within the mainstream, although I will also give examples of work that fall outside of it.

A few other terms may be helpful here. The term *psychodynamic* is often used when speaking of therapies that deeply explore the childhood roots of behavior; when such therapies focus on the reparative effects of the relationship with the therapist, the terms *relational therapy* and *attachment-based psychotherapy* are sometimes used. These are all very different from *attachment therapy*, a controversial therapy used primarily with adopted children who have not attached to their new caregivers.

The discussion that follows relates to long-term depth therapies attuned to early attachment.

Parallels with the Good Mother

Therapy parallels the mother-child relationship in that it exists to meet the client's needs, not the therapist's, just as the mother is there to meet the child's needs and not vice versa. Like the Good Mother, the therapist attends to you in an attuned way, giving you the space to express anything and everything, being interested in your inner experience, helping you negotiate what is difficult. Some researcher-clinicians even suggest that just as the mother functions as part of the baby's nervous system (albeit an external part) and is a platform for the child's growth, the therapist plays a similar role with a client, offering a taste of new states of consciousness and new ways of relating by entering into shared states in the course of therapy.[1] (Remember limbic resonance.)

The psychiatrist and pediatrician D. W. Winnicott talked about the therapist providing a holding environment, just as the mother provides for the infant. He believed the therapist needs the same patience, tolerance, and reliability as a mother devoted to her infant; must treat the client's wishes as needs; and has to put aside other interests in order to be available.[2] Just as the Good Mother must at first be very accommodating to the baby's needs but over time allows natural frustrations to arise (although in a calibrated fashion), the therapist can back off a little as the client becomes more independent.

Another parallel between therapist and Good Mother is that the relationally attuned therapist keeps a two-pronged awareness, always paying attention to what is happening between them at the same time that he is helping the client deal with any given problem. While attunement to the feelings of the client is standard in all therapies, not all therapies keep an eye on the relationship dance, especially as it relates to attachment issues. The problem-solving focus of most behavioral, cognitive, and brief forms of therapy generally isn't paying attention to this more subterranean aspect.

For clients who had the types of mothers described in this book, a therapist not paying attention to attachment-related issues is akin to a mother who is somewhat clueless about the child's relational needs. The emotionally absent mother has room in her awareness only for the immediate task at hand, and those who are highly stressed may barely be doing that. She may be responsive to outer needs (to some degree) but not to inner feelings and needs. The emotionally present therapist must be attuned to both.

Unlike the mother who is relationally "blind," the relationally attuned therapist knows that he is an important source of constancy for the client. This is something that was missing for those who have been undermothered. They haven't had someone there in that consistent way that you can count on and which is the basis for a sense of security. Therapists who are willing can become this source of constancy and help fill the hole of what was missing in the early environment and missing in the client's psyche.

Often an undermothered adult child will have a great need to feel that the therapist is not just providing care because it's his job (like Mom), but that this time the caring is personal. Many adults who were undermothered don't have a sense that their mothers really knew them and consequently didn't have a sense of their mothers liking them. They may have felt their mothers somewhat dutifully loved them (on a superficial level), but people can't feel truly loved (or even liked) if they don't feel seen for who they are. For such a client to feel genuinely liked by the therapist, she must know that her potential as well as her pain is seen.

All of this requires great skill on the part of the therapist. The therapist must show that she genuinely cares yet must keep certain boundaries in order for the relationship to stay clear, professional, and not become enmeshed in the therapist's needs.

Special considerations in attachment-oriented work

In attachment-oriented therapy, the therapist serves as a new attachment figure, allowing an opportunity to form an attachment bond and work through some of the unresolved issues from earlier relationships. This is a very deep form of work, requiring a number of special skills on the part of therapists.

First, it must be understood that clients with attachment injuries will often be unaware of much of what is affecting them. Because so much of our infant experience is preverbal, it doesn't get encoded and stored as explicit memories do and isn't something we can talk about or are even consciously aware of. These unconscious patterns will likely be lived out by the client both in therapy and in life.

A skilled therapist watches for replays of patterns and reactions, reads the body language of a client, and pays careful attention to his own experience as information about what is going on for the client and what is happening between them. As psychotherapist and author David Wallin writes in *Attachment in Psychotherapy*, "That which we cannot verbalize, we tend to enact with others, to evoke in others, and/or to embody."[3] The quality of our attachment relationships is largely determined by the nonverbal interactions that make them up, he explains.[4] Eye contact, facial expressions, and moving toward or away from are all part of an exquisite dance between infant and mother, between lovers, and between therapist and client.

Because of the regression that will happen at times (the client going back to very early states), there may be feelings of merging in the relationship; these can blur the normal boundaries. Therapists need to be impeccable in not furthering dependency beyond what is healing and to not use touch or any aspect of their relationship to meet their own needs for affection, power, contact, and so forth. As you can imagine, a codependent therapist who needs to be needed could become entrapping and wounding rather than healing.

In most intensive forms of therapy there will be some idealization of the therapist, who, for a time, will be seen through rose-colored glasses. The therapist is being seen through the eyes of the client's love and need for love. Because we so need this love to fill in for what we missed as a child, we fill in for what may be missing in our therapists, attributing to them more than they actually possess. We see them not as they are but as we need them to be.

This idealization is, for a time, advantageous in that it helps us attach to the therapist, just as a child's idealization of parents is believed to help them attach to parents. While some would posit that all children, out of necessity, idealize their parents, I'm not so sure of this. One woman shared with me that her first remembered experience of her mother was of someone with very limited capacity. At three years old, she felt smarter than her mother. Naturally a three-year-old is not going to have more life knowledge than her mother, but something about this experience is eerily prophetic. The woman grew up to become a doctor, while the mother was a woman of very limited maturity.

Although all forms of therapy involve some vulnerability on the part of clients, dealing with our earliest abandonment wounds and allowing feelings of neediness and dependency to arise in the therapeutic relationship really accentuates this feeling of vulnerability. It takes tremendous trust on the part of the client to tolerate and express these feelings, and therapists must know how to deal with this respectfully and skillfully.

As you can see, working with early attachment issues is very delicate business, and clearly not every therapist or form of therapy is suited to it. In the attachment-oriented work I am describing, the relationship becomes the vehicle for healing. In other therapies, the relationship has to be sturdy enough to hold the other elements, but the various interventions are believed to be the more specific vehicle for healing.

Touch in therapy

Most therapists are trained to restrict or avoid touching their clients. In psychodynamic therapy, the need for touch is explored, but it is considered "acting out" to bring those touch needs into the relationship rather than help the client "work through" them. Therapists who are more "body-centered" or whose training has been less traditional often feel differently about it. Some will employ touch to help calm a client who is extremely agitated; others may use touch as part of helping clients tune in to their experience, and yet others may feel that offering an occasional touch is important for clients who, because of their history, have so often felt untouchable. One trauma expert remarked that there may come a time when *not* touching your client becomes unethical, because it is withholding such an essential element of healing.

When dealing with early attachment injuries, the issues related to touch are heightened more than usual. Often clients may come with higher-than-average touch deprivation and touch hunger. They feel a greater need for touch, and touch has greater impact with them.

One therapist allowed her client to express her needs for contact and support by allowing the client to take hold of her hand or make contact with the therapist's foot by reaching out with her own foot. The primal need for contact was met, and the client's fears about rejection and constraints about reaching out were easily accessed without the kind of body contact that could have been confusing.

Adults who have had touch sexualized inappropriately as children or who are overstimulated by touch or tactilely defensive will have specific vulnerabilities. Touch may feel too powerful to them or too threatening. It's a very complex issue.

Most therapists whose training includes touch have learned to always ask permission before touching and to verbalize what they are going to do. ("Is it okay if I touch your shoulder as we do this? I'm just going to touch you right here, like this. How does that feel?")

A therapist might accept a client initiating touch when it reflects an important step for the client, as for example, the client above who would reach for her therapist's hand when working through issues from her early life where it felt too dangerous to reach out or to have needs. If a client's touch feels seductive, manipulative, or as if the client is not respecting boundaries, the therapist will need to confront this.

Re-mothering

Occasionally one will find a therapist who is willing to more directly take on the role of "surrogate mother" and also more willing to touch. One such therapist offers "re-mothering therapy" to adult women. She encourages her clients to relax into their dependency and attachment needs and let them be met. "Instead of shaming undermothered women for being hungry for love, I take their hunger for love seriously," therapist Soonja Kim writes.[5] She is there, as the Good Mother, willing (most radically) to love them. This includes holding clients who want to be held and affirming them with what I have called Good Mother messages.

Soonja Kim invites her clients to settle back and take in this loving attention:

> Passive love is the kind of love where care is offered, without your having to do much to elicit it. It requires more intuitiveness and empathy on the part of the giver, and more receptivity of the taker. Receiving passive love can be deeply healing for undermothered women, who had to be so active in trying to earn love. They have so much shame around their emotional neediness, that to be given, without having to disclose their needs directly, feels extremely comforting.[6]

Kim goes on to say:

As you feel your dependency and attachment needs sweetly embraced by a mothering figure, and allow yourself to receive passive love, there proceeds a gradual relaxation in your body, heart, mind, and spirit. In that relaxation, you may first go through the grieving period of not having the care and the sweet love you needed growing up. However, as you allow the grieving to flow and to be released, you can move to a deeper level of relaxation, where you can access who you really are. You also may experience the truth of your interconnectedness with all beings that releases you from the deep sense of aloneness you have felt.[7]

Many would agree that relaxing into a deeper connection and one's underlying essential nature is a much needed healing. Some would say it is our birthright, lost when mothers can't support a baby's presence.

Work of this nature sometimes requires something outside the traditional fifty-minute hour. It may require sessions that are several hours and that may on occasion take special forms. One woman, nearly fifty, recounted a series of sessions she had with her therapist after working for over a year by phone on issues related to her emotionally absent mother. She traveled to her therapist's town and stayed in a nearby motel so she could do several long sessions, even including some nonsession time with the therapist's family. (Keep in mind that we are talking about loving human contact and inclusion for a person who never felt wanted by her mother.)

Here is the woman's description of breaking through to her deepest core of infant pain and what it meant to be held by her therapist.

I was weeping from my core and the depth of my being, and at that moment more than anything, I needed the

embrace of love to hold me, contain me, which my thera-
pist did. After a while, it was as if it wasn't just my thera-
pist holding me, though I know she was there.

[Later] I would feel an amazing sense that I had been
held by Love itself, that it went beyond my therapist
and her family, and was something so much deeper. We
had touched a core reality, and that embrace of love, for
me, is a metaphor of the love and embrace I needed my
whole life. The longing to be wanted, really wanted; to be
acknowledged that I even exist and don't have to earn the
right to exist and be alive; that I am beautiful and lovable
(to be held and not treated like poison)—well, what more
can be said?

This early re-mothering is powerful medicine that is not always handled well. I've heard of a number of therapists who provide holding, sustained eye contact, healing verbal messages, and sometimes even a baby bottle. Clients have reported mixed results, and I've heard of some serious injury when the therapist abandoned a client who had previously been encouraged to regress into a dependent state. Other times the work has been benign but not always on target for the client. The first rule of good mothering is attunement, so even well-intentioned and compassionate therapists who are not quite in sync with a client aren't going to have the best results.

I believe it is authentic, attuned, trustworthy, and respectful connection that heals, and that is not something a therapist can pull out of his pocket like certain other kinds of interventions. I thus place more trust in needs and responses that organically arise in therapy rather than those that are applied in a formulaic way.

This was how it was in my own experience of being re-mothered by a therapist. The felt need for re-mothering arose from deep within me after working on other early trauma for several years. As others have reported, it felt like a hole in my heart where Mother was supposed to be. When I indicated to my therapist that I wanted her to stand in for my mother, she was momentarily reluctant. (It goes against so much of our professional training.) But then she responded in the way her heart dictated and really showed up for me. She did not offer to hold me (and I never asked), but she wasn't afraid of touch, which was really healing for me. I think our deepest bonding happened through gazing deeply into each other's eyes. The connection went through the eyes and straight into my heart. It was a profound experience for me, and this bonding (which I reinforced internally) resulted, over time, in reorganizing my entire experience of myself and of life. It provided me the chance to experience the essential ingredients I had missed, which allowed my development to move ahead by leaps and bounds. Speaking about it later, I said the most important element in that therapy had been the fact that in a very tangible and real way I felt loved.

From isolation to secure attachment

When things go well in therapy, we grow and develop new options. People who have sworn off vulnerability may learn to tolerate vulnerability enough to actually let someone in. Here is an example of the progression that a person with a self-sufficient strategy might go through with a therapist:

1. PROTECTIVE ISOLATION

The self-protective stance is not letting others in. This is a defense against the pain of possible rejection. The self-sufficient person has concluded that love isn't going to be there, so it's better not to want it. Any expression of warmth and affection unsettles this stance.

2. CRACKS IN THE ARMOR

The therapist who is patient and attuned will eventually find ways to help the client feel seen and understood, melting some of the protective armor.

3. AMBIVALENCE AND LONGING

As more contact is tolerated, repressed longings come to the surface and fight with the old defenses. Now there is both a "stop" and "go" message, with attending ambivalence.

4. MELTING

Because the longing has been so repressed, it is very strong when it breaks through. Indeed, it's strong enough to melt the resistance, leaving the client feeling exposed and vulnerable.

5. FEAR

Feeling vulnerable and dependent may set off tremendous alarm bells. This is something the self-sufficient have learned to avoid at all costs.

6. INSECURITY

If the fear can be navigated, more attachment continues to form, and the therapist becomes very important to the client. This is often hard for the client to tolerate. Therapists go away (on vacation or for work) and are available on a limited basis. The adult part of the client understands this, but the attachment needs of the infant that are aroused go far beyond an hour a week. Absorbed into the feelings of the infant self, the client may feel as if she needs the therapist for her very survival. When the therapist goes away, the client caught in these states may fear that the therapist will not return or perhaps won't care about her in the same way.

7. DRINKING IN THE NURTURANCE

Even with feelings of insecurity, the client increasingly is able to take in and enjoy the nurturance that is offered, feeling gratitude and satisfaction.

8. INCREASING SECURITY OF THE BOND

As the bond between therapist and client continues to strengthen, it becomes sturdier and more resilient. Disruptions to the relationship (a vacation, a misunderstanding) are more easily tolerated, and the client needs less reassurance.

9. HEALTHY ENTITLEMENT

In time and with consistently positive response, the client begins to feel more confident and deserving and to ask for what she wants. This has a positive effect on self-confidence and on other relationships.

10. INTERNALIZING THE ATTACHMENT FIGURE

Both the attachment figure's presence and the good feelings that constitute the relationship become part of the client's psyche and structure. In a secure attachment, that person becomes part of your heart. (See "Your portable Good Mother," p. 171.)

Although I am describing a self-sufficient style that begins with protective isolation, it's an isolation that isn't always obvious. Attachment wounds can stay hidden for a long time. The client going through these stages may have comfortable and close friendships that do not stir up and do not have the same power to heal the attachment wounds that lie under the surface. An adult with a self-sufficient style may even have a stable marriage that lasts for decades but is just distant enough not to rock the attachment boat. Although I have described this process in the context of a close therapeutic relationship, a similar process could happen with any potential attachment figure who stays consistently present and supports this evolution.

From frustration to satisfaction

For those with a preoccupied (anxious) attachment style, the progression will be different. Rather than needing awakening, the attachment system is "too on." It is fixated on connection, obsessed with it. The task here, according to Diane Poole Heller (see reference on p. 214), is taking in the contact offered so that a state of satisfaction can be reached. Although always looking for connection, those with this attachment strategy dismiss or don't register the connection that is offered, so their attachment hunger is not quenched and they stay in a state of heightened anxiety. It's not unlike a fussy baby who is so upset that she can't take in soothing. The upset gets in the way of the taking in. Once more, attunement, consistency, patience, and finding a way for this client to "feel felt" and to take in caring (both in the therapeutic relationship and in other significant relationships) are critical. Eventually, these feelings allow the person to arrive at an earned secure attachment.

Therapist as "Teaching Mommy"

One of the most difficult things for clients in an intensely relational process like this is to understand that even though the therapist is providing a yummy, long-desired experience of the Good Mommy, one that the client might wish to bask in forever, the therapist is there as a temporary stand-in. The therapist is standing in while you develop your own Good Mother inside. The therapist in all her tenderness, wisdom, and patience is simply showing you how it is done, when it is done well. She is what I call the Teaching Mommy, meaning that she is there to model this, to show your adult self how to do it.

It is the inner mother that will be there on Christmas Day or a long weekend or the middle of the night, not the therapist. Of course to the extent you have internalized the therapist, you can pull her up anytime.

Even without referring directly to an inner mother, we could say the therapist jump-starts aspects of yourself that haven't been working, like being able to provide support or appropriately protect yourself. We don't want these to be available only in the therapist's office. A skilled therapist will help the client incorporate these capacities so that they are available 24/7.

Advice to therapists

Working with emotional neglect and abuse, in my experience, is rather slow work, which is often heartbreaking. It's important that you have the emotional resource within yourself to meet the demands and the emotional pain that comes with the territory. Clients can be badly injured by therapists who don't have the emotional bandwidth needed and who end up replicating a rejecting or unavailable mother.

The work takes gentleness and patience: gentleness because we're dealing with incredibly tender young places inside our clients, and patience because rebuilding one's foundation is long-term work. You may have even worked for several years in therapy before the most severe examples of abuse or neglect come up. It takes time for the client to trust you, and time for the client to be ready to take on what was most overwhelming in her past. In the meantime, you never quite know when there is a land mine beneath something you thought was innocuous.

In addition to knowing you have the necessary patience, internal strength, knowledge of the issues, and therapeutic skills, it is important to understand your own attachment dynamics. Most therapists have a history of insecure attachment; how much you've worked through this is critical. You need to be available for clients to securely attach to you and to help promote this attachment through your welcoming stance, warmth, empathy and attunement, and ability to deal with clients' needs and their frustrations with you.

It's good to know how your own attachment sensitivities may get activated, for example by a client who clings to you or, alternatively, by one who can't let you in. Your strengths will play more to some types of clients than to others. For example, I recognize that clients with a more preoccupied attachment strategy who need a lot of verbal reassurance are less satisfied with me than those who need to learn to trust. My presence is generally more spacious and not so much reaching out, as some clients need.

You might find it helpful to pursue training focused on working with attachment-related issues. Diane Poole Heller offers several levels of training and certification for therapists using her DARe method, the Dynamic Attachment Re-patterning experience. This includes learning about the various attachment strategies and therapeutic interventions helpful with each.[8] You can also find information about working with the various attachment styles in David Wallin's *Attachment in Psychotherapy*, or through his in-person trainings.[9]

Authors and therapists who work with particular kinds of parents may also offer trainings. For example, Karyl McBride offers brief training for therapists based on her work around healing from narcissistic mothers.[10] The more familiar you are with the territory of emotional neglect and abuse and the types of poor parenting, the more helpful you can be in general.

It's rewarding but demanding work, so it is important to know your capacities and limitations. Being in supervision may help you extend your skills and work through the inevitable "growth opportunities" that come your way in putting yourself on the line in this type of work.

As always in this work, your own degree of healing and wholeness is the most important element that you bring. All the book learning in the world won't make up for a system that is reactive rather than calm, or an ego that can't be found lacking in any way. There is nothing better than continuing to "do your own work," which may happen informally through your own ways of processing, through a therapeutic relationship, and even through spiritual work. As David Wallin says, "We are the tools of our trade."

13.

More Healing Steps and Practical Strategies

I'VE GIVEN YOU MANY OPTIONS for working with your mother wound, but I would be remiss if I didn't include this proactive approach built on needs we've identified. Consider the following:

- Not everyone is going to be lucky enough to find someone who is willing to serve as a replacement for the Good Mother they missed in childhood.

- Not everyone has a partner who wants a conscious relationship and is willing to let that relationship be a place to work on childhood wounds and unmet needs.

- Not everyone is going to be drawn to the Great Mother or to working on the archetypal realm.

- Not everyone has the resources, commitment, or inclination to do psychotherapy.

- Not everyone is comfortable working with the child within.

- *But everyone can*, in addition to any of the above, employ the perspective of this chapter to proactively identify and meet needs that are left over from childhood.

Identifying specific "holes"

For the undermothered child, the hole where Mom should have

been can feel as big as the universe. When we come back to it as an adult, we may feel that there is no way to fill that hole.

It is essential to recognize this as a feeling (not an actuality) and realize that the hole *can* be filled. It helps when we remember that this spot in our psyche is simply a place where pieces of ourselves have not yet filled in because they didn't have the support they needed. It is not an endless abyss but rather is made up of specific holes where the functions of the Good Mother were not met. Between these spaces is dry land! Despite what was missing, there are places where your development was supported and consequently there are pieces of yourself that are solid and real. It's important to feel what is there as well as what is still missing or underdeveloped.

Here is a list of ten needs we all had as children. You'll notice a great deal of overlap with the ten functions of the Good Mother listed in chapter 2.

- to feel that you belong somewhere and are part of the larger web of life

- to attach to others in a secure way and know it is safe to be vulnerable and show your needs

- to be seen for who you are and have your feelings met (mirroring)

- to have help and guidance that is calibrated to your needs

- to receive encouragement and support, to feel that someone is behind you

- to have others serve as a model for you and teach you skills that you need to succeed

- to have needs met in a timely way and to be comforted and soothed when you are upset, thus establishing an ability to soothe yourself and bring your system back into balance (self-regulation)

- to have adequate protection so that you are safe and are not overwhelmed

- to be treated in a way that communicates respect (for your boundaries, needs, feelings, and so on)

- to feel loved and cared for

Another universal need is to feel valued, but I did not include this as a separate item because I think the sense of value is the result of, and comes with, all of these. Value comes when we feel that we belong and are part of a positively valued group. Value comes with secure attachment. Value comes with positive mirroring that helps us know and accept all parts of ourselves. When others take time to guide, support, and encourage us, it communicates that they value us. When others provide appropriate protection and want to keep us safe, it tells us that we are precious to them. Likewise, when people treat us with respect, it helps build a sense of value. And certainly being loved gives us a sense of being lovable and having value.

Identifying your needs (an exercise)

Look at the list of ten needs above. For each need, consider how well it was fulfilled in your childhood and where you are now with it. If it helps to use a numerical rating system, here is one you can use:

1 – strongly unfulfilled
2 – somewhat unfulfilled
3 – somewhat fulfilled
4 – strongly fulfilled

However you choose to do the exercise, the goal is to end up with a list of needs that are still active.

Taking a proactive approach

Rather than look back at an absent mother and get caught in the feelings of the unfillable hole, it is more fruitful to step back from the feelings, assess what specific holes need to be filled, and responsibly go after what you need in each of these areas.

In *Growing Up Again: Parenting Ourselves, Parenting Our Children*, authors Jean Illsley Clarke and Connie Dawson talk about healing one hole at a time. "There is no quick fix," they write. "There is no magical, sudden way to borrow the needed skills and to reclaim our self-confidence and self-esteem. We must do it ourselves step by step; we must build it from within."[1]

Building it starts with identifying what we need. So, for example, if you know you never had much encouragement and you recognize that you often avoid doing things that are new or that you haven't developed skills for, you might ask yourself, "What do I need for support? Do I need someone to mentor me? Do I need some cheerleading? How can I work on developing more self support?"

If you feel disconnected and as if you don't belong anywhere, you could look for places to develop relationships and eventually experience a sense of belonging. You might also consider how work or volunteer activities can give you a place in the web.

Many of these will have both an outer and inner level. So, for example, if you feel as if you'd benefit from more love, you can consider both how to cultivate loving relationships and ways to nurture your own self-love.

The point I want to make is that we can be proactive. In general, I think there are three ways we can go after the pieces that we've missed:

- We can identify what we need and ask for it directly.

- We can look for people and situations where whatever we seek is easily found (e.g., a situation in which safe touch is plentiful).

- We can provide ourselves with what was missing.

I find that when I am specific in my needs with others, asking precisely for what I want (in a nondemanding way) works quite well. Sometimes I even give people their "lines" (often making a joke about it) and then ask that they use them only if they can do so sincerely. Often people respond by saying, "Absolutely I can say that," and then repeat what I've asked to hear. When others start off in a direction that's not helpful, I gently try to steer them to what I'm looking for. So I might, for example, tell someone this isn't the time when I want to hear their critique of my next book idea and all the challenges that might come with it; right now I need their support. I might say something like, "I want you to say it's an exciting idea and you're behind me."

If we can tell people when we want to be held, when we need our feelings mirrored, when we need verbal support, and so on, then we won't feel so powerless. Another advantage is that we don't look like "unfillable" holes to other people, who will likely respond with some kind of pulling away from what is perceived as endless need. Specific needs are generally less threatening and overwhelming to everyone.

The hole of support

The hole of support is one of the most common in children of emotionally disengaged parents. Often we didn't have a person who provided support for our efforts and support for us when our efforts failed. There was no one jumping up and down, saying, "Yes, you can do this!" or "I'm behind you." In the desired situation, that person is the mother, joined by the father and others as well. Without people who communicate that they believe in us, it is harder to believe in ourselves.

This lack of support often means that our confidence doesn't develop normally or fully. We can feel as if we are missing a piece—and we are! We're missing something inside us that develops when a child receives consistent support. We're missing our sense of capacity and inner support. This leaves us feeling intimidated, inadequate, and insecure. When we feel the hole of support, we say things to ourselves like, "It's too big. I don't think I can do it," or "I feel so alone with this."

Issues of support often come up when we are tackling something new and the outcome is not guaranteed, or when we come up against challenges. We often need support when we have a "failure" of some sort.

Rather than blame yourself for your lack of confidence and wonder why you can't just push ahead like others seem to do, it may be helpful to take a look at how much support you had growing up. I'm going to keep the questions broad so you can answer them with whatever parental figures you had.

- How often did a parent come to any performances or events you were involved in? What did they say afterward? What did their body language convey? Did it feel supportive that they came?

- How did your parents respond to your accomplishments? Were your achievements acknowledged and celebrated?

- Apart from accomplishments, did you have a sense of parental support just for being you and for the inherent challenges of growing up?

- How did your parents respond to feelings of fear, insecurity, or inadequacy? What about times you were a little down and just needed to know that someone cared?

- Did you have a sense that there was a parental figure you could go to in times of need?

As with almost any area we explore, we see the family legacy at play. We reject or fail to support in ourselves and our children what was not supported by our parents, which, in turn, generally wasn't supported by theirs. We can break this chain by consciously deciding to.

Getting support now

If you want to reverse a pattern of inadequate support, you need to first examine what your needs are and commit to building more support. You will also want to notice how well you take in support when it is offered. Often when we didn't receive much when we were young, our ability to receive gets blocked by defenses that we developed.

There are many approaches to bolstering your sense of support both in the self-help literature and therapy. Here is my list of helpful strategies:

Ask for support from others.
This is not an optional skill but an essential one. You must be able to ask for support and encouragement in whatever form you need from people who have a decent chance of providing it.

Learn to access others even when they're not there.
When others aren't available, you can take the process inside. You can do this either as internal dialogue or as a dialogue that shows up in your journal. If you are journaling, simply imagine what that person would say. You can do this with anyone, including a Good Mommy figure or imagined guide or Higher Self.

Find supportive structures.
Get creative about collecting or developing supportive structures, including support groups, classes, work groups, an exercise buddy, an accountability partner, or whatever would be helpful in a particular situation. Consider how you can set up a series of goals and rewards and what routines and learning situations can help you.

Step away from your feelings and get objective.
Remind yourself of your actual capacities. The sense that you don't have enough support is, in the end, only a feeling. As a

feeling, it can limit you, but only if you are paying more attention to that feeling than to your capacities to meet a situation.

Support your inner child.
Since often it is an inner child state that gets caught in feelings of fear and insecurity, you can step into your own Good Mother and dialogue with the child, listening to her fears, providing empathy, holding, and reassurance.

Say nice things to yourself.
Notice if you're repeating deflating messages to yourself and replace these with positive statements. Ask yourself, "What would a Good Mother say in this situation?" Here are some statements you might work with:

- I have faith in you.

- I know you can do this

- I'm behind you, whatever happens.

Make it real through imagery.
Imagine having the support you need. Feel this as vividly as possible. See yourself moving easily through whatever feels challenging.

Feel the fear and do it anyway.
If there is a particular task that is difficult, it may help to dive into it. The engagement itself and any progress you make can provide support. If fear leads you to back down and cave in, the fear has won, and will be used again.

Access the support of your body.
Not everyone feels their body as a resource, but if you can, it's a great asset. For example, sensing your bones can provide a sense of solidity. There may be other subtle cues you can use as well, like pressing your lips together. Feeling your muscles can feel good, and getting some exercise may help break the spell of inadequacy.

Reach to Spirit for help.
Millions of people turn to Spirit for help in times of need. This may take the form of spiritual beings outside yourself or contacting the part of your own being that is far beyond what you normally experience. I can say unequivocally that support is definitely available.

For the undermothered, support is often an issue that requires continued attention. It is worth the effort it takes, however. As we learn to seek out and take in external support and slowly develop more internal support, we find that we move forward with more ease. There aren't the same limits then, and life becomes less of a struggle.

A sense of confidence

What is confidence, and where does it come from? Confidence is not all or nothing, but rather something we feel more of or less of in different areas of our lives. As adults, we may feel confident about our relationship skills but not our computer skills or confident in our decision making but not in our ability to aggressively go after what we want.

I've observed that for some people confidence is more closely associated with doing (and is dependent on skills and performance), while for others it is related more to their felt security with others. My suspicion is that confidence gets tied up with doing when parents put a lot of emphasis on competence. When children are not shamed for undeveloped skills but rather are loved quite fully just for being who they are, then competence becomes less important. The secure person simply says, "I don't know how to do that," and looks on with curiosity. A child's competence at whatever level needs to be mirrored for the child to take that into his identity; otherwise the child will often feel inadequate.

Although it would be a mistake to make our confidence as an adult dependent on how others feel about us (just as it is a mistake to make it dependent on how well we perform), having a secure attachment serves as a foundation for a child's sense of confidence. A secure attachment gives you a place in the world, the sense that someone values and is invested in you, and the sense that you have a right to be here and take up space. One way to define confidence is as the courage to show up and express yourself. That's easier when others have supported this.

We can look at our list of needs and say confidence comes with almost all of them. It comes when we feel wanted and are an accepted part of a larger group that we feel good about. It comes when we are seen and accepted for who we are and when we are treated with respect. When others encourage and praise us, it builds confidence. When we know we'll have the help and support we need, it builds confidence. When we can regulate our own physiology, our ups and downs, and bring ourselves back to balance, this gives steadiness and confidence.

You can ask your inner child what he or she needs to develop more confidence. One such child said she needed to feel safe, to feel liked, to have someone excited about what she could do, and to have someone see her strength.

What do you need to develop more confidence?

Finding your power

It's hard to be successful in life when you don't have your full power. Without your power, you're hindered in your attempts to compete on the many stages of life, whether the athletic field, the marketplace, or even the dating arena. Therapists sometimes refer to the sense of power as self-efficacy or a sense of "agency" (as in being an agent acting on your environment). Often we think of this in terms of the power to change our circumstances, but it is also empowering to know that we can change our internal experience, such as our mental patterns or our mood. When you know you can change things, you are no longer a victim.

There are an untold number of ways you can increase your sense of empowerment, including:

- Developing communication skills that help you advocate for needs and defend boundaries.

- Finding the power to say no (through assertiveness training or self-defense classes, for instance).

- Selecting situations where you can make a difference and minimizing situations where you can't. Some situations are inherently disempowering.

- Noticing when you do have an effect on a situation. You can't grow your sense of power if you keep overlooking times when you are effective. You must take in experiences of success so they get braided into your self-concept.

- Learning to change your self-talk. Self-talk is the running dialogue you have in your head about things, and especially about yourself. There are classes, books, blogs, and articles that can help you move from a pattern of negative assessment and commentary to something more positive, compassionate, and objective.

- Sensing strength in your body. This doesn't mean bodybuilding, although it could include that. Often just feeling our muscles or feeling the support of bones gives us a sense of solidity and power. There is also a felt empowerment that comes with "embodiment," which is simply having more of your consciousness in your body. Body-centered therapies can help with this, as can anything that increases your awareness of your body, such as a good yoga practice.

- Working through the issues that have blocked your power, utilizing avenues such as psychotherapy.

- Learning how to locate resources to help with specific needs. Being empowered doesn't mean you have to do everything all by yourself. Think of the CEOs of the world!

Protecting what is precious

As we've learned, one of the functions of the Good Mother is to provide a safe place, a protected environment in which her child can grow and blossom. We continue to need this as an adult. We need an environment that safely and comfortably holds us and that feels nourishing. Just as the Good Mother provides this for the infant, we must learn to provide it for ourselves as adults.

There are several aspects to a holding environment and the sense of safe, protected space. One is our home, where we live. Does your home feel both safe and nourishing? Is it a place you like to be? What happens when you move one level farther out to the surrounding area? Do you feel at home in your neighborhood?

How about boundaries, both as it relates to others touching your body and to psychological boundaries? Can you keep others at the right distance? Do you let others intrude on your privacy or in your psychic space, with nosy questions and unwanted advice? If someone moves into your personal space either physically or emotionally in a way you don't want, can you push them back to a more comfortable distance?

Boundaries will generally be more difficult for those who have had intrusive parents and whose families were enmeshed rather than emotionally disengaged, but even families that are emotionally distant can have boundary violations. In order to let out the more hidden and vulnerable parts of you, it's essential that you feel you can protect yourself as needed.

Just as the Good Mother arranges the environment for the young child so that nothing will be experienced as harsh or invasive and what the child needs is available, part of cherishing ourselves is to pay attention to what is too much and what is just right for us. So, for example, it is knowing what is too much social contact, what is not enough, and what is most satisfying. Obviously it's not just a matter of quantity but quality, so we look at what kinds of contact are satisfying and what is not and then adjust our lives accordingly. Here the protection role and modulation role are combined. Modulation is making things just right. Not too much and not too little.

Here are some questions to help you assess how well you are fulfilling the Good Mother roles of protector and modulator:

• Where in your life, if anywhere, are you not protecting what is precious in you?

• If you were creating a "holding" that was just right for you, what would be different than it currently is? Consider as many levels as you can, including the physical environment, social environment, and emotional environment.

Showing up and being seen

Often when we're not mirrored, we lose contact with parts of ourselves. It's a journey to recover these, a journey that involves being seen now. Of course seeing yourself is part of it, and any kind of self-exploration will help, but having others see and acknowledge these lost parts helps cement them in place.

While the invisibility may have started with parents too busy, too checked out, or not capable of really seeing you, it may be maintained by our own habits and a certain turning away from the world. Often to survive the emotional barrenness of emotionally absent parents or any early environment that did not feel welcoming, we turn into ourselves. Rather than reach out in relationships, we withdraw. Part of healing is coming out of the cloister and back into the world.

In expanding your opportunities to be seen, you might consider expressive and even performance activities, such as theater, group singing, and dance. My mother is a very conventional woman who shows little of herself, and I have found it very freeing to participate in activities that pull me out of a similar tendency to hold back, activities where people are spontaneous and uninhibited.

Some groups provide an opportunity for a person to have the stage (the group's full attention) for a moment and just be seen. The person in the center can express anything he wants. Often what is most healing is simply to be transparent in that moment, showing true feelings.

Having emotional intimacy with even one other person, someone you can show all of your inner world to, also provides a sense of being seen.

A place in the web

Many who did not experience a strong connection with their mother also feel a lack of connection with other family members or with the family as a whole. That leaves a hole, something missing. We rely on family to connect us with the world in a meaningful way by giving us any number of things: a port in the storm, a sense of belonging, identity, support. We look to family to find a place where we are known and held.

If you have your own mate and/or children now, this may help compensate for the earlier disconnection, but what if you have only your family of origin, to which you feel so thinly tethered? What if you have no place that is home in the sense of tribe or family?

I find that some people feel totally bereft when they don't have a sense of a family around them. While certainly both family and partner are seen as an important part of a safety net, neither are as essential as we might believe. Our safety net and sense of community can change over time. We need to see that people can step in and fade out of that regularly, and that, most importantly, in the hour of need someone—even a stranger or a near stranger—can step up to help.

I heard a touching story from a friend of mine. A woman my friend had recently met had contacted her, saying she needed help. This woman was new in the community, was having surgery, and was writing to eight women to see if any could help her. She knew none of them well and felt a little embarrassed to be asking, but she didn't have anyone else to ask. All eight said yes.

People who seem constantly busy and not as attentive as we want them to be will often respond to a specific need. In general, people like to be helpful. True, when the period of need stretches out for months, they may fall away, but this is not necessarily because they don't care. It's because they have other things to attend to.

The fears I see in those of us who feel so vulnerable, so unprotected, so exposed without parents or siblings to rely on are primarily the fears of our child parts. We are not endangered by not having that protective net of family around us if we have the capacity to reach out and ask for help, like the woman new to her community. The more we feel rooted in our adult selves, the less adrift we feel without surrounding kin.

The nuclear family has taken on disproportionate importance as the larger sense of tribe or community has diminished in Western culture. In some cultures, the whole village takes on the role of family, but here we're talking about a very limited number of individuals. Instead of being connected by dozens or hundreds of threads, we're held by half a dozen—or maybe only one or two. That is not enough to sustain a healthy sense of connection and belonging.

The solution is to build additional strands of connection and belonging. Some of the primary ways we do this are through the following:

- A circle of close friends may serve as a "family of choice," being there in times of need and celebrating important passages in our lives with us.

- Ties to groups help give us a place in the web of life. These may be interest groups, healing groups, social groups, or any other. For some, their community is one whose interactions take place across the World Wide Web. While a virtual community alone may miss some important aspects, it does provide a sense of connection that is meaningful to many.

- Meaningful work (volunteer or paid) gives us a place and purpose in the world.

- Ties to places anchor us in a physical way to the planet, so that we're not simply wanderers or "lost in space." This could be a sense of connection with your home or the area surrounding your home. Many people feel a strong connection with the land around them.

Navigating the world of emotions

Humans live in a world filled with emotions, but for many who are undermothered, this world is more uncomfortable than not. Learning to navigate these waters is an important part of functioning successfully in the world and being a full human being.

John Bradshaw explains how many get cut off from this world: "Children growing up in dysfunctional families are taught to inhibit the expression of emotion in three ways: first, by not being responded to or mirrored, literally not being seen; second, by having no healthy models for naming and expressing emotion; and third, by actually being shamed and/or punished for expressing emotion."[2] He continues, "The earlier the emotions are inhibited, the deeper the damage."[3]

When emotions have been cut off in this way, becoming part of the world of emotion may require significant learning. We

have to break the spell of our own "still face" and become transparent. This may be harder to do with some emotions than with
others. The feelings that our parents had a particularly hard
time tolerating will usually be the ones that we have the hardest time tolerating if we have not yet healed in this area.

Expanding your repertoire (an exercise)

- Which of the following emotions are hardest for you
  to accept and express?

○ hurt	○ desire
○ sadness	○ love
○ joy	○ awe
○ anger	○ disappointment
○ fear	○ remorse
○ vulnerability	○ envy
○ pride	○ jealousy
○ bewilderment	○ confidence
○ hatred	○ happiness

- Which were hardest for each of your parental
  figures?

- Using this list as a jumping-off point, make a
  list of emotions that you want to add to your
  emotional palette.

- For each of the emotions you have just named,
  write about what would support you in
  developing it.

Just as we can be proactive with the other deficits identified in this chapter, we can be proactive in claiming or reclaiming emotions we have not been able to easily express. For example, perhaps in your family of origin, there was no room for you to show disappointment, and you notice that you are still shy about expressing it. It might help to select a trusted person, share some disappointments, and ask for validation. Ask to have the disappointment mirrored and normalized. An example of normalizing might be, "Of course that would be hard! I would be disappointed, too." If you were shamed for showing disappointment, this could be a powerful corrective experience.

EMOTIONAL STYLE AND CARETAKING PATTERNS

Remember that many who are undermothered will need to work on continuing to get in touch with their feelings. When Mother didn't notice or respond to feelings, we often don't have a strong connection with them ourselves. We may even have learned to turn them off in order to keep what thread of connection we felt with Mother.

Our individual style, whether we suppress feelings or exaggerate them to get attention, generally develops in response to our caretaker's style. It makes sense that when caretakers are consistently uninterested in a child's feelings or act punitively toward the child for expressing feelings, children learn to suppress their emotions. We can also see how when caregivers are sometimes responsive in an attuned way and other times just don't get it, children are more likely to exaggerate feelings in order to get help, which is what the research finds.[4]

Take a moment to reflect on this.

- Are you more likely to hide your feelings out of fear of rejection or to "whip them up" when you want a response from someone?

- If you do some of both, which feelings or in which circumstances do you tend to conceal your feelings, and when do you let them get really big? What do you expect will happen when you let your feelings get big?

Embracing your needs

When it comes to our needs, we tend to adopt the attitude our parents had toward them, at least initially. So, for example, if your mother was impatient with your needs or rejecting, you'll tend to have little tolerance yourself. I remember a time in my own therapy when I had just expressed a fair amount of neediness and suddenly felt very apologetic. I was, in essence, rolling my eyes as if to say, *This is way too much!* Fortunately, I noticed it and recognized it as a hand-me-down from my parents. "I'm glad you caught that," my therapist told me, "because I don't feel that way at all."

For many whose needs were not met in their early years, needs feel humiliating and dangerous. One woman disclosed that putting herself in a dependent position vis-à-vis another felt like handing them a knife to cut her throat. Feeling dependent was associated with feeling raw and unprotected and about to get clobbered.

Moving through this is not easy. We need to learn that it is no longer dangerous and that there are people who *want* to meet our needs! Learning this involves some risk, because we won't know until we try. That risk can be hard to tolerate.

Beliefs will not change without new input. When our needs are ignored when we're young, we often feel rejected for having needs. This can lead to a belief that our needs are too much or that our needs will drive others away. The belief gets dismantled by showing our needs and having them met.

It's helpful if you can start by reaching out in small ways to people who are safe. The risk is less this way, and you can slowly build your tolerance for the vulnerability as well as a reservoir of experiences where you are successful.

For those with a self-sufficient style, it's a long journey from "I'll do it myself" to "I'm so happy for your help." It means learning that your needs can actually be the place where others are responsive to you.

Knowing your needs and being able to express them is an important developmental achievement that supports intimacy, which authors Jett Psaris and Marlena Lyons acknowledge in their book *Undefended Love*. Yet, it's not the whole story. We want to feel okay even when our needs aren't met by partners. As Psaris and Lyons note, "The earlier the unresolved need, the less capable we are as adults of sustaining our sense of well-being when that need is not fulfilled by another."[5] When our early dependency needs weren't met as infants, our consciousness often fractured in that moment. We didn't have the resources or maturity to "hold it together," meaning to hold ourselves together. That intolerable rawness and sensitivity around need comes from these very early injuries.

It can be embarrassing to expose these unpolished aspects of ourselves, but it is part of the process. We bring to our intimate relationships everything we didn't work through or complete in childhood. From the perspective of those who see relationship as a path of growth, that is a blessing.

To explore where you are in your healing journey, consider the following questions:

- How do you feel about having needs? Can you see how this mirrors how early caregivers felt about and responded to your needs?

- Do you generally expect that others will be available when you need them, or do you carry more sense of deprivation in relation to this?

- Which of your needs is hardest to express?

- Can you expose a need, have it only partially filled, and be okay with that? Do you have room to, in essence, "hold" your needs rather than pass them off like a hot potato or suppress them altogether?

Cultivating a capacity for intimacy

Intimacy requires emotional openness, a willingness to see and be seen, and letting your needs be a place where you are met. This will be challenging if you haven't worked through the residues left by unresponsive parenting, but it is worth working toward. Although you may have carried deep disappointment about relationships over many years, you also likely carry a deep longing, and you can use this longing to help propel you forward when you're hanging back, caught in a self-protective posture.

One way of proactively working with this is to think about what you do to foster intimacy. What are the "attachment behaviors" that are part of your repertoire, and how can you increase these? Consider the following:

- Can you accept comfort at times of threat or when in distress? (This is an "attachment behavior.")

- How do you respond when someone reaches out to you? Can you allow someone to need you?

- Can you touch in caring ways? Sustain intimate eye contact?

- During lovemaking, can you keep emotional contact?

- What fears and defenses come up when you get really close to a partner?

One therapist reports that when a couple is able to increase their attachment bond, it helps each partner self-regulate and resolves some of their individual problems. For those with a self-reliant style, the task is to wake up the attachment system, which can then function more normally, as nature intended it. Consider what you can do to cultivate the capacities that allow for intimacy.

Receiving good touch

Caring touch often brings the warmth that has been longed for. There are many situations where safe touch is available—more than we generally imagine. Consider various forms of dance, interactive movement, athletics, massage or bodywork, and of course hugs!

If you want to be more comfortable touching others, you might take as a model someone who touches easily and natu rally, as often it's more a matter of permission than anything else. Taking on child care responsibilities or playing with children also affords opportunities, although we need to make sure we're not imposing an agenda but rather responding to the child. This is true of other types of caregiving, too, as with the elderly and sick and those who are grieving.

Stepping out of deprivation consciousness

Mother is our first environment, and how we experience her has great impact on how we subsequently experience the world and what we expect from it. If Mother was not responsive to our early needs, we generally don't expect the world to be. If Mother was not welcoming, we don't perceive the world as welcoming. In fact, a major part of healing is seeing that the world is not the same as Mother, changing both our perceptions and our relationship with it.

I have found many who were undernurtured as children to have what might be called *deprivation consciousness*. It is a sense of lack that is carried within and becomes the unconscious filter through which we receive experience. We might go so far as to say some of us create a "deprivation story" that becomes the repeating theme of our life. A deprivation story is filled with thoughts such as "There's never enough for me" or "I'll never get what I want." Often this will be in contrast with how you see others. It's as if you're the last baby in the row at the orphanage, and they always run out before they get to you.

If you resonate with this sense of deprivation, consider the following:

- What's the flavor of the deprivation you feel? Is there an image or a metaphor that captures it?

- Can you see how this flavor has run through your life?

Only after you metabolize the pain in the experiences that generated this story will you be able to eventually let go of the story and have a different experience.

As part of that process, you may also want to do some exploration of any barriers that may be present to having a different experience now. Try to imagine what abundance would feel like. Where does it rub up against self-images that block it? How would it change your sense of you to feel there is plenty rather than not enough?

When we experience something totally unfamiliar, it can bring a sense of shock at first. If you've essentially never had good support and then have someone who behaves in a totally supportive way with you, you may find yourself feeling rather disoriented, wondering if this is real. Think of the people who win the lottery, gain instant riches, but a few years later are back at the level they were beforehand. That instant and drastic change wasn't ever integrated.

- Can you think of a time when your sense of deprivation was challenged by something quite contrary to it?

- List five examples of times when you had everything you needed or more than you could wish for. What did that feel like?

Sometimes the sense of deprivation is deeply branded into our psyche, but we try to displace it by steeping ourselves in symbols of abundance. This may be preferable to the earlier experience, but even better still is when the old imprint dissolves and we leave deprivation consciousness altogether. Then, even in the midst of a very ordinary life, we feel rich.

Taking in the good

One practice that can help with dissolving the effects of deprivation is to consciously take in positive experiences. This has been a focus in positive psychology, which is supported by modern neuroscience. My go-to resource for this field is psychologist Rick Hanson, whose writing is very accessible.[6] The brain is like Velcro for the negative and Teflon for positive experiences, he explains, so even if your life is filled with positive experiences now, they will flow right through—without nourishing you—if don't learn to pause and take them in.

Hanson created a model that he has written about extensively. He calls it the HEAL process and often writes about it as "taking in the good." It begins with deliberately noticing a positive experience and then staying with it. You want to steep in it, paying particular attention to what feels good about it. You can even deliberately accentuate or enrich the experience by bringing in as many senses as possible as well as adding emotions and personal meaning. This savoring of experience, lingering with it, is what it allows it to actually change us.

Positive emotions have been found to have far-reaching effects: lifting mood, increasing optimism, and helping develop a resilience that is an antidote to the emotional collapse that so many adult children of emotional neglect and emotional abuse feel.[7]

Another practice backed up by research is working with gratitude.[8] The following exercise is one place to begin:

Counting your blessings (an exercise)

At the beginning of the chapter, I said that between the holes is dry land; between the deficits and places we are underdeveloped are places where we have what we need. Part of empowerment and stepping out of deprivation consciousness is being solidly anchored in our strengths and resources. We'll look at this as three different lists, one dealing with capacities that you have developed, the second as assets or blessings in your life, and third (perhaps the hardest) of positive things about your childhood.

Make a list of twenty capacities that you have developed. Here are some examples:

- I know how to be a good friend and provide support to others.

- I am resourceful and know how to get the information I need.

- I am compassionate with myself as well as others (maybe not all the time but a good deal of the time).

- I have learned to recognize my feelings and can verbalize them rather than simply act them out.

- I am able to feel my own preciousness.

Make a list of at least twenty things in your life that you might consider blessings. For example:

- I live in an area that has very little crime and where my neighbors know and like me.

- Judy has been very generous with me, lending me equipment so I don't always have to buy it.

- I sleep well at night.

- I have a great massage therapist.

Make a list of twenty positive things about your childhood. Make at least half of these about your mother. For example:

- My brother protected me at school when I was little.

- My mother took me for medical care when I needed it and was proactive around my headaches.

- My father introduced us to wild areas in nature.

- We used to sing in the car on road trips, and this was enjoyable.

- My mother cared about how I looked without being too controlling about it.

If you keep these lists available for reference, then, when a pervasive sense of deprivation starts setting in, you have something to counteract it.

Practicing good self-care

As I mentioned above, we tend to treat ourselves as we have been treated. For some this leads to a marked lack of good self-care. Often this comes out of lack of awareness. Adults with emotionally absent mothers don't have a model of what attuned, attentive care looks like and have often learned to override distress signals. I think of a woman who came to see me wearing no socks on a snowy day. She didn't notice that her feet were cold.

Less frequently this lack of self-care is an expression of aversion and self-rejection. A woman told me that she had the distinct feeling "I hate taking care of you" when prompted to start paying attention to her skin. She would wait until her skin was cracking before applying moisturizing lotion.

Other times we don't want to take care of ourselves because we secretly want others to take care of us. I've heard the belief *If I take care of my needs, then no one else will, and I'll never be taken care of by another.* One woman told me that she would only get holding if she fell apart (so meeting her own needs was in opposition to getting holding).

It's not true that meeting our own needs is exclusive of having needs met by others. I find that in my social circle, I prefer meeting the needs of friends who show that they care about themselves. Meeting some of your own needs makes you less dependent and clingy. It models how you want others to treat you.

A client with a history of emotional neglect looked at me blankly and asked, "What is self-care? I don't really know what that means. Eating well, sleeping, and exercising?" Yes, and so much more.

- Good self-care is being responsive to your needs rather than shutting out anything that is painful or inconvenient and gets in the way of normal functioning. Your feelings and needs are important and deserve to be attended to with respect and loving care.

- Good self-care is finding (healthy) activities that give you a moment of pleasure or are a time-out from what is stressful.

- Good self-care is not pushing yourself to function at your optimal level when you're going through a rough patch.

- Good self-care is holding with compassion the person who is suffering and has suffered so much. In this case, that person is you. Can you have as much compassion for yourself as you would have for your best friend going through what you're going through?

- Good self-care is being kind to yourself. Can you speak to yourself with as much empathy and caring as you would to a loved one? Can you touch your face or your arm with tenderness? Can you give yourself a break when you need one?

- Good self-care is finding things that feel good to your heart, whether holding a favorite stone, listening to a song, sitting somewhere special, or calling someone special.

Caring for someone recovering from an illness often means bringing food and helping out so that the person can rest and heal. In a similar way, caring for yourself when recovering from emotional pain means supplying nourishment and doing what you can to make your life easier. It means that *you*—and your well-being—come first and are more important than keeping up with expectations. It's nice to keep up as best as you can, but it's not as important as your healing process.

Just as you might protect an injured finger with padding, good self-care provides a cushion to your nervous system. It is paying attention to all those things that affect you: sound, temperature, light, the effect of different food and drink on your digestive system, the effect of various people on your emotional system. When we are healing emotional wounds, our nervous system is doing extra work and starts with the disadvantage of already being compromised.

Knowing this, you allow yourself a little more "margin" than usual: an extra hour in bed, time to journal rather than attend to your to-do list, the option to leave the obligatory social gathering (or to not go) because you just want to be alone.

Practicing good self-care gives an important message to your system. It says, "I care about you. You are important." For a child of emotional neglect or abuse, this message is medicine.

- What are the ways that you neglect your physical or emotional well-being? (Be as detailed as you can.) What are you willing to do to change this pattern? You might also think of ways you can do a better job in areas you are not currently neglecting.

- Create a list of things you can do when you need to feel nurtured. Look for healthy things, perhaps things a Good Mother would suggest or provide, like a hot bath, a foot rub, curling up in a comfy chair with a comforter and a good book, or making a pot of soup or a nourishing hot drink.

Self-care is a practice—one in which we keep growing. Although you may start out feeling handicapped, remember that you get feedback in this process. When you feel your body relax or you have a little more space emotionally, your self-care is working. Keep it up!

General tonics

There are some things that are just plain healing, regardless of the particular deficit or injury. They are "general tonics" that strengthen the system, including things like creativity and self-expression, cultivating a friendly relationship with your body, nurturing self-talk, and time spent in nature. Many have found in Mother Nature the holding that was missing for them earlier.

Pay attention to what is "good medicine" for you. Just as the Good Mother stays attuned to the needs of her child, your job is to stay attuned to your needs and to provide what is nourishing.

In this chapter I've encouraged you to take responsibility for meeting some of the deficits of your childhood. In combination with the preceding four chapters, it gives you enough material to work with for a long time. Enough to change your whole experience, transforming your story.

14.

Changing the Story

THE TERM *STORY* CAN be used in a couple of different ways. One is to refer to our account of something, the story we tell ourselves about it. This story that we tell ourselves may be very different from the objective facts and often makes it hard to see the objective facts. Caught in a deprivation story, for example, we fail to see how we do have what we need.

The word *story* can also be used to refer to a more objective account of events, as when we think about someone's life narrative. Here we are looking at the sequence of events that compose that life.

In this chapter we'll look at our mother's story (second meaning) and see how that impacts our story (first meaning). We'll see how these influences pass along to the next generation. We'll also consider what all of this reparative work means for our actual relationships with our mothers now, as adults, and the ongoing nature of healing.

Your mother's story

Our own subjective story, maintained by our childhood feelings, is by nature, self-centered. We interpret the world according to our experience. We know Mother by who she is to us.

When we stop there—who she was and still is to us—we miss a big piece. If you are a parent, can you imagine being known only through your interactions with one of your children? There are so many more aspects to you, so many other parts of your life that deeply influence who you are as a parent.

A large part of healing is stepping out of the limited story we replay about our mother and actually letting her emerge as a person. We need to see her life as it was. This exercise may help.

Telling your mother's story (an exercise)
There are several ways you can do this exercise. One would be to ask a friend to listen as you tell your mother's life story. Another option is to write it on paper. You can do this in any length and detail that you want. You can do this without the aid of the questions below, or you can use them as a prompt. Not every question may be relevant or something you can answer.

- What do you know about your mother's childhood, including family circumstances? Was she close to her parents? What were they like? How many siblings did she have, and where was she in the lineup? Was she enrolled in any responsibilities, like taking care of younger siblings?

- Was her childhood happy? How do you think she experienced it?

- What seemed important to her as she emerged into young adulthood? What did she want out of life?

- How much do you think she had "found herself" before starting a family?

- How did she negotiate intimate relationships?

- Why did she have children?

- What was it like for her to be a mother of young children? What about this might be particularly hard for her? What kind of support did she have?

- What else was going on at the time? What was happening in the household and in the world? What social and economic stresses were present?

- What do you know about her health and overall energy level?

- What were the circumstances of your birth? How may these circumstances have affected your bonding with your mother?

- If she worked outside the home, what was her job like? Did she enjoy it? Was she empowered there?

- How was it for her to be a parent of adolescents?

- Was there a childhood age or stage that seemed hardest for her to show up for as a parent? What do you relate this to?

- What other events in her young and middle adulthood were important?

- What were her greatest assets? Her greatest deficits?

- What do you think were the biggest struggles in her life?

- Do you think she felt satisfied with how she parented you?

- What aspects of her life were most unfulfilled?

- What regrets might she have, if she could be totally honest?

- Now think of a title for her life story. What would capture the essence of it?

The stepping-stones of your mother's life (an exercise)

Here is an alternative (or supplemental) way to paint your mother's story with broad brushstrokes. It is based on a journaling technique developed by Ira Progoff, inventor of the Intensive Journal, and is called a stepping-stone list. Progoff used the term stepping-stones to refer to major life markers, although they are not always events per se. An item on a stepping stone list could refer to a whole period of life that has a certain atmosphere or quality to it.

Progoff suggests limiting stepping-stone lists to eight or ten items and never more than twelve. It is not necessary to put them in chronological order or even order of importance. Creating a stepping-stone list is simply a process of letting these markers come to mind and writing them down. A quiet, receptive state can facilitate this more easily than thinking too hard.

With this instruction in mind, make a list of eight to twelve significant markers in your mother's life.

A letter from Mother (an exercise)

Here is a third exercise that might be revealing. Write a letter to yourself from your mother. It doesn't matter if your mother is alive or has passed on, or even if you are still in touch with her. Imagine what she might say to you if she were able to be genuinely disclosing. The letter may be about your relationship, a problem, what she wants for you . . . anything that comes to mind as perhaps unsaid. Note after this exercise how you feel.

There are also therapeutic techniques for taking Mother's perspective. In Gestalt therapy, role-playing, Psychodrama, and Family Constellation work, you or another might take Mother's perspective, speaking and acting as her, although sometimes from a deeper soul perspective than the persona shown to the world. In one of these stand-in experiences, a "mother" disclosed that she was empty and had nothing to give. It was painful for her to look at her daughter because she recognized her daughter had needed more.

Understanding Mother's experience is important. It helps you not personalize her behaviors so much. You can more easily slip out of feeling unlovable, for example, when you see that Mother had limitations in expressing love. Rather than simply feeling lost and unshepherded, you can see that Mother had absolutely no experience guiding anyone, and probably had received no guidance herself.

The more we see our mothers clearly, the easier it is to find some compassion for them.

Your story

"Developing compassion for the wounded mother does not preclude honoring the pain of the hurt child within oneself," writes therapist and author Evelyn Bassoff.[1] Mother's story is just part of the picture. There's also our story of what we've been through.

As I mentioned in the last chapter, our story is not always fully conscious, although we can make it conscious. Just as I invited you in the first exercise of the chapter to tell your mother's story, I invite you now to tell your story, either to another or on paper. It can be the long or the short version. An advantage of the abbreviated version is that it's often easier to see the themes. What stands out when you consider your entire life experience?

When I first worked with my story, it was too hard for me to begin in childhood. It was too captivating, too tragic, too sad, and I found it hard to move on from there. I decided to start from the point of leaving home at age eighteen and to continue the story past the present time into the future, and that story made me smile. I liked the ending, and I could feel my empowerment and healing. I think now I could go back and start it in childhood, stating the truth of it but no longer so snared by the feelings that they overshadow everything else.

As you heal, your story changes. As you more objectively understand why your mother failed in the ways she did and take responsibility for mothering yourself along with taking in mothering from others and seeing that your needs are met, you change your life.

The dance between you

The intersection of the two stories, your mother's and your own, creates the dance between you. This is very important to keep in mind and helps explain how our siblings can have experiences so different from our own. Siblings come in with different sensitivities, have different needs, and are a different match with Mother. The hardier the baby and the closer the match, the easier it goes, all else being equal. But all else is not equal. For example, a child who is the tender age of twelve months will experience Mother grieving the loss of a parent or spouse differently than a child who is six. So the dance between each child and mother is unique.

* What adjectives describe your relationship with your mother? Is it cool? Adversarial? Have there been particular points of conflict? Is it perhaps superficial and obligatory? Are there points in the dance where there is closeness? If so, how do you feel at such moments? Do you like the closeness, or is it uncomfortable in some way and hard to fully accept?

We used stepping-stones when looking at Mother's life. Now let's make a list of stepping-stones for your relationship with her. Limiting your list to eight to twelve items, note the major markers in this relationship.

Assessing what is possible

It may be shocking to consider that your current relationship with your mother can be quite separate from your journey to heal your mother wounds. It would be a mistake to think, *I can't heal this load I carry unless she can understand my feelings and make up for past mistakes.* That is trouble for three reasons:

1. You give her power over your healing process. It's not true that you need her in order to heal.

2. You likely can't navigate a new relationship with your mother from an open place if you're still marinating in sadness, resentment, or anger. It is important for you to have made some headway with difficult feelings.

3. You can't assess what she is capable of if you are too blended with your undermothered child inside. You'll need your strong adult for that and for being prepared to do any confrontational or reparative work.

In considering your next step in this dance with Mother, it's important to ask yourself what you want, to objectively assess what is possible, and to know what kind of risks you are willing to take. Here are some questions that may help you:

- What do you want? Do you have some *should*'s operating—for instance, that you *should* be close to your mother? What if you set these aside for a moment? As you contemplate various possibilities, do any of them bring a feeling of relief?

- If things never improve, how would that be?

- What do you think is your mother's capacity to have a warmer, more genuine relationship? (Support this with what you see in her other relationships.)

- From her perspective, what would be a desirable relationship between you? (Generational and cultural factors also play a part in her expectations, desires, and capacities. Is closeness for her more about showing up on a holiday or about sharing feelings and being there for each other?)

- What is your capacity for more emotional closeness with her? What would need to be different inside of you?

- Are there fears you have about the relationship becoming more real?

- If she sometimes responds to your overtures and at other times does not, how would that be for you?

- How is this timing? Do you have the emotional energy and does she to attend to this relationship?

There is no one template for the optimal relationship between adult children and their mothers. It has to be a fit that takes into account your personalities, capacities, history, needs, and current situation.

Maintaining a civil but distant relationship

Most common, it seems, with mothers who are emotionally shut down and disengaged is simply to continue a superficial relationship. This is a relationship with minimal contact, which stays on the surface, one which never was and never will be close. This fits for those adult children who don't want to hurt mother or lose family contacts and aren't actively being hurt as long as they maintain an emotional distance.

With mothers who were intrusive or enmeshed or overly helpless, moving into a more boundaried relationship with less contact may be a new move, intended to protect you from the ongoing hurt that you experience in the relationship. It is a demotion of sorts for Mother as it moves her out of your inner circle where she had too much influence.

Strengthening boundaries

Having good boundary skills helps us feel that we don't need to give up ourselves to be in a relationship. Being able to say "No," we are then more free to say "Yes."

What kind of boundaries we need with aging mothers depends on the type of mother. Let's start with helpless-acting mothers. Helpless mothers depend on their grown kids for all kinds of assistance. They may call frequently asking for advice, but seldom follow it. It's not the advice they want so much as the contact. These mothers can be infuriating, as they step over their adult children's boundaries on an ongoing basis. Tell them not to call you at work, and they'll disturb you time and time again with one perceived crisis after another.

In *Understanding the Borderline Mother*, Lawson's advice for dealing with the Waif is widely applicable when helplessness is Mother's calling card (see p. 134). Lawson's advice is to give a consistent message that Mom can and must help herself. You might say, "I'm sorry I can't help you; I know you can handle this yourself." Don't let general helplessness and need control you, but rather force her to ask directly for what she wants. I think this is a good guideline in general. When the request is owned in a very specific way, you can then decide whether you want to meet it and are not sucked into taking it on yourself to solve all of Mother's problems.

With many of these mothers it is important to show that you will not be manipulated (guilt being the major strategy) and will not allow intrusions. Lawson advises her readers to warn and follow through with logical natural consequences for inappropriate behavior. Just like we do with kids.

It's very different with a mother who takes on the Queen role. She is in many ways more brittle, so although you need to point out each time she violates your boundaries, you have to say it in a very careful way. If she feels blamed, watch out! The most dangerously abusive mother, Lawson's "Witch," is much like the vindictive narcissist, and I've heard similar advice given. Leave the field as soon as possible. Any verbal defense or hitting back will just bring more abuse. That doesn't mean you have to play dead, but you need to not feed the fire in any way.

With more non-harming emotionally absent mothers you don't have to be as excessively careful, but it's still good to not make any situation more adversarial than it needs to be. I have a client whose mother lived thirty minutes away and would start with a demand that her adult daughter take her somewhere on Saturday. When the daughter learned to say, "Saturday doesn't work, but I could do it on Friday afternoon," she noticed that her mother seemed to treat her with more respect. We teach people how to treat us by our response to them.

Setting a boundary can be as simple as "that doesn't work for me." You don't need to justify and you certainly don't need to feel bad about saying no.

Our boundaries are part of what creates a sense of being intact and in charge of our life. The more you feel both an energetic boundary and know that you can keep these outer behavioral boundaries, the easier it is to feel relaxed and not threatened around people who are insensitive or even abusive.

Setting boundaries is often an important stage in separating from intrusive family members. Having your voice is important in establishing a sense of being your own person and having rights. You need to be ready, however, for dealing with the hurt and anger that will likely arise if your family doesn't respect these boundaries. Unfortunately the people you most need boundaries with are those who aren't used to respecting them, so you'll want to be ready with your natural consequence. If you tell your mother you'll hang up if she doesn't stop yelling and she continues to yell, you must hang up.

Speaking your truth

I have known many adults who desperately want Mother to know how abandoned, misunderstood, or poorly treated they felt as a child. They want to at last be able to speak their truth.

Sometimes speaking your truth and asking for what you want leads to better understanding that then allows more warmth to flow between you. If done right, confrontation is an act of engagement and an act of intimacy. It is letting another person into your vulnerable interior.

Most of us are not well-practiced at confrontation and tend to lead with our complaints. Others respond to this defensively because they don't want to feel that they are wrong. My best rule of thumb in confronting people is tell them how to please you rather than hammer them with what they're doing wrong. Give them a way to feel good about themselves and to get out of the doghouse and into your good graces.

Unfortunately, the most unloving mothers cannot and will not hear you no matter how skillfully you present your case. In my therapy practice I've seen how heartbreaking it is when Mother cannot move toward you. You can cry, plead, offer suggestions, and tell her what you need, and the most you may get back are responses such as, "Are you having a bad day?" There is no taking in of your feelings and experience. They hit a wall and ricochet back. In worse cases they become fodder for an attack.

I find that most of us do not understand how strong our psychological defenses are. It takes a flexible ego to take in what will make us feel bad. In mothers who are not healthy, what you will receive instead is denial (it didn't happen), minimizing (it wasn't so bad), playing victim, or going on the attack.

In choosing the option to speak your truth you need to be honest with yourself about where you're coming from. Is the motivation to heal and bring closeness, or is there hidden or not-so-hidden anger wanting to hurt Mother like you've been hurt? Where you stand inside yourself will be critical for the outcome.

Unfortunately, if you approach Mother from your inner child, there's a good chance she'll respond as she did with you as a child. Of course your inner child is the one who really wants to know Mother is sorry and that she cares, but it's risky to bring your child into confrontations where she may be retraumatized by another abandoning or attacking response. Better to let your inner child speak privately and in therapy, where she can be met with empathy. If you decide to bring to Mother some inconvenient truths, let your adult do the talking.

Leaving Mother

Some authors and therapists when speaking of leaving the relationship use the term *divorce*. This term may seem more apt when there has been a high-conflict or an enmeshed relationship than when there was never much of a relationship to begin with. I can hear some of you groan. "Divorce? We were never together!"

Usually leaving the relationship is seen as a last resort and follows much individual healing work as well as failed attempts to "make it work." When you can't get Mother to respect your boundaries or stop hurting you, sometimes you need to leave so that you can get on with creating the life you want.

Like divorce, there may be a number of attempts to leave before you're successful. As Peg Streep, author of *Mean Mothers*, points out, you may return to the relationship when your own emotional neediness and wishful thinking trumps what you otherwise know to be true: Your mother can't give you what you want from her.

Writing of her own experience, she shares a critically important insight: "It didn't occur to me until years later that never once did my mother initiate a reconciliation, and I now understand why: She was relieved by my absence. From her point of view, I was the mirror that reflected her greatest fear and failure: her own unloving nature as my mother. Keeping that secret was, I believe, more important to her than I was."[2]

Best-selling author Susan Forward, PhD, in *Mothers Who Can't Love*, advises those who want to leave the relationship to write a short, very direct letter that they mail to their mother. It simply states that you want no further contact, what that includes, and a request to please respect your wishes. This is not an emotive letter, not getting into the issues or laying blame. Just stating the new facts of life. Using the vehicle of a letter saves you from immediate confrontation and getting pulled back in. I've worked with clients who prefer not to send such a letter but after repeated boundary setting simply stop responding to any contact.

It's a hard step to leave Mother, and most will feel guilty for a while, although most will also feel a sense of relief at being free from the relationship. It's certainly a step in one's independence, although it may also involve mourning the loss of any hope of getting the love you wanted.

A concern I've heard many times is how this change will reverberate through the extended family. It is not uncommon that more narcissistic and unhealthy mothers will share their distorted side of the story, hoping to get sympathy and to punish or vilify the adult child who has left them. You can't control what Mother will do. This is part of the really hard letting go of trying to manage what Mother, or anyone else, thinks or feels. Mother will do what Mother will do, and those who have eyes to see will put it in perspective. You can also share with those family members you are most close to what you've done, though better to assure them you are not trying to get them entangled in it. A few may become a source of validation or support.

Feeling internally separate

If Mother is not currently harming us, leaving Mother in the sense of cutting off the relationship may be less important than separating from her internally. Many people, however unsatisfied as they are in the relationship, are still negatively merged with Mother. They are still fighting inside, still pushing against her, caught as if in an undertow in this all-pervasive sense of Mother they want to get away from.

An exercise I give clients who are either worried about being just like Mom or are caught in her script is to make a list of ways you and Mother are different. It becomes a list of contrasts, and these contrasts have the effect of revealing that "Mother and I are not the same." This is generally a great relief.

From this place of separation, and with boundaries protecting you from invasion and enmeshment, you may be freer to move toward a more healed, or at least a more peaceful relationship. Most importantly, you have more of yourself.

Toward a more healed relationship

Of those in my initial interview group whose relationship with their mothers improved, I noticed that it was generally the grown child who initiated the changes. It seemed to come with the adult child's capacity to extend warmth to the mother who, for the most part, had failed to extend warmth to her child. It came as these healed adult children were able to understand Mother's limitations, forgive, and want to include Mother in their lives.

Our understanding of reconciliation is greatly expanded by Laura Davis, one of the two authors of the best-selling *The Courage to Heal* who later wrote *I Thought We'd Never Speak Again: The Road from Estrangement to Reconciliation*. This was informed not only by her own reconciliation with her mother after an eight-year estrangement but also one hundred interviews with others who had either restored severed relationships or achieved a sense of inner peace when reconnection wasn't possible. It is a good book that I recommend. It helps us go beyond the idea of a single heart-to-heart that will make things good again, and to see reconciliation as a process that happens over time. Usually there are setbacks. Progress is slow as trust is reestablished. Davis found that for some, talking about wounds of the past was essential, while for others it was not.

Davis named her individual healing as the most critical element in her reconciliation with her mother. She had worked through the wounding and let go. This letting go involves an "earned autonomy," we might say, in which you are truly detached from outcome and not needing anything from Mother. It comes only when you accept that "I may never get an apology, Mother may never know what I went through, but I know what I went through and I am solid in that and don't need her validation. This is my hard-won healing, not dependent on her."

"When you are desperate for the relationship, you can't get it," Davis writes. "You have to let it go, and then you may find it slipping in later through the back door."

I have seen reconciliation come with this "dropping of old accounts." Julie's story is a good example. Julie grew up with a narcissistic mother who, like most narcissists, couldn't reach beyond herself. It was always about Mother. Julie's relationship with her was of the civil-but-distant type described above. It's hard to be close when there is no room for you in the relationship.

When Julie's mother was diagnosed with melanoma and was ill in her later years, Julie traveled cross-country frequently to help care for her. These trips started out as obligatory, but over three or four years they became more rewarding as her mother warmed up to her. Julie was shocked the first time her mother stood up as she was leaving and asked for a hug. "You're the only person who's ever been there for me," her mother confided. While we may have heard of this sort of thing with mothers who are manipulating, Julie heard it as vulnerable and sincere. Within the larger context of their time together, Julie experienced it

as "mother letting me in." As she helped her mother on practical levels, Julie listened. The more she understood her mother's
experience of early abandonment, the easier it was to feel compassion for this old, dying woman. As her mother continued to
become more vulnerable, it made it safe for Julie to let down her
guard and become more open. In this case, Julie's being open
led to being seen in an appreciative way. A moment Julie trea-
sures is when her mother said, "You're the kindest person I ever
met." Julie now truly misses the mother she discovered in the
last years of her mother's life.

Should I forgive?

Most of us are aware of an *ought* that says we should forgive
any harm done to us. We certainly hear this in religious and
moral teachings in which forgiveness is consistently presented
as the high road. With so much social support around forgiveness, it promises to at the very least help others feel good about
us. You've perhaps noticed how uncomfortable many are with
the depth of your pain. They're hoping if you can forgive, all of
that will simply disappear.

We may hold that fantasy for ourselves as well. The idea of
banishing all bad feelings through a simple act of forgiveness
sounds like a pretty slick move.

Unfortunately, it doesn't seem to work that way. As Susan
Forward reported in *Toxic Parents*, she noticed that forgiving
didn't create any significant or lasting change for her clients
and they didn't feel any better about themselves. In fact, since
the blame wants to go somewhere, it will often get turned
inward if that's the only direction available, leading you to feel
worse about yourself.

This raises the question of what exactly forgiveness is and
where it is coming from. Does it come from trying to be good,
from desperately wanting to get beyond your pain, or from
accepting *what is*?

My own view aligns with those who have seen forgiveness less as something we do than as something that evolves under certain conditions when we have done our work. It is letting go of old accounts and allowing someone back into our hearts, usually after we've worked through our anger, hurt, and disappointment. When we've run through all of this, the blame sputters to a halt and we just want to be done with it. The feelings that once consumed us are now a burden to maintain. We're moving on to more interesting things.

Others view forgiveness as coming by way of grace. Either way, when forgiveness comes, what we forgive is the flawed human being who did very bad things as a consequence of their own wounding. It is not saying that what they did was okay, and not saying they are not at fault. Forgiveness is simply acknowledging, "Yes, you messed up, and I still have a place in my heart for you."

Part of what makes this possible is understanding why people hurt you as they did. Laura Davis explains, "When we accept another person's inadequacies, compassion arises. Rather than see their weaknesses as *something malicious directed at us*, we begin to recognize them for what they are—human frailties."[3] (Italics added.)

This is a significant turnaround from where we started. It's natural to view what people have done to us as malicious, especially as children. Children don't have the sophistication to know that this wounding behavior was because of the Other's brokenness. It is by healing our own brokenness that we see how hard it is to be healthy and whole, how hard it is to be with emotional pain full-on, how imperfect we are.

Also very striking in Davis' book was an admission by a mother who always disappeared when her adult child was in a really bad spot and needed her. The mother said, "I can't stand it when you're hurting." So when what would naturally be seen as the most heartless indifference and selfishness can be seen in a larger context, what comes into view is the mother's lack of capacity, not a malicious "I don't care one speck about you."

Forgiveness comes with maturity, with an opening of the heart that comes as we work through our pain. Yes, sometimes innocent, young beings seem to forgive without this, because it is a capacity latent in us all; yet, the more there is to forgive, the more healing is necessary to return to this openheartedness. My experience is that when forgiveness comes, it happens slowly, and you notice it only in retrospect.

Perhaps one more clarification is useful here. Having worked through a process where you've come to forgiveness for someone who has deeply harmed you does not guarantee you'll never return to older feelings. For example, coming out of a trauma memory, you may strongly feel rage. This is part of the natural fight/flight response that is suppressed when we go into what the trauma literature refers to as a freeze state or state of immobility. This is what a wild animal does when it is captured by a predator. It plays dead. Many times in an attack by another person, we cannot flee or fight and the best we can do is to go limp and often dissociate—stop the movie, so to speak. But when that movie starts again, when the immobility state wears off, what was there immediately before—although suppressed— is there again. The rage that was part of the fight response is now accessed. This rage is natural from both a physiological perspective and a psychological perspective. Rage is a healthy response to violation that is wired into us.

Both in terms of working through previous traumatic experiences and because we are made of internal parts that are often dissociated, we may at any given moment be blended with a younger part of us stuck in the past that does not feel forgiving, although our adult selves have come to some kind of forgiveness.

For these complicated reasons it is important to hold an open, fluid view around this topic of forgiveness.

Can I be a good parent if I didn't have good parenting?

While it is true that most parents who are emotionally neglectful or abusive are passing along poor parenting that they experienced, I have been heartened over the years to see what good parents my clients who were poorly parented have become.

Of women who choose not to have children, most are undermothered and fear they won't know how. Sometimes they fear they will "mess up" their kids like they feel they have been messed up. (Although let's not forget that there are other important reasons someone may choose not to become a parent.)

What I would say to women who are worried about this is that you can do it differently. First, there seems to be a maternal instinct that kicks in if not interfered with. I've known women to be in awe at the Good Mother energy pouring through, the love enveloping them when they became mothers.

Second, you are likely more sensitive than your mother, in a good way. Many of those who parent so much better than they experienced as children are more sensitive to begin with and then more tuned in because of what they went through. They want their children to have what they missed.

Third, you can learn. And I encourage this. Good parenting requires a lot of understanding of developmental levels and how to deal with hundreds of events new to you. Why not consult the experts, whether authors, clinicians, or those who have earned their stripes taking care of children either as parents or nannies. It's probably the most important job on the planet, as I remarked at the beginning, so doesn't it make sense to get help?

To be sure, parenting will require taking good care of yourself so that you stay awake and don't go on automatic pilot. It's then that we are more prone to repeat the family legacy, acting in ways we swore we would never do. The more we heal from our dysfunctional families, the more we deconstruct those old tapes.

While I've heard it said that giving your children what you wished you had is healing for you, it doesn't always work this way. I've mentioned a few times that it can be harder to provide what rubs up against your own raw places, activating latent pain. I've also seen many women doing a great job with their kids without doing much to heal the wounds they carry related to their own mothers. This is partly because of our complex organization—encapsulated wounded child parts that aren't themselves healed until we take on the task of mothering them directly. So although being a good parent to your own kids is of course something that supports growing your own healthy structure, it's only part of the picture.

Although I've been speaking directly to women here, this holds true for men becoming good fathers as well.

Holding your process/holding your self

If you've been working this process, if you are on this journey of healing, you know that it is hard work. It is major reconstruction. We are reworking ourselves on so many levels from the hardwiring of the limbic brain to our core beliefs, from our self-concept to how we relate to others, from the anxiety in our chest to our ability to love, make money, and get a good night's sleep.

Most likely this process will take several years if not decades. I hesitate to say this out of concern that you'll find that discouraging. But you may also be discouraged if you think this is going to be a quick process, and it's not. No one I know who has worked through this wound has done so quickly.

It is thus important to pace yourself, to take breaks, to be able to see your progress and take pride in that. You don't want to mimic the mother who never saw your accomplishments, let alone celebrated them.

The process of growth is not a straight line but a spiral. You'll cycle through similar issues many times. If you experience each cycle without change, that's a signal to get more help, but otherwise expect to need to lament what was missing, grieve the injustices, and fulfill the unmet needs multiple times. It won't be forever. There is grace in the healing process, so although it's not like one good cry can make up for years of repressed sadness, it can take you further down the field than you might think.

A Good Mother understands that the process of growth is uneven and doesn't shame or scold her child when she falls back. It is important to have that kind of compassion and patience with ourselves. We're doing the best we can, and some days are simply harder than others.

Does healing ever end?

Although the process of healing never really ends, the hurt can end, and the feeling of being a motherless child may disappear completely. The reason healing doesn't end is that we're always changing. Even just the simple passage of time changes our perspective, once we have become unglued from the past. So how we feel the first year or two after the bulk of our healing has occurred will be different than ten years later, when the past feels even further away.

When there has been significant injury, it's never as if that didn't happen. There is always at least the memory of the wound, if not some remaining sensitivity. But the power of that wound diminishes with healing, and our response to any poking in that area changes. Rather than get caught in childhood feelings that are triggered, we can learn to turn our attention slightly and ask the child inside what it needs now. We can *respond* to the feelings rather than stay trapped in them.

As we work through these wounds, our identity slowly changes. After all, our story has changed. Our life has changed. And it's time for the internal narrative to change as well. As one person told me, "There's still a wound, but it doesn't run my life. It doesn't define who I am."

For those who are able to receive the care of someone standing in for the Good Mother or who are able to become that Good Mother to their own inner child, the feeling of being unmothered can be replaced by a feeling of being well mothered. You can feel loved, supported, and cared for. No, you can't go back and relive the past, but you can have now what you deserved to have then. As novelist Tom Robbins said, "It's never too late to have a happy childhood."

Appendix

Three Mothers, Three Messages:
A Guided Visualization

To get a sense of how powerfully various types of mothers shape a child's experience, let's play with a taste of three types of mothers: the prickly mother, the emotionally absent mother, and our archetypal Good Mother. Your first task is to cast the three characters. The following may help.

For the first character, we've all had experience with someone who is prickly, so that shouldn't be hard to imagine. Prickly people are critical, quickly irritated, and harsh. Prickly mothers, by the way, will fit the profile of the emotionally abusive mother described in chapter 7. For the emotionally absent mother, think of your own if this fits, or do your best to imagine it. And for the last character, the Good Mother, you've likely experienced a nurturing person somewhere in your life that you can use as a model. If you haven't personally experienced this, you might be able to call up a loving mother you saw in a movie.

This works best as a guided imagery exercise, which requires putting yourself in a relaxed state at the beginning. You might have someone read the instructions so that you can more deeply sink into the experience. Another option is to record the instructions on a tape and play them back for yourself, and a third is to simply go back and forth between the book and your inner experience. Some people can just read, close their eyes, and be there.

This exercise can bring up some strong feelings, so you might want to choose a time that allows for reflection afterward. Certainly you'll want to make sure there won't be any interruptions in the environment, so turn off the phone, and let others know you are unavailable for half an hour at least. After each question there should be enough of a pause for your experience to unfold without feeling rushed. We'll imagine each type of mother from the perspective of three different ages, starting with the prickly mother.

🖋

Find a position in which you are comfortably supported. You can lie down if you like. Take a couple of deep breaths, feeling your body relax as you release each breath. Enjoy the sense of relaxation that comes as you give yourself this time to settle in. Allow your eyes to close gently if that is comfortable.

This is not an exercise where you need to do anything. It's a chance to relax and follow, allowing feelings, images, and sensations to come to you as you fall into a deeper and deeper state of relaxation and well-being.

We'll start with the prickly mother. Tune in to whatever feelings and image you associate with this mother. Get a good sense of her energy.

Imagine that you are lying on a blanket in a sunny nursery or room. You are about six months old, and you hear birds singing in the background. Notice the colors of the walls and blanket and the temperature in the room. Your mother comes in to feed you. How do you feel as she approaches? What is her voice like? How does she move? What is it like when she picks you up? How does she interact with you? What do you notice in your body? What happens to your breathing? (long pause)

Now imagine being any age between four and six years old. You're at home, playing. What are you doing? What is she doing? Does she play with you? Notice the quality of her voice, movements, and the expressions on her face. How does it feel to have her here? What do you notice in your body? Pay careful attention to your inner state right now. What thoughts, images, and sensations are you aware of? What emotions? (long pause)

Move forward in time to an age between eight and ten. Imagine yourself in an environment of your choosing with Mother not far away. What are you doing? How far away is Mother, and how does it feel to have her in this scene with you? Notice how it feels in your body.

Bring yourself back to the present for a moment. You might want to write down a few words to remind you of this experience.

Now we're going through the sequence with the emotionally absent mother. Take a moment to tune in to what she feels like.

First imagine yourself at six months, lying in the sunny room. This mother comes in to feed you. Notice the qualities that are present in her interactions with you and especially notice how you feel in your body and your emotions. What is this time with your mother like? (long pause)

Now imagine being any age between four and six years old. You're at home, playing, with Mother not far away. What are you doing? What is she doing? Does she play with you? Notice the quality of her voice, her movements, the expressions on her face. How does it feel to have her here? What do you notice in your body? Pay careful attention to your inner state. (long pause)

Move forward in time to an age between eight and ten. Imagine yourself in an environment of your choosing with Mother not far away. What are you doing? How far away is Mother, and how does it feel to have her in this scene with you? Notice how it feels in your body. (pause)

Bring yourself back to the present and write down a few words to remind you of this experience.

We'll go through one last time with the Good Mother. Put yourself back in the nursery. Hear her voice as she approaches. What sounds does she make? How does she look at you? What expression is on her face? Notice how she reaches out to touch you and what qualities are there in her movements. Notice what her touch feels like and how you feel with her. How do you feel in your body? (long pause)

Now imagine being any age between four and six years old. You're at home, playing. It can be anywhere you want, inside or outside, with Mother in the environment. When you want to engage her, she is there. How does she play with you? Notice the quality of her voice, movements, and the expressions on her face. How does it feel to have Mommy playing with you? What do you notice in your body? Pay careful attention to your inner state right now. (long pause)

Now we're going to experience one more age with the Good Mother. This time you're somewhere between eight and ten. Notice where you are and what you're doing. How far away is Mother, and how does it feel to have her in this scene with you? Notice how it feels in your body.

Bring yourself back to the present and write down a few words to remind you of this experience.

What did you notice? How did you feel being around each of these mother figures?

Often prickly mothers (and prickly people in general) cause us to tighten our muscles, hold our breath, and hold back our spontaneity. Since almost anything we do could be wrong, we're more inhibited around them. The phrase *walking on egg-shells* describes how many of us feel around someone with this disposition. We often much prefer not to have them around.

In contrast, we like being around nurturing mothers. It brings out our affectionate side. We smile and feel happy, and we have lots of permission and support to try new things and to be silly.

Emotionally absent mothers often leave us feeling absent. People may feel spaced out, disconnected, and less here with this type of mother. You may have found yourself more serious and alone in the imagined scenes with her. Some find themselves angry and want to do something big to get her attention.

Is there really any question that a mother's basic disposition and energy profoundly affects her child?

Notes

INTRODUCTION TO THE SECOND EDITION

1. Robert Karen, PhD, *Becoming Attached: First Relationships and How They Shape Our Capacity to Love* (New York: Oxford University Press, 1998), p. 230.

CHAPTER 1: MOTHERING

1. David J. Wallin, *Attachment in Psychotherapy* (New York: Guilford Press, 2007), n. 1, p. 24.

2. Diana Fosha, *The Transforming Power of Affect: A Model for Accelerated Change* (New York: Basic Books/Perseus Book Group, 2000), p. 64.

3. Ibid., p. 65.

4. Ibid.

5. Most of this list is my creation, although some are also noted in Jack Lee Rosenburg with Marjorie L. Rand and Diane Asay's book *Body, Self & Soul: Sustaining Integration* (Atlanta: Humanics, 1985), pp. 207–14. Also, Pamela Levin has affirmations similar to these for every developmental stage in her book *Cycles of Power: A User's Guide to the Seven Seasons of Life* (Deerfield Beach, FL: Health Communications Inc., 1988 and later self-published by the Nourishing Company). Her affirmations were first published in an earlier work, *Becoming the Way We Are: An Introduction to Personal Development in Recovery and in Life* (Berkeley, CA: self-published, 1974).

CHAPTER 2: THE MANY FACES OF THE GOOD MOTHER

1. Harville Hendrix, PhD, and Helen Hunt, MA, MLA, *Giving the Love That Heals: A Guide for Parents* (New York: Pocket Books, 1997), p. 214.

CHAPTER 3: ATTACHMENT

1. Cesareans have been correlated with a mother-baby attachment gap. Mothers who give birth by C-section have been found to "take longer to begin to interact with their babies, have less positive reactions to them after birth, and interact less with them at home. In one study, a month after cesarean birth, the mothers had much less eye-to-eye contact with their babies." Susan Kuchinskas, "The Mother/Baby Attachment Gap," retrieved from www.hugthemonkey.com/2006/10/the_motherbaby_.html on April 25, 2008.

2. This is based on a study of maternal levels of oxytocin (sometimes called the love hormone) during pregnancy, which revealed that mothers with higher levels "gazed at their babies longer, touched their babies affectionately, had positive expressions while interacting with their baby, and reported checking on their baby more often than moms with lower oxytocin levels during pregnancy." Miranda Hitti, "Hormone May Help Mom and Baby Bond: Pregnancy Levels of the Hormone Oxytocin May Influence Mother-Child Bonding," *WebMD Medical News*, October, 16, 2007, retrieved from webmd.com/parenting/baby/news/20071016/hormone-may-help-baby-bond on April 25, 2008.

3. This is modified some with infants who have significant sensory and neurological issues that interfere with their ability to demonstrate attachment behaviors. With the right intervention, these differences can be overcome and, once more, the mother's behaviors become key.

4. Allan Shore, reported in Sue Gerhardt, *Why Love Matters: How Affection Shapes a Baby's Brain* (New York: Brunner-Routledge, Taylor & Francis Group, 2004), p. 41.

5. Mario Mikulincer and Phillip R. Shaver, *Attachment in Adulthood: Structure, Dynamics, and Change* (New York: Guilford Press, 2007), p. 38.

6. Karen, *Becoming Attached*, p. 238.

7. Susan Anderson, *The Journey from Abandonment to Healing* (New York: Berkeley Books, 2000), pp. 77–78.

8. Daniel J. Siegel, "Toward an Interpersonal Neurobiology of the Developing Mind: Attachment Relationships, 'Mindsight,' and Neural Integration," *Infant Mental Health Journal* 22, no. 1: p. 77 (citing Cassidy and Shaver, 1999).

9. Wallin, *Attachment in Psychotherapy*, p. 22.

10. Ruth P. Newton, PhD, citing 2005 research by L. A. Sroufe, B. Egeland, E. Carlson, and W. A. Collins, in *The Attachment Connection: Parenting a Secure and Confident Child Using the Science of Attachment Theory* (Oakland, CA: New Harbinger Publications, 2008), p. 27.

11. Shirley Jean Schmidt, MA, LPC, citing Siegel, "Toward an Interpersonal Neurobiology," in *The Developmental Needs Meeting Strategy* (San Antonio: DNMS Institute, 2006), p. 17.

12. Siegel, "Toward an Interpersonal Neurobiology," p. 77.

13. Gerhardt, *Why Love Matters*, pp. 65–79.

14. The books detailing this tend to be quite technical. Authors to see include Allan Schore, PhD, and Daniel J. Siegel, MD. The most readable version of the research can be found in *Why Love Matters* by Sue Gerhardt.

15. Gerhardt, *Why Love Matters*, pp. 38, 44.

16. Studies of middle-class children show slightly lower rates of insecure attachment and hover around 30 percent, while studies of all American children come in at closer to 38 percent. Karen, *Becoming Attached*, pp. 220, 224.

17. Ibid., p. 329.

18. Ibid., pp. 156, 373, reporting on both Ainsworth and Main.

19. Gerhardt, *Why Love Matters*, p. 93.

20. Mary Main, reported in Karen, *Becoming Attached*, p. 224.

21. Fosha, *Transforming Power of Affect*, p. 52.

22. Kathryn Black, *Mothering Without a Map*, (New York: Penguin Books, 2004), p. 64.

23. Karen, *Becoming Attached*, p. 387.

24. This was a pattern identified by attachment pioneer John Bowlby.

25. Malcolm L. West and Adrienne E. Sheldon-Keller, *Patterns of Relating: An Adult Attachment Perspective* (New York: Guilford, 1994), p. 75.

26. Newton, citing 1999 research by Belsky in *Attachment Connection*, p. 29.

27. Main and Hesse, 1990, cited in Siegel, "Toward an Interpersonal Neurobiology," p. 78, and also described in other places.

28. Newton, *Attachment Connection*, p. 30.

29. Siegel, "Toward an Interpersonal Neurobiology," p. 78.

30. Daniel J. Siegel, "Attachment and Self-Understanding: Parenting with the Brain in Mind," in *Attachment and Human Survival*, ed. Marci Green and Marc Scholes (New York: Karnac, 2004), p. 34.

31. Joan Woodward, "Introduction to Attachment Theory," in *Attachment and Human Survival*, ed. Marci Green and Marc Scholes (New York: Karnac, 2004), p. 16.

32. Newton, *Attachment Connection*, p. 30.

33. Ibid.

34. Siegel, "Attachment and Self-Understanding," p. 29.

35. Gerhardt, *Why Love Matters*, p. 147.

36. Fosha, *Transforming Power of Affect*, p. 54.

37. These items come from a variety of scales and descriptions, including a measure of adult attachment style developed by Hazan and Shaver (1987) found in Mikulincer and Shaver, *Attachment in Adulthood*.

38. Karen, *Becoming Attached*, p. 227.

39. Ibid., p. 228.

CHAPTER 4: MORE BUILDING BLOCKS

1. As Diana Fosha reports, "Anxiety is a reaction to the nonavailability or nonresponsiveness of the caregiver and is rooted in the feeling of being alone in the face of psychic danger." *Transforming Power of Affect*, 47. Earlier in the same book is this support: "Just as the feeling of safety has its origins in a secure attachment relationship with an available and responsive caregiver (Bowlby, 1988; Sandler, 1960), similarly anxiety and the defense mechanisms to which ... anxiety gives rise have *their* origins in an attachment relationship with an unavailable or unresponsive caregiver," pp. 39–40.

2. Michael St. Clair, *Object Relations and Self Psychology: An Introduction*, second edition (Pacific Grove, CA: Brooks/Cole Publishing, 1996), p. 79.

3. Ashley Montagu, *Touching: The Human Significance of the Skin*, third edition (New York: Harper Paperbacks, 1986), p. 126.

CHAPTER 5: MOMMY, WHERE WERE YOU?

1. Karen, *Becoming Attached*, p. 340.

2. Ibid., p. 339.

3. Daniel N. Stern, MD, *Diary of a Baby* (New York: HarperCollins/Basic Books, 1990), p. 61.

4. Black, *Mothering Without a Map*, p. 60.

5. Stern, *Diary of a Baby*, p. 62.

6. T. Berry Brazelton, MD, and Bertrand G. Cramer, MD, *The Earliest Relationship: Parents, Infants, and the Drama of Early Attachment* (Reading, MA: Addison-Wesley/A Merloyd Lawrence Book, 1990), p. 109.

7. Gerhardt, *Why Love Matters*, p. 124 (citing research).

8. Ibid., p. 21.

9. Brazelton and Cramer, *The Earliest Relationship*, p. 110.

10. I do not work in the field of early intervention, where there may be some exceptions. In cases where the baby has a neurological or sensory disorder, mother and baby often need interventions to help the baby attach.

CHAPTER 6: LIVING WITH AN EMOTIONALLY ABSENT MOTHER

1. Rose-Emily Rothenberg, "The Orphan Archetype," in *Reclaiming the Inner Child*, ed. Jeremiah Abrams (Los Angeles: Tarcher, 1990), p. 92.

CHAPTER 7: CHILDHOOD EMOTIONAL NEGLECT AND ABUSE

1. Catherine Robertson Souter, "Psychologist Examines 'Childhood Emotional Neglect,'" *New England Psychologist*, March 1, 2015, nepsy.com/articles/leading-stories/psychologist-examines-childhood-emotional-neglect.

2. "Childhood Psychological Abuse as Harmful as Sexual or Physical Abuse," American Psychological Association press release, October 8, 2014, apa.org/news/press/releases/2014/10/psychological-abuse.aspx.

3. Centers for Disease Control and Prevention, "About the CDC-Kaiser ACE Study," cdc.gov/violenceprevention/acestudy/about.html.

CHAPTER 8: WHAT'S WRONG WITH MOTHER

1. Fosha, *Transforming Power of Affect*, pp. 54–55.

2. Lindsay C. Gibson, PsyD, *Adult Children of Emotionally Immature Parents: How to Heal from Distant, Rejecting, or Self-Involved Parents* (Oakland, CA: New Harbinger Publications, 2015).

3. Christine Ann Lawson, PhD, *Understanding the Borderline Mother* (Northvale, NJ: Jason Aaronson, Inc., 2000), p. 9.

4. Ibid.

5. Diane Dweller, *Mom, Mania, and Me* (Tucson, AZ: Writing Ink, 2017).

CHAPTER 9: THE PROCESS OF HEALING

1. John Bradshaw, *Homecoming: Reclaiming and Championing Your Inner Child* (New York: Bantam, 1990), p. 75.

2. Ibid., p. 78.

3. Gibson, *Adult Children of Emotionally Immature Parents*, p. 41.

CHAPTER 10: CONNECTING WITH GOOD MOTHER ENERGY

1. Dennis L. Merritt, PhD, "Brief Psychotherapy: A Jungian Approach," retrieved from dennismerrittjungiananalyst.com/Brief_Psychotherapy.htm on June 24, 2008.

2. Anderson, *Journey from Abandonment*, p. 76.

CHAPTER 11: INNER CHILD WORK

1. I believe Freud used this; certainly his student Theodore Reik did. Also the poets William Wordsworth and Gerard Manley Hopkins did in the 1800s, and it has more recently been used as the title of a song, an album, and even a TV episode.

2. Cited in Bradshaw, *Homecoming*, p. 205.

3. Nancy J. Napier, *Recreating Your Self: Help for Adult Children of Dysfunctional Families* (New York: W. W. Norton, 1990), p. 151.

CHAPTER 12: PSYCHOTHERAPY

1. Edward Z. Tronick, "Dyadically Expanded States of Consciousness and the Process of Therapeutic Change," *Infant Mental Health Journal* 19, no. 3 (1998): pp. 290–99.

2. "Donald Winnicott," retrieved from en.wikipedia.org/wiki/Donald_ Winnicott on April 12, 2008.

3. Wallin, *Attachment in Psychotherapy*, p. 121.

4. Ibid., p. 119.

5. Soonju Kim, "Sweet Re-Mothering for Undermothered Women," first published in *Open Exchange Magazine* and retrieved from the author's Web site, motheringwomen.com on January 27, 2017.

6. Ibid.

7. Ibid.

8. dianepooleheller.com.

9. "David Wallin's Schedule of Upcoming Public Presentations, Workshops, and Conferences," davidjwallin.com/calendar.cfm.

10. "Workshop Overview: Therapist Training," Web site of Dr. Karyl McBride, willieverbegoodenough.com/workshop-overview-therapist-training.

CHAPTER 13: MORE HEALING STEPS AND PRACTICAL STRATEGIES

1. Jean Illsley Clarke and Connie Dawson, *Growing Up Again: Parenting Ourselves, Parenting Our Children* (Center City, MN: Hazelden, 1999), p. 8.

2. Bradshaw, *Homecoming*, p. 71.

3. Ibid., p. 72.

4. Gerhardt, *Why Love Matters*, p. 26.

5. Jett Psaris, PhD, and Marlena S. Lyons, PhD, *Undefended Love* (Oakland, CA: New Harbinger, 2000), p. 141.

6. At rickhanson.net, you'll find all kinds of programs and can sign up for his newsletter.

7. Rick Hanson, "Taking in the Good," Greater Good Science Center, November 1, 2009, greatergood.berkeley.edu/article/item/taking_in_the_ good.

8. Alex Korb, PhD, "The Grateful Brain: The Neuroscience of Giving Thanks," *Psychology Today*, November 20, 2012, psychologytoday.com/ blog/prefrontal-nudity/201211/the-grateful-brain; "Thanks! The Beneficial Effects of Expressing Gratitude," Positive Psychology Program, March 23, 2014, positivepsychologyprogram.com/beneficial-effects-expressing-gratitude.

CHAPTER 14: CHANGING THE STORY

1. Evelyn Silton Bassoff, PhD, *Mothering Ourselves: Help and Healing for Adult Daughters* (New York: Dutton/Penguin Group, 1991), p. 175.

2. Peg Streep, *Mean Mothers: Overcoming the Legacy of Hurt* (New York: William Morrow, 2009), p. 28.

3. Laura Davis, *I Thought We'd Never Speak Again* (New York: HarperCollins, 2002), p. 213.

Resources

HEALING MOTHER WOUNDS

Mothers Who Can't Love: A Healing Guide for Daughters
Susan Forward, PhD, with Donna Frazier Glynn (New York: Harper Collins, 2013)
> Using a lot of case description, Dr. Forward describes five types of hurtful mothers, the effects of such mothers on their children, and offers suggestions for managing difficult mothers as an adult, along with self-care advice, including working with the hurt inner child.

Mean Mothers: Overcoming the Legacy of Hurt
Peg Streep (New York: William Morrow, 2009)
> A well-researched book that includes moving personal stories gathered outside the therapy context.

Difficult Mothers: Understanding and Overcoming Their Power
Terri Apter (New York: W. W. Norton & Company, 2013)
> Describes several types of difficult mothers and offers suggestions.

Adult Children of Emotionally Immature Parents: How to Heal from Distant, Rejecting, or Self-Involved Parents
Lindsay C. Gibson, PsyD (Oakland, CA: New Harbinger, 2015)
> Describes characteristics of emotional immaturity and offers strategies for dealing with parents who fit this pattern.

Running on Empty: Overcome Your Childhood Emotional Neglect
Jonice Webb, PhD, with Christine Musello, PsyD (New York: Morgan James, 2013)
> Describes types of neglectful parents, effects of emotional neglect, and self-help strategies focusing on feelings. Many case stories.

Warming the Stone Child: Myths and Stories About Abandonment and the Unmothered Child
Clarissa Pinkola Estés, PhD (Louisville, CO: Sounds True [audiobook], 2004)
> Jungian therapist, bestselling author, and poet Dr. Estés is a skilled storyteller, and many will find this audiobook enchanting. Focuses on the unmothered child's need for guidance.

I Am My Mother's Daughter: Making Peace with Mom—Before It's Too Late
Iris Krasnow (New York: Basic Books, 2006)
> Focuses on adult daughters repairing the bond with Mother; includes a large number of interviews.

Note: There are a number of books (often in ebook format) that are memoirs of dysfunctional mothers. I have not included these, but checking on online retailers, you may easily find them.

BORDERLINE PARENTS

Understanding the Borderline Mother: Helping Her Children Transcend the Intense, Unpredictable, and Volatile Relationship
Christine Ann Lawson, PhD (Northvale, NJ: Jason Aaronson, Inc., 2000)
   In addition to describing the borderline personality, Lawson delineates four types of borderline mothers, details the effects of each, and offers guidelines for how to best deal with them.

Surviving a Borderline Parent: How to Heal Your Childhood Wounds and Build Trust, Boundaries, and Self-Esteem
Kimberlee Roth and Freda B. Friedman (Oakland, CA: New Harbinger, 2004)
   Provides useful information and guidance on how to overcome the devastating effects of growing up with a parent who suffers from BPD.

NARCISSTIC PARENTS

Will I Ever Be Good Enough?: Healing the Daughters of Narcissistic Mothers
Dr. Karyl McBride, PhD (New York: Atria/Simon & Schuster, 2009)
   Nicely structured book about recognizing the narcissist mother and having tools for dealing with her as an adult.

Children of the Self Absorbed: A Grown-up's Guide to Getting over Narcissistic Parents
Nina W. Brown, EdD, LPC (Oakland, CA: New Harbinger, 2nd edition, 2008)
   After describing narcissism and its effect on children, this book focuses on healing strategies. Contains test for NPD and useful scale assessing your separation from Mother.

daughtersofnarcissisticmothers.com:
Many readers will find this a good source of information.
   Danu Morrigan began this website and later wrote *You're Not Crazy—It's Your Mother!: Understanding and Healing for Daughters of Narcissistic Mothers* (London: Darton, Longman & Todd Ltd, 2012), available only on Kindle.

INNER CHILD

Recovery of Your Inner Child: The Highly Acclaimed Method for Liberating Your Inner Self
Lucia Capacchione, PhD (New York: Simon & Schuster, 1991)
   Practical, enchanting, and heartwarming, this guide will help you work with your inner child. Includes over forty exercises.

Homecoming: Reclaiming and Healing Your Inner Child
John Bradshaw (New York: Bantam, 1992)
A guide to working with the wounded inner child. Along with a general description of the process, includes developmental stages and the needs in each. There are also videos and audio books of Bradshaw's work, which you can find online.

Reconciliation: Healing the Inner Child
Thich Nhat Hanh (Berkeley, CA: Parallax Press, 2006).
Those who love Thich Nhat Hanh or come from a Buddhist perspective will appreciate his focusing compassion on the wounded inner child.

ATTACHMENT, EARLY LIFE

Why Love Matters: How Affection Shapes a Baby's Brain
Sue Gerhardt (New York: Routledge, 2nd edition, 2014)
This book makes accessible the latest findings in the neuroscience of attachment. Highly recommended.

Becoming Attached: First Relationships and How They Shape Our Capacity to Love
Robert Karen, PhD (New York: Oxford University Press, 1998)
An engaging, well-written book detailing the history of attachment research and ideas. More for professionals.

Mothering Without a Map: The Search for the Good Mother Within
Kathryn Black (New York: Penguin, 2005)
An excellent book for women who were undermothered and who are or are contemplating becoming mothers. Includes interviews with women who grew up without adequate mothering and a review of attachment research. A Yahoo! discussion group is available: groups.yahoo.com/group/mothering_without_a_map.

Growing Up Again: Parenting Ourselves, Parenting Our Children
Jean Illsley Clarke and Connie Dawson (Center City, MN: Hazelden, 2nd edition, 1998)
This is a relatively short self-help book written in a simple, direct style. It may be helpful to any parent who was underparented.

ATTACHMENT, PARTNER RELATIONSHIPS

Attached: The New Science of Adult Attachment and How It Can Help You Find—and Keep—Love
Amir Levine, MD, and Rachel Heller, MA (New York: TarcherPerigee, 2012)
Focuses on the two insecure attachment styles plus secure attachment, helps you identify your style and your partner's, provides guidance for working out conflicts and moving toward health. Note: Many with more

severe emotional abuse and neglect may have a disorganized attachment style not included here.

Wired for Love: How Understanding Your Partner's Brain and Attachment Style Can Help You Defuse Conflict and Build a Secure Relationship
Stan Tatkin, PsyD, MFT (Oakland, CA: New Harbinger, 2012)
  Drawn from neuroscience, attachment theory, and emotion regulation, this book presents ten guiding principles that can improve any relationship.

Insecure in Love: How Anxious Attachment Can Make You Feel Jealous, Needy, and Worried and What You Can Do About It
Leslie Becker-Phelps, PhD (Oakland, CA: New Harbinger, 2014)
  Focuses on the anxious (preoccupied) attachment style in partner relationships and using compassionate self-awareness and relationship skills to improve relationships.

Hold Me Tight: Seven Conversations for a Lifetime of Love
Sue Johnson (Little, Brown and Company, 2008)
  Sue Johnson is the developer of Emotionally Focused Couples Therapy. This guide, an adjunct to therapy (or perhaps replacement), teaches couples how to sort through the usual conflicts that happen in partnerships and identify the attachment needs underneath.

The Journey from Abandonment to Healing: Surviving Through and Recovering from the Five Stages That Accompany the Loss of Love
Susan Anderson, CSW (New York: Berkeley Books, revised and updated edition, 2014)
  An insightful book about how our need for attachment informs our intimate relationships and the painful process that occurs when such relationships fail and the abandonment wound is stimulated.

SELF-ASSESSMENT

You can find tests (formal and informal) online for all kinds of things, from attachment styles to emotional neglect to personality disorders and informally identified conditions such as being a highly sensitive person. Some of these self-assessment devices are more reliable than others. Remember that many conditions overlap. Bring results to your therapist, if you have one.

Acknowledgments

Every book, like every child, needs a good home. My deepest appreciation to Matthew Lore and The Experiment for providing such a welcoming home and such expert care. I was thrilled when in 2016 they invited me to do an expanded edition of the book. I have learned so much in the eight years since the first edition was constructed and so appreciate the chance to share more of that knowledge in this second edition. Thank you to Batya Rosenblum for shepherding this new edition through the process of becoming a book and Ana Ban for helping it achieve a greater reach through the various translations and audiobook formats.

I have been honored over the years to have a great many people share their inner lives with me, including the joys and disappointments of their childhood. Thank you to clients, students, and friends who have shared their stories with me and to those who generously gave their time to be interviewed for this book. May your suffering and your hard-earned lessons enrich the lives of others on this journey. I have grown through my work with clients in the years between editions, and my respect and appreciation for those who've chosen to work with me is enormous. Thank you! You teach and inspire me.

Thanks to those who helped with the first edition: Sara Lynn Swift, Willow Arlenea, and Betsy Kabrick, who offered valuable insights and feedback; Raji Raman for her editing suggestions; and Amber Vallotton for her enthusiasm and help with the initial online support group (now discontinued).

Finally, I will always feel deep gratitude to Konstanze Hacker, my therapist for many years, who provided me with an experience of the Good Mother, helped the sweet child within me develop and emerge, and who so patiently and capably guided me through the process of healing.

Index

About the Author

JASMIN LEE CORI, MS, LPC, is a licensed psychotherapist in private practice in Boulder, Colorado, whose specialty is working with adults who experienced childhood emotional neglect and abuse. An experienced educator, Jasmin taught over a dozen different psychology courses in a variety of colleges and professional schools, including training therapists in counseling skills. She has also worked in human service agencies.

Jasmin is the author of *Healing from Trauma: A Survivor's Guide to Understanding Your Symptoms and Reclaiming Your Life* (2008), *The Tao of Contemplation: Re-Sourcing the Inner Life* (2000), *The Tarot of Transformation* (with Willow Arlenea; 2002), *The Magic of Your True Nature: A Sometimes Irreverent Guide to Spiritual Development* (2013), as well as a book of mystical poetry. She has written articles published through various print and online sources and blogs at her website: jasmincori.com.

In her free time, Jasmin enjoys hiking, expressive movement groups, communing with nature and Spirit, political activism, and creativity and play with friends.